"While attention is finally being paid to victims of international trafficking, their sexually exploited American counterparts as young as eleven are criminalized for their heinous victimization. Rachel Lloyd's memoir should be mandatory reading for every cop, prosecutor, judge, and 'john,' but also every mainstream American who thinks racism, classism, and misogyny don't exist."

—Sarah Jones,
Tony Award–winning playwright/performer
and UNICEF Goodwill Ambassador

"*Girls Like Us* is a life-changing book, in every sense of the word. Rachel Lloyd changed her life to help change the lives of thousands of others—read her incredibly powerful story, and your life will be changed too."

—Janice Erlbaum,
author of *Girlbomb: A Halfway Homeless Memoir*
and *Have You Found Her: A Memoir*

"*Girls Like Us* is a powerful and eloquent recounting of the lives of children and young women caught up in the ravages of sexual exploitation by someone who has 'walked the walk.' This introspective and reflective book offers valuable insights into understanding the complex emotional and economic factors that contribute to the exploitation of children and youth. Lloyd is to be congratulated."

—Richard J. Estes,
professor of social work,
University of Pennsylvania

D0035290

Praise for Rachel Lloyd's
GIRLS LIKE US

"Riveting. . . . [Lloyd] describes with introspection and honesty the unfortunate circumstances and decisions that led her into 'the life.'. . . Lloyd's passionate, persuasive arguments for recognition and protection give a voice to the thousands of girls all around us who work and suffer in near invisibility."

—Corrie Pikul, *Elle*

"Extraordinarily inspiring. . . . [*Girls Like Us*] illuminates the complexities of the sex industry. . . . I hope that Lloyd's important and compelling book will be a reminder that homegrown American girls are also trafficked, and they deserve sympathy and social services—not handcuffs and juvenile detention."

—Nicholas Kristof, *New York Times*

"Powerful, superbly reasoned, and articulate. . . . Tackles a sensitive subject with clarity, compassion, and a biting sense of humor. . . . *Girls Like Us* tells the whole story with visceral power. . . . It is a page-turner, an eye-opener, a call to action, and a moving and inspiring story. . . . Lucky for us there are girls and women like Rachel Lloyd."

—Jane Wells, *Huffington Post*

"Heartbreaking. . . . But the book is also at times funny, bawdy, and optimistic, as is Lloyd herself."

—Jennie Yabroff, *Daily Beast*

"A brutally honest and disturbing look at sex trafficking, challenging society's indifference and offering portraits of the occasional victory of girls who, like [Lloyd], heal and recover from their abuse."

—*Booklist* (starred review)

"This book will burn a hole in your heart. The beauty of Rachel Lloyd's searing memoir is how she exorcises the pain of her own troubled girlhood by connecting with hundreds of young women on a brutal path. The truth and power of her writing takes us to a place where common humanity becomes the ultimate healer."

—Mira Nair, film director

"*Girls like Us* is powerfully raw, deeply moving, and utterly authentic. Rachel Lloyd has turned a personal atrocity into triumph and is nothing less than a true hero. Exposing the complexities of 'the life,' she takes you inside a world most prefer to pretend doesn't exist, and puts you front and center with the realities of the commercial sex industry and the modern-day slave trade right here in America. Never again will you look at young girls on the street as one of 'those' women—you will only see little girls who are girls just like us."

—Demi Moore, actress and activist

"Harrowing. . . . A painful yet powerful book that asks readers to examine personal prejudices, find compassion for those most view as throwaways, and recognize child abuse however it manifests."

—*Kirkus Reviews*

"With this moving new memoir, Rachel Lloyd takes her rightful place next to groundbreaking authors and activists like Dorothy Allison, Sapphire, and Jeannette Walls. She gracefully weaves together her own personal story of surviving 'the life,' the stories of the forgotten and fierce girls she has mothered and mentored, and big picture analysis of domestic trafficking. I turned the last page feeling like I'd just earned a PhD in injustice, but also a profound and rare sense of hope."

—Courtney E. Martin,
author of *Do It Anyway: The New Generation of Activists*,
and editor, Feministing.com

"With empathy and intellect, Rachel Lloyd brings to light the heartbreaking stories of these lost, forgotten, and abused girls. Her own life story is a source of inspiration and hope. She is an important new voice of conscience to which America needs to pay attention."

—Geoffrey Canada,
President and CEO,
Harlem Children's Zone

RACHEL LLOYD

GIRLS LIKE US

Fighting for a World Where

Girls Are Not for Sale:

A Memoir

HARPER PERENNIAL

NEW YORK • LONDON • TORONTO • SYDNEY • NEW DELHI • AUCKLAND

HARPER ● PERENNIAL

A hardcover edition of this book was published in 2011 by Harper, an imprint of HarperCollins Publishers.

The names of certain individuals have been changed to protect their privacy.

GIRLS LIKE US. Copyright © 2011 by Rachel Lloyd. All rights reserved. Printed in the United States of America. No part of this book may be used or reproduced in any manner whatsoever without written permission except in the case of brief quotations embodied in critical articles and reviews. For information address HarperCollins Publishers, 10 East 53rd Street, New York, NY 10022.

HarperCollins books may be purchased for educational, business, or sales promotional use. For information please write: Special Markets Department, HarperCollins Publishers, 10 East 53rd Street, New York, NY 10022.

"The Movie in My Mind" from the musical *Miss Saigon*, by Alain Boublil and Claude-Michel Schönberg. Music by Claude-Michel Schönberg. Words by Alain Boublil and Richard Maltby Jr. Copyright © Alain Boublil Music Ltd. (ASCAP). Used by permission.

"I Loves You, Porgy" from *Porgy and Bess*. Words and music by George Gershwin, DuBose and Dorothy Heyward, and Ira Gershwin. Copyright © 1935 George Gershwin Music, Ira Gershwin Music, and DuBose and Dorothy Heyward Memorial Fund. All rights administered by WB Music Corp. Used by permission of Alfred Music Publishing Co., Inc.

"Someday We'll All Be Free." Words and music by Donny Hathaway and Edward U. Howard. Copyright © 1972 by Universal Music—MGB Songs, Kuumba Music Publishing, and WB Music Corp. All rights on behalf of itself and Kuumba Music Publishing Co. administered by WB Music Corp. and Universal Music—MGB Songs International copyright secured. All rights reserved. Used by permission of Alfred Music Publishing Co. and Hal Leonard Corporation.

FIRST HARPER PERENNIAL EDITION PUBLISHED 2012.

Designed by Fritz Metsch

Library of Congress Cataloging-in-Publication Data is available upon request.

ISBN 978-0-06-158206-6 (pbk.)

12 13 14 15 16 OV/RRD 10 9 8 7 6 5 4 3

For Falicia and Adam. I miss you both.

To all the GEMS girls and young women,
past and present, who all hold a place in my heart.
I love you more than you will ever know.

And to all the girls like us.

Hang on to the world as it spins around.
Just don't let the spin get you down.
Things are moving fast.
Hold on tight and you will last.

Keep your self-respect, your manly pride.
Get yourself in gear.
Keep your stride.
Never mind your fears.
Brighter days will soon be here.

Take it from me, someday we'll all be free.

Keep on walking tall, hold your head up high.
Lay your dreams right up to the sky.
Sing your greatest song.
And you'll keep going, going on.

Just wait and see, someday we'll all be free.
Take it from me, someday we'll all be free.

—DONNY HATHAWAY AND EDWARD HOWARD,
"Someday We'll All Be Free"

CONTENTS

PROLOGUE

She likes swimming, SpongeBob, Mexican food, writing poetry, getting her nails painted (light pink is her favorite color), and Harry Potter books (plus she thinks Daniel Radcliffe is "fine"). This Christmas, she really wants an iPod but would settle for some sweat suits, preferably pink. Sometimes she's petulant—pouting and sullen—but mostly she's open and eager to be loved. When she smiles, huge dimples crease her chubby face and are still capable, as she moves into awkward adolescence, of melting hearts. She's much like any other eleven-year-old girl in America, except for one critical difference. Over the last year of her life, she's been trafficked up and down the East Coast by a twenty-nine-year-old pimp and sold nightly on Craigslist to adult men who ignore her dimples and her baby fat and purchase her for sex.

It's late on a Friday night and I'm still in the office. As the executive director of Girls Educational and Mentoring Services (GEMS)—the organization I founded to help girls and young women who have been recruited and trafficked into the commercial sex industry—I have a lot of late nights at the office. During the day, the office functions as a drop-in center, filled with teenage girls who are meeting with their case managers, coming for poetry or cooking or a boxing group, using the computers, or simply hanging out on our old and overused couch. It's frequently noisy; someone always needs something and while I love the energy of the space that we've created, it can be tough to get much paperwork done in this environment. After-hours, when all the girls and staff have left, is often my time to finish writing that grant that's overdue or respond to the never-ending stream of e-mails that I can never seem to stay on top of. Tonight, though, I have no plans to be here till the wee hours; I've promised myself that I'm leaving in ten minutes. *The Soup* is on and I have a new *InStyle* magazine to read. After a long day and a long week, it's a perfect Friday night plan.

When the office phone starts ringing, I'm almost tempted to ignore it and run out the door, but instead find myself answering and agreeing to a request to come to a foster care agency to meet a fourteen-year-old who's just been picked up off the streets. Since we're the only nonprofit in New York State designed to serve commercially sexually exploited girls, calls like these are common. Tonight the on-call staff is already at home in Brooklyn, so I figure it's easier and quicker for me to just grab a cab downtown, do a quick assessment, try to make the girl feel safe and comfortable, and then transfer the case on Monday to one of my staff members. I figure I can still make it home in time for *The Soup*'s 1 a.m. rerun and my weekly date with Joel McHale.

Ten minutes after arriving at the agency, though, I'm grouchy and wishing I actually had let the phone ring; the security guard gives me a hard time about getting into the building and the two staff workers on duty act as if I'm invisible. I'm deposited on a bench in the hallway by another staff person who then disappears for almost an hour, time well spent writing furious e-mails in my head to the agency's supervisor detailing what constitutes an emergency call on a Friday night and what doesn't.

I'm struck as always by the sterile, clinical atmosphere of the agency. This newly renovated center had been unveiled with much fanfare from the city. In fairness, it stands in stark contrast to the prior building, which had been Dickensian in its disrepair, yet I can't help feeling that they've really missed the boat with this new facility. Though it is clean, the harsh fluorescent lights and pale green walls, with the long hallways decorated with nothing more than a few child abuse hotline posters, don't really add up to a warm feeling. I couldn't imagine being a child who was brought here (actually, I could and that was worse). If you ended up here, it was likely after repeated abuse or neglect. You would probably just have been removed from your home, a terrifying experience even if you did feel lucky to escape. Now you were in unfamiliar territory, with strangers, in one of the most child unfriendly spaces in the city. I guess this thought had occurred to people other than me, because at least the living areas for the infants and toddlers had a wall mural and some brightly colored plastic furniture. Someone must have figured that the older kids didn't need color or a semblance of warmth, as the only thing that decorated the walls of the girls' unit were some pictures ripped out from *Essence* and *Honey* magazines. Clearly one of the staff had tried, but the effort is almost comical: a few magazine pictures, curled at the edges, of happy black women and girls, fashionable and beautiful, eating, laughing, celebrating life. I guess that a concerned woman of color who worked there desperately wanted the children of color, the overwhelming majority, who came through the doors to see images that looked like them in vastly different circumstances. Yet the sparseness of the unit in contrast with the staged, golden-lit happiness of the models makes their picture-perfect lives seem all the more unachievable and remote. I decide to once again offer my five decorating cents (warmer, brighter paint; colorful pictures; curtains; lamps; throw pillows) to the director before I leave.

I sit there redecorating in my mind, alternating between frustration (with waiting so bloody long) and sadness (that there even needs to be a place where kids can go when they can't live at home), when finally two staff workers appear flanking a child, I presume the Danielle I've been told about, who is obviously fresh from a shower. Her wet black hair is swept back into a ponytail framing a very pretty, slightly chubby, but extremely pissed-off-looking face. I'd been informed that the clothes Danielle had been wearing when she was brought in were considered "inappropriate," so her new attire consists of a plus-size shapeless black pantsuit, the type favored by larger women in their sixties and probably purchased at Walmart or Talbots. The outfit swamps her short frame, her hands hidden in the sleeves, the pants bagged around her ankles, creating a bizarre Aladdin look that is enhanced by an incongruous pair of black open-toed heels. Despite encouragement from the staff to put on socks and slippers, she has vehemently refused to let go of her shoes and clatters down the hallway with the familiar gait of a girl whose feet are killing her.

The staff members introduce me to Danielle as "someone who wants to talk to you," which unsurprisingly is met with a completely disinterested look from her, and then leave us alone in the interview room. Given the staff's bored and vague introduction, I figure I'll give it another go.

"Hey, my name's Rachel and I'm from a program called GEMS that works with teenage girls who've been in the life, and I'm just here to see how we can support and help you. I know you've had a pretty rough day, how are you doing tonight?"

Pause. Silence. Danielle sits eyeing me warily, with her arms folded tightly across her chest.

"Guess they didn't tell you I was coming, huh?" I roll my eyes at the door. Cheap trick, bond against the system when all else fails. Silence.

"I'm just here to talk to you a little bit and see if there's anything we can do. I'm not from the cops or child welfare or anything like that. What you tell me will be confidential."

Silence. If she is at all relieved that I'm not a cop, she doesn't show it.

"You know, the reason I started GEMS is cos I used to be in the life, too, so I wanted to have a place for girls who'd been through the same thing."

Silence. That admission normally at least provoked a question: "Really, miss? How old was you?" "What track you worked?" "You had a daddy?" But nothing, not even a raised eyebrow or a show of interest.

"Can you tell me what brought you here today?"

Silence. This is a little tougher than I'd expected or, to be honest, wanted, particularly at the end of a long week. A lot of girls I encountered in these situations started chatting right away and it was harder getting them to be quiet.

"So I know that your name's Danielle. Can I ask how old you are?"

I'd already been told over the phone by the intake worker that she is fourteen and it is a close-ended question (bad move in the counseling process), but I'm not really getting anywhere so I figure that this will at least get her to respond.

She breaks her silence. "Eleven."

I'm so mentally prepared for a different answer that it takes a moment to register.

Double take.

"I'm sorry, how old?"

"Eleven."

"Really?" I say, with far too much incredulity in my voice, and, I'm sure, on my face. Wow . . . dumb response.

She looks at me like I'm a little dense and just nods.

I wonder if perhaps she is lying. Lots of girls lied about their age in order to be older but I'd never met anyone who'd lied to be younger. While it probably isn't hard to believe that one of the staff had erroneous information, I really don't want to believe what she is telling me. Fourteen was bad enough, but eleven?

I try again, desperate to find her mistaken. "What's your date of birth, hon?"

"Twelve, eleven, ninety-five."

Yup, we are in June 2007. I take a hard look at her, past the shapeless outfit and the wary eyes, to the puppy fat and the fear, and I know that she is telling the truth. I want to throw up. I can't seem to find my protective wall, my shut-down switch that ten years of working with sexually exploited children has taught me to internally access. Meeting girls ages twelve, thirteen, fourteen years old had become routine, however sad and horrific. But eleven? Not even a teenager, still very much a child. A child being bought by adults? Shit. I'm hoping that the Port Authority police were wrong and that she hadn't really been sold as they suspected.

A million emotions jostle for control, but since I'm in a session, I try not to feel anything. If I act shocked or horrified, which of course I am, she might think that I'm horrified *by* her instead of *for* her and shut down even more than she is now. I pull myself together for the moment and continue the interview. I ask a few more basic questions and she continues to give one-word answers, arms still firmly crossed. I'm still struggling and beginning to get a little frustrated with myself. My engagement skills are pretty dead-on, normally, and yet I'm being outwitted by an eleven-year-old. I feel old and out of practice as I struggle to connect with this child. And then somehow it just comes, somewhere between asking her about music (and gratuitously throwing in Beyoncé and Jay-Z to earn some cool points . . . listening to Hot 97 pays off when you work with teens) and talking about our organization's upcoming summer trip to Great Adventure amusement park. Slowly her arms begin to relax and eventually drop to her sides and I learn that she likes swimming, wants to be a singer, and enjoys writing lyrics. I also learn that she has a boyfriend, who's twenty-nine. She fingers the costume jewelry around her neck. "He gave me this," she says as she leans forward to proudly show me a heart necklace made from what looks like pink glass. She vigorously denies that he knew she was eleven (despite the fact that I haven't asked), and claims he thought she was eighteen. I nod as if I believe her, but I'm not convinced.

She warms up as we talk about safer subjects but when I begin to bring up the circumstances that led her to the Port Authority Bus Terminal, the wariness comes back. She's been well trained to give standard answers (her boyfriend didn't know her age, she was just in D.C. visiting family, she has no idea why the cops thought she'd been sold) but it doesn't take long to engage her in conversation about hotels in D.C. I throw out a couple of generic chain names and she's excited to tell me which ones she's stayed in, all the while adamantly sticking to her story that she was just "hanging out, chillin" in the hotels with "friends."

"Do you know the Days Inn on Connecticut Ave?"

She nods proudly. "Uh-huh, I stayed there one time."

"You know how I know that hotel?" She shakes her head, interested in spite of herself.

"Well, remember how I told you that the program I run works with girls who've been in the life? One night, we got a call from a girl that we knew and she was in D.C., but her man—" I pause. "Her pimp was beating her and she was scared to leave cos she had her baby with her. So me and one of my staff drove down in the middle of the night and ran in and got her out."

Her eyes are widening.

"It was kinda crazy and a really long drive. We pulled over and fell asleep on the way and got yelled at by some cops who woke us up."

I pantomime being woken up unexpectedly, and Danielle laughs aloud.

"Anyway, that's how I know that hotel and that whole strip.

It's kinda rough over there. You weren't scared when you stayed there?"

"Nope." Danielle makes her best tough-girl face to demonstrate how unscared she was. "I kept weapons, in case the tricks acted up. So I wasn't never scared of them. They stupid. Especially the white ones. They be the ones that want to do the dirty stuff but I wasn't having none of that. . . ."

And finally, Danielle begins to tell me about her experiences in the sex industry. Now she's animated, confident to be the expert, schooling me on which johns are the best paying, which hotels are the nicest, which tricks you have to be careful of. I'm trying to reconcile what she is saying with the fact that I know that she's eleven and a minute ago we were talking about her favorite rides at Great Adventure, but I can't. She asks me about other hotels in Virginia and Maryland, naming districts I've never heard of, showing off her newfound knowledge as a seasoned traveler. Any hope or wishful thinking that Danielle has not been in the sex industry is pretty much crushed. She's been trafficked up and down the East Coast from Holiday Inns to Best Westerns by her boyfriend, who bought her a cheap heart-shaped necklace and, no doubt, the stilettos on her feet.

I want to cry.

I ask again about safety on the streets. Regardless of her bravado and claims, I know how dangerous the tracks are for any girl, let alone one this young.

"Oh, I didn't work the track." She looks slightly disdainful. "I worked through the computer. I had ads."

I take a guess. "Craigslist?" She nods approvingly.

"Yup. That's how you do it now." A nineties baby sold cyberstyle.

I flash to men sitting, pointing, and clicking to buy girls, not caring who they really are. Turning up at Danielle's hotel room, not seeing or caring how old she really is.

Now that we're apparently engaging in an open conversation, I'm curious how she met her pimp, although I'm still careful to follow her lead and call him her boyfriend.

"My sister introduced us. He was friends with her boyfriend." She leans forward, confidentially. "Her and my other sister do the same thing that you and me did," she whispers.

"How old are your sisters, hon?"

"Elizabeth's fourteen and Annette's sixteen."

The room just keeps getting smaller and smaller and I feel like I need air, immediately. A family of girls sold? On the Internet? I don't know if I still want to cry or throw the institutional beige couch at the institutional green walls. I take a deep breath.

"That must be really tough for you, hon. It seems like you've had a lot to deal with in your life."

She shrugs, but then looks sad. "I miss my mom," she says quietly.

"I know, sweetie, I know." Except this time I really don't.

After we wrap up the interview (Danielle actually gives me an awkward, brief hug when I leave), and I give my basic assessment (PTSD, needs far more support than the foster care agency can give), I rush out, unable to stay in the building one second more. I find myself walking along 8th Avenue with tears streaming down my face. I've walked forty blocks, enraged, before I realize that my sandals are cutting into my feet and creating blisters across my toes. I just can't go home, though. My original Friday night plans are dead. I need to process. I need to breathe.

I sit down at a sidewalk table at an almost deserted Italian restaurant and immediately order a glass of wine. I drink my first glass like a shot of liquor before the waiter comes back to take my order. From my outdoor seat, I watch the Upper West Side Friday night crowd walking by, girls in groups, couples old and new, solos coming from the gym. I fight the urge to interrupt their leisurely night out. "Do you have any idea what kind of world we live in? Children are being sold!" I want to yell, perhaps for the more placid ones a vigorous shake of the shoulders. I'm disgusted by their ignorance, by their carefree attitudes. I feel ridiculously and irrationally angry at the whole world. I rapid-dial three friends back-to-back and effectively ruin their Friday nights by unleashing all the vehemence and frustration that I've just carried forty blocks. "Eleven?" I hear each of them say incredulously in succession. "Yeah, eleven." If I say it enough, maybe it will feel better.

Righteous anger and honest sadness apparently take a couple more glasses of wine to temper. I feel woozy and numb, which was definitely the plan, and the desire to accost perfect strangers subsides. I take a cab home and think I'm sufficiently zoned out to sleep soundly, to leave the day behind, and yet I cannot shake Danielle's face. It stays with me, guarded and silent, as I try to fall asleep. When I dream that night, I'm chasing her, trying to protect her against some shadowy, dream-real, unspecified threat, and yet I can't save her, and each time she slips from my grasp and closer toward the shadows.

The trafficking and exploitation of children for sex is a global problem. UNICEF, the international nongovernmental organization for the protection of children, estimates that 1.2 million children and youth are commercially sexually exploited each year worldwide. While globalization has led to an increased number of children and adults who are traded and trafficked internationally, and to a growing business of sex tourists who journey to developing countries for the sole purpose of purchasing sex, the majority of sexual exploitation occurs within a country's own borders and involves native children and women with native men. Places like Thailand and the Philippines are often pointed to as the worst offenders, yet the issue affects every continent, particularly those regions that are already vulnerable due to war, famine, and natural disasters. In recent years, people have paid increased attention to the plight of trafficking victims and a growing awareness that slavery, in multiple forms, still exists.

Yet it's easier to imagine a Danielle on the streets of Calcutta, or in a brothel on the border of the Czech Republic, than to imagine her waiting for a man on the bright, floral, polyester bedspread at some motel in Virginia. Easier, too, to think of her story as an unfortunate but isolated incident, rather than a story representative of potentially hundreds of thousands of children and youth throughout the United States. Yet according to a 2001 University of Pennsylvania study, an estimated 200,000 to 300,000 adolescents are at risk for commercial sexual exploitation in the United States each year.

When I tell people that the agency that I run serves over three hundred girls a year in the New York City metro area alone who've been trafficked for sexual purposes, they're invariably stunned. When I tell them that the girls and young women we serve are predominately U.S. citizens, their shock and sympathy turn to utter incomprehension. "How?" "What do you mean? "From here?" "How?" "Where?" To talk about trafficking conjures images of Thai girls in shackles, Russian girls held at gunpoint by the mob, illegal border crossings, fake passports, and captivity. It seems ludicrous and unthinkable that it's happening in America to American children.

It's often not until you explain that this phenomenon is what is commonly called "teen prostitution" that recognition dawns. "Oh, that . . . but that's different. Teen prostitutes choose to be doing that; aren't they normally on drugs or something?" In under three minutes, they've gone from sympathy to confusion to blame. Not because the issue is any different, not because the violence isn't as real, not because the girls aren't as scared, but simply because borders haven't been crossed, simply because the victims are American.

I'm not sure why Danielle's story particularly got to me that night. After all, this is what I *do.* I've spent the last thirteen years of my life working with girls just like Danielle, girls who've been bought and sold. I don't cry after meeting every girl I meet, nor do I drink several glasses of wine after every tough story. Over the years, I've learned to develop some distance, a basic ability to hear, to absorb varying levels of horrific detail without taking it all home with me every night. As any cop, emergency worker, or first-line responder will tell you, sometimes something unexpectedly sneaks in, getting through the wall that you've so carefully constructed in order to stay sane. Perhaps what got to me was the ease with which men had been able to buy Danielle, right there on their laptops. No lurking about in the streets, no curb-crawling in shady areas. They bought sex online from a child like they were paying a bill, ordering a pair of shoes, booking a vacation. Perhaps it was the insidious nature of her recruitment, the fact that she never stood a chance. A foster care kid, bounced from place to place, with two "older" sisters who had also been trafficked. Or was it the cheap necklace that she so lovingly fondled and the realization of how easy it had been for this adult man to lure her, to seduce her, to become her "boyfriend." Maybe it was the fact that just a month before I had met her, the New York State Senate had refused to pass a bill that would have created services and support for girls just like her, who were normally treated as criminals, not victims. Perhaps what cracked my armor that night was her age. Even though I frequently recited the statistic that the estimated median age of entry into the commercial sex industry was between twelve and fourteen years old, and had worked with lots of very young girls over the years, there was something about her eleven-year-old puppy fat, her love of roller-coaster rides, that shook me.

Ultimately, it was all of it. Meeting Danielle that night was a harsh reminder of how much work there was still to do. All the work I'd done for the last thirteen years, everything I'd committed my life to, still wasn't enough. I thought back to my arrival in New York in August 1997, a wide-eyed and eager-to-help twenty-two-year-old. Danielle was about to turn two years old. When I was meeting sixteen-, seventeen-, and eighteen-year-old girls who'd been raped, tortured, bought, and sold, Danielle was still a toddler, perhaps still sucking her thumb, learning to talk. I can see her, a chubby baby, all curly hair and smiles. A few months later, just after her second birthday, Danielle would be placed in the foster care system, due to her mother's substance abuse. Danielle would never get to live at home again but she would search for a family in the arms of a man she now calls Daddy, whom she tells me she feels "connected" to. As I started GEMS, learning how to run a program, getting my first office space, Danielle was bouncing from foster home to foster home. As GEMS began to grow, hiring staff, adding programs, Danielle was being groomed and prepared for her recruitment into the sex industry. As I started to feel as though we finally were making progress, Danielle was being sold to her first "customer." As I advocated for change in New York State laws, Danielle's pimp was beating her with a belt and leaving scars across her back.

I felt like the little Dutch boy with his finger in a dam. No matter how hard I tried, it didn't prevent a whole new generation of children from being bought and sold, from being ignored and vilified by their families, the system, the media, the legislature. Just around the corner were the next round of Danielles, girls who didn't know what a pimp was, didn't know what a track was, girls who hadn't been trafficked yet.

That night it seemed insurmountable, a Sisyphean task that I'd never be able to conquer. Yet in the light of the next morning, as I prepared to visit Danielle again, I reminded myself that progress had been made. The cops she'd met that night hadn't arrested her on prostitution charges, and although that outcome wasn't the norm for the majority of trafficked girls, it did indicate that there were law enforcement officers who really believed that these girls were victims. The foster care agency had actually called GEMS, a huge step forward, and they'd even described her as an "exploited child," not a "prostitute." A few years earlier that would have been unthinkable. It was major progress that GEMS even existed, that there was even an organization to call. When I started GEMS as an unlikely and unprepared executive director, I really had no clue about what I was doing. Yet I'd still managed to create something that continued to benefit and serve girls all these years later. It was for girls like Danielle that I'd founded GEMS, when all I really had to offer in the beginning was compassion and love. I remembered how important that still was, even in the face of the overflowing dam. I decided to pick up a journal and some SpongeBob socks on the way to see Danielle. It would not solve the problem but it would make her smile, and for today, that would have to be enough.

1

LEARNING

Child sexual exploitation is the most hidden form
of child abuse in the United States and North America today.
It is the nation's least recognized epidemic.
—Dr. Richard J. Estes, University of Pennsylvania

FALL 1997, NEW YORK CITY

As soon as I step through the gates of Rikers Island, the air seems to change. If air can smell oppressed, thick and heavy with misery, this is pretty much it. I feel like I'm suffocating. Rikers is the world's largest penal colony, encompassing its 413-acre island and housing over fourteen thousand inmates on any given day, and going there is not a trip to be taken lightly. Once that heavy door slams behind you, visitor's pass or not, there's a sinking sensation that you'll never be able to leave. On all my visits, I slide my bag onto the X-ray machine, get yelled at by a guard for putting it on the wrong way/too soon/too late/something, try not to be bothered that even as a visitor I am treated like an inmate, and pray that I haven't forgotten to take any change out of my pockets before I get humiliated by the guard again. Getting in, while I'm sure not quite as arduous as trying to actually get out of Rikers, is an ordeal in itself. Once inside, getting to the high school for the adolescent girls is even harder. While it is less than a two-minute walk from the inside gate to the school, you can potentially wait an hour for a "ride," a guard to escort you, as is required for visitors. The general rule of thumb is that male guards will escort you, not female guards. In a women's facility, female guards outnumber the male ones, so there is a lot of waiting quietly on the bench for someone to take pity on you and walk you a hundred-yard distance. Impatience gets you yelled at, as does requesting the front gate guard to assist you. So I shut up and wait.

I'd been coming to Rikers to do outreach for a few months and was getting used to the routine. At first, the walk through the jail had intimidated me. On my first day, a few leers from some of the women, curious stares, and a couple of mean looks had my heart pumping. My ideas about women's prison came primarily from the Australian soap opera *Prisoner: Cell Block H*, a female version of *Oz* in which characters were disposed of weekly in all types of violent ways. Perhaps I'd be shanked; perhaps there'd be a riot and I'd be killed by COs by mistake. There were endless variations of the bloody-end-in-jail theme, but after my first presentation to a group of adults in the drug unit, the fear left and all that remained was sadness and a sense of hopelessness. Women in their thirties and forties stuck in a revolving door of addiction and jail, women in their sixties who should have been spending time with their grandchildren instead of facing yet another incarceration, women in their twenties who looked so much older, just starting out on their path already branded with a record. I quickly grew to have empathy for these women, understood that our lives could have been reversed, that it was a major miracle that I wasn't stuck in the jail cycle myself. At one time, during my teenage years, I'd even considered going to prison a badge of honor, a way of proving myself. I'd taken the risks, hadn't "grassed," and had even been willing to take a multiple-year sentence for my bank robber boyfriend. It turned out, though, despite my loyalty and Bonnie and Clyde mentality, that the police had scant evidence on me and then had violated my rights as a juvenile, thereby ensuring that the charges were eventually dropped. My time in jail had ultimately amounted to a couple of overnights for theft and three days for the bank robbery conspiracy, and even that had been limited to being held in the bookings of our downtown local precinct. The older I'd gotten, the less jail had seemed like a good idea, until I simply stopped doing things that might've sent me there. Still, though I had no legitimate jail experience to speak of, I did know what addiction felt like, both to substances and men. I knew what it felt like to live on the edges of society, to feel hopeless and to be homeless. I understood confusing domestic violence with love and always having to hustle to make the next buck (or in my case, pound). Once I shared my story with the women, they'd shown me so much love that there was nothing left to be scared of. Now as I walked down the hallways, I'd see a few familiar faces who would greet me respectfully. "Hey, miss. You coming to see us today?"

"Nah, adolescents. Friday I'll be there."

"Good. Those little bitches need somebody to talk to. They hardheaded."

I laughed. The older women were forever complaining about the teenagers, but even in the way they'd called them *little bitches*, *knuckleheads*, *them loose asses*, there was maternal concern and identification. They could see themselves at that age, remember what it was like to think they knew it all only to discover twenty years later that there was nothing cute about being in jail. Even when I would do street outreach at night, the older women would point me in the direction of a younger girl and say, "She's a kid, she needs help. You should talk to *her.*"

Implicit in their admonishments to focus on the younger girls was the unspoken belief that it was too late for them, but that there was still hope for her/them/those little bitches. In fairness, too, I knew that while the women who knew my story both accepted and respected me on some level, I was still some fresh-faced twenty-two-year-old without a criminal record, without decades of substance abuse, without kids I'd lost to the system. I did my best not to come across as a know-it-all, a kid who'd gotten lucky and who was now, as my own grandmother used to say, "trying to teach my grandmother to suck eggs." Some of the women I worked with had daughters older than me; most had addictions older than me. So I understood why they pushed me toward the teenagers though inside I felt a little relieved, but also a little guilty, that I, too, felt more optimism and passion for the adolescents and young adults than perhaps I did for them.

That fall of 1997, the best-known British import to these teenagers is, sadly, the Spice Girls, who've just come out with their movie and yet another stuck-in-your-head song. With my long dark hair in a ponytail and my accent, according to the girls, I look "just like Sporty Spice, miss." I'm not thrilled about being compared to the Spice Girl I think is the most awkward-looking, but after my initial horror, I see it as a workable hook. The girls are excited about this tenuous connection to a pop group, so I play it up and do my best British accent. "Say *blah, blah girl power.* Pleeeeeeease, miss." There's a chorus of plaintive "please"s and "yeah, do it"s, so I oblige the fans, giving the peace sign as I've seen on the group's ubiquitous commercials. The crowd goes wild. "Do it again, do it again." Although we started out with a group of just three or four girls, they're now calling their friends, "Ay yo, come listen to the lady that talks like a Spice Girl." Just another day at Rikers Island High School for Girls. One of the most notorious and largest jails in the country, and here I am Spice Girling it up, using my accent to the max. I had just started coming to the high school and had run a couple of small groups with some girls who'd been identified by the social worker as "really needing to talk to you," plus a few individual sessions. That day I am doing a presentation for all the girls and the teaching staff and I'm nervous. The girls are loud and raucous, nothing like the boot-camp-trained adult women who lockstep in single file, sit quietly, and apparently recite the Serenity Prayer at every opportunity. These high school adolescents are sixteen to twenty-one and are charged with everything from shoplifting to murder although most, I'll learn, are in for some type of drug charge, invariably holding for, copping for, or trafficking for a man or a boy who has escaped prosecution and is now suddenly too busy to visit or send commissary money. The classroom is packed, standing room only, and now, after a few months of speaking to the adult women, I've gotten more comfortable at telling my story. Over the years I'll learn to edit out more and more to preserve my own sanity and to avoid some of the offensive and often stupid questions that will inevitably come up. But these are the early days, so after I've told my story in much of its raw and painful detail, the stupid questions come and, interestingly, none of them are from the girls. I try to deflect a few of the more offensive remarks coming from the teachers, and mercifully the girls jump in to save me from more embarrassment, with sincere, thoughtful questions and comments. The whole group is quiet and subdued; a few girls are sniffling, trying to be unobtrusive with their tears.

"Miss, do you and your moms get along now? Cos me and my moms is still beefing cos she getting high again."

"Yo, did you ever hear from your pimp again? Is he sorry?"

I answer the questions as honestly and carefully as I can and as I do, the girls begin to share their own stories, their own pain. The teachers are quiet.

"I got abused, miss, when I was little and now I just be so fuckin angry at men and I can't help it."

"I've been in foster care since I was five and my family knows I'm locked up and they don't even visit."

"My boyfriend tried to shoot me and I grabbed the gun and now I'm here cos I shot him by accident. But he was beating me every day and I was scared of him. I don't understand why they didn't lock him up before this all happened. I didn't mean to kill him, I just wanted him to stop."

Girls are crying as they speak. The girls sitting next to them cry, too; their backs are rubbed, some compassionately, some awkwardly. Soon most everyone in the room is crying. I'm wiping away tears, too, as the group continues. Teachers drift out quietly and yet the girls don't want to move. Something's happening in the room that was unforeseeable an hour ago when the rowdy, boisterous group had sauntered their way in pushing, cursing, cracking on each other. The room has let down its guard, without the defenses, the anger, the front that has been carefully erected often for years prior to their incarceration, if not hastily built as soon as they hit the island. "Weakness" is not accepted in an adult correctional facility, despite the fact that most of these girls are not even of the age of majority and should be experiencing high school in a very different environment. Yet here we sit together listening, allowing each other to share raw emotions, to be scared, to be hurt, to be girls just for a few minutes. Even in my naïveté, I'm clear that once we leave this room their defensive fronts have to return, which is perhaps why they seem so reluctant to leave.

A girl with a scarf covering her mousy hair and pockmarked skin who's been sitting near the front, tears streaming, finally speaks.

"I've been in the life too—I was on heroin, and I had a man who was pimping me out to everyone to buy drugs. I can relate to what you were saying about nearly dying cos I nearly died too. They tied me up in a bathtub and stabbed me in the head with a screwdriver."

She leans forward and pulls her hair back. The wounds are horrific—fresh and red; her whole head is littered with lumps of raw flesh and there's a collective gasp from the rest of the group.

"I thought I was going to die, but somehow I lived and managed to get out. And now I feel like you came here for a reason to tell me that I was supposed to live. I never heard no one talk about this stuff, about the stuff you did, that I did." She chokes up. "I'm glad you came."

The room murmurs assent and I'm choking up, too.

A petite Latina with long black curls, who's been the most silent and reserved of the whole group, finally speaks up and looks directly at me. "She's right, you was sent here, miss, for us. God sent you. Everyone else, the counselors and stuff, they can be nice, but they had a luv-luv life. You feel me? A luv-luv life, they read about the shit we went through in some book—that's good 'n' all but you lived this shit. It's different, your life was like ours, some the same, some different but you been there, you feel me? And look, you came all the way from a whole nother country to here. To New York, to Rikers! That's kinda crazy, if you think about it, you feel me? So that's why I know. God sent you. To us. To help us be strong. To let us know we not alone and we can be all right too." She finishes her pronouncement and sits back in her original spot against the wall.

Later I'll learn her name, Miranda, and that she's incarcerated for murder. Over the months that she's incarcerated, before she's finally sentenced and sent upstate, we'll connect occasionally but we'll never be particularly close, yet her words will reverberate for months and then years to come. I'll never really hear the term *luv-luv life* again but it will stay in my mind as a perfect description of those who seem untouched by life's horrors and tragedies, for whom childhood memories conjure up joy and innocence, for whom the thought of family evokes comfort and safety and for whom the word *love* remains undistorted and untainted by disappointment, by violence, by fear. Over the years I won't meet many girls who've had luv-luv lives, yet thanks to Miranda, I'll remember that that's the whole point of my being here.

For most first-time visitors to New York City, there are a few essential tourist spots: the Statue of Liberty, the Empire State Building, Rockefeller Center, Times Square. However, for the first six months that I live in New York, the only place I can cross off my "must-see" list is Times Square and that is only because, at the time, it was still home to a burgeoning sex industry. My list of places visited went something like this:

Hunts Point market—creepy industrial area at night in the
    Bronx
Long Island City/Queensboro Plaza (under the bridge)—
    creepy industrial area at night in Queens
Flatlands—creepy area at night in Brooklyn
A few other assorted deserted areas
A youth homeless shelter
Rikers Island jail

I came to New York City in August 1997 to work as a missionary for an agency that works with adult women in the commercial sex industry, a job I've obtained not based on my sparse résumé, which consists of being a waitress and a nanny, but rather on my rare admission that I've worked in the sex industry, too. Given that I have moved from Germany to the States for work, I don't really expect to be living it up in tourist hot spots, but I don't know that I'm really prepared for night after night of street outreach to some of New York's most notorious tracks. The first night in Hunts Point, located in the poorest congressional district in the country, the South Bronx, I'm horrified by the quiet, deserted industrial landscape. All I can think as I drive around is *serial killer's paradise*. So many dead-end streets, Dumpsters, the absence of streetlights, no one around for miles to hear you scream. Over the next few years, the Disneyfication of Times Square pushes sex stores, strip clubs, and the street-based sex industry farther and farther into neighborhoods like this, areas where no tourists from Iowa want to visit and residents' concerns about crime and safety are largely ignored.

It is in these dark, desolate areas that I do outreach, talking to women and girls on the street, although in the beginning, these conversations are often fairly one-sided.

"Hey, how you doing?"

"Would you like some hot chocolate/coffee/candy/a toiletry pack?"

"So, my name's Rachel. . . . I'm from an agency that works with women on the street."

Often they ignore me, so casually and easily, as if I am simply an annoying fly that is buzzing near their ear. Sometimes they give me the once-over and weigh up quickly that this little girl with a funny accent isn't po-lice and doesn't have much to really offer. And once in a while, on a slow night, they begin to talk to me and I learn names, street names but still; whether they have children and where they got that cute jacket/shoes/earrings. It isn't deep but it's a start. The more I'm out there, though, the more they learn about my story. And soon they introduce me to others, particularly the younger girls. I learn not to bother them too much on a busy night, to be aware if we are being observed by their pimps, to not take up too much of their time if we are. For months, the only people I really meet are girls and women who are being sold on the streets.

Nights are for street outreach. Daytimes I go to detention centers, shelters, and Rikers, where the girls and women who come in are scorned by staff and the other residents or inmates alike.

"Whatcha daddy gonna do for you now, huh?"

"Nasty ho."

If the other girls and women didn't know what the girl was in for, the guards or staff made sure to announce it. To have been on the street, to be in "the life," as the girls called it, was to be on the lowest rung. It didn't matter how old they were; they were shunned and mocked as dirty, nasty, hos, whores, hookers, dumb bitches. In this environment, it is jarring to go public for the first time about my own experiences: The looks, the snide comments—particularly from the adults, who are supposed to know better—make me flush with shame and cry at night. It isn't surprising to me then that the girls go back to the familiar, where they are at least accepted, even if that means being sold and abused. Most of them really didn't have anywhere else to go. The girls are surprised, and then relieved, when they realize I won't judge them. In the beginning, simply not judging them and my own story are about all I have to give, and while we develop some good relationships, I know that I have to be able to offer them more.

The first girl that I really work with one-on-one is Melissa, a strikingly beautiful seventeen-year-old who towers over me even in her sneakers. Melissa is an angry young woman who is often frustrated by my lack of knowledge about the welfare system, the housing system, the subway system, and anything else even remotely useful. I'm woefully naive in thinking that I just need to be supportive and caring and offer encouraging platitudes, which Melissa often throws back in my face as she struggles to leave her one-year-old daughter's father, who has also been her pimp since she was fourteen. With Melissa, I negotiate the bureaucratic nightmares that are endemic to every public system and grow angry right along with her that caseworkers look bored with her plight and have no answers for her situation. It is on these long, tedious trips to the clinic, to the welfare office, to the housing offices that we begin to bond, albeit reluctantly on Melissa's part. While she and I share a common understanding about the general workings of the life, she is frequently impatient, often downright scornful, of my lack of knowledge about street slang—"What's the track?" "What's a wife-in-law?"—and the intricate rules of "the game." "Why do you have to walk in the street and not on the sidewalk?" "Why can't you look a man in his face?" Melissa becomes my teacher, and I begin to make the connections between the things that I'd experienced and the stories she's telling me. The area where girls worked on the street is called the track; the girls I tried to recruit to work for my "boy-friend" would've been my wives-in-law; the money I had to give my "boyfriend" was my quota; oh, and my boyfriend, yeah, he was actually a pimp. This was probably one of the hardest things for me to verbalize and it would take a while for me to really accept that reality.

Jennifer, my next tutor, is a moonfaced Latina who would call me at 6 a.m. after a beating. I'd meet her at the train station and let her sleep on my couch. After a night or two, Jennifer would find her way back to her pimp, although eventually she stayed with me three, four nights, then for almost two weeks as I searched desper-ately for a program out of state that would take her. From Jennifer I learn that leaving the life takes practice, that girls need to try mul-tiple times without having someone give up on them.

Tiffany, who weighed about eighty pounds, ran up a ridiculous phone bill at our office calling psychic hotlines. Her pimp had cut off half of her hair and it was so badly matted that I had to take her to the hair salon to have her head almost completely shaved. No program would take Tiffany: She didn't have a drug problem, a prerequisite for most programs that cater to her age. One night she disappeared for a few hours and returned proudly announcing that she'd smoked crack and was now eligible for the drug program, but we had to hurry cos she wasn't sure how long it would be in her system. From Tiffany I learn how few resources are available to meet the needs of these girls, and how few people understand what they've experienced.

I meet Aisha at Rikers. One day she rolls up a leg of her sweat-pants to show me the crude tattoo of her pimp's name that he'd hand-carved into her inner thigh as he sat between her legs holding a gun to her head. From Aisha I learn about the systematic violence of pimps, and make the connections to my own experiences. Kim-mie, who is stabbed in the vagina by a group of men and left to die in the street, reminds me about the violence of johns.

Then there's Katherine, my first successful intervention, which I can't really take full credit for. Katherine—soft-spoken, with delicate features—and I spend a couple of court-mandated days together and then talk on the phone a few times before she decides to return to her family in Houston. She goes back to school and eventually gets a Realtor's license. Throughout it all she sends me cards and e-mails thanking me for our brief time together. I post her picture proudly over my desk. Katherine, I believe, comes into my life simply to encourage me that support does make a difference.

Mostly, though, it is just tough, sad work. I listen and listen to story after story of fatherless girls; motherless daughters; parents lost to the streets; drugs; prison; domestic violence turned murder; sexual abuse by an uncle, a cousin, a neighbor, a teacher; running away; being put in foster care; meeting a man—that was central to every story—meeting a man who made promises, who made them feel safe. After a while, everywhere I look I see pain. Every teenage girl on the subway is a victim, or at least a potential victim. Every man, particularly middle-aged white men, the ones I most closely associated with johns, is a predator. I am both numb and oversensitive, overwhelmed by the need, the raw and desperate need of the girls I am listening to and trying to help. I'm overdosing on the trauma of others, while still barely healing from my own.

I cry for hours at home and have fitful nights of little sleep. My nightmares resurface as my own pain is repeated to me, magnified a thousand times. It feels insurmountable. How can you save everyone? How can you rescue them? How do you get over your pain? How do you ever feel normal?

I don't have many answers, for myself or for the girls. So I listen and listen, doing my best to learn as much as I can, to make the connections, to be open and honest about my own experiences, to be sincere, to love them and not judge. And while that isn't much to offer, it becomes the basis for some amazing relationships. I learn to be honest during that first year about what I can't specifically relate to; while we share many common experiences, I can never claim to have lived someone else's life. I wasn't and never will be a thirteen-year-old black girl from Bed-Stuy who is sitting in a juvenile detention center. I have experienced different privileges and supports that sometimes leave me with a sense of survivor's guilt. Yet still, despite the difference in cultures and even continents, in ethnicities and slang, threatened with guns or threatened with knives, sold in a club or sold on the street, our experiences are consistently more similar than different. The themes are common: the lack of family support; the need for love and attention; the early stages that felt almost good; the pain that kept us trapped; and the long, slow journey back to life, feeling all the while that we'd never quite be normal, that we'd never fit in—a message reiterated through family, through loved ones, through society's view of us. Over and over it is clear for all of us that our backgrounds had prepared us for this. In one way or another, through abuse, neglect, abandonment, we'd been primed for predatory men, for an industry that would use us up and spit us out.

Every new encounter provides a new mirror for me to view my own experiences through, and there is a level of selfishness during this period as I hunger to understand more about the girls' lives in order to understand mine. If I could figure out what had happened to them, perhaps I had a better chance of explaining it all to myself.

RISK

There can be no keener revelation of a society's soul
than the way in which it treats its children.

—*Nelson Mandela*

My room is the "isolation" room, windowed on three sides, where children who have contagious diseases and require constant supervision from the nurses are kept. Yet as our local hospital does not have a pediatric psych department, this is where I'm placed. Initially I'd been placed in a regular room, but when the nurses realized that every time I was left alone I would utilize all my creativity in finding new and inventive ways to attempt suicide, they moved me. I'd pretended to want to shave my legs so a gullible friend from school brought me razors. I'd developed a sudden craving for R Whites Lemonade, which was conveniently sold in a glass bottle. I'd used bandages to tie my neck to the plug hole in the deep sink and then filled it up. While none of these attempts has been successful, I'm left with sliced and diced wrists and a realization that no matter how much you want to die, the human body will not simply relax and let itself be drowned, especially not in a sink.

My initial and most serious attempt, the one that has landed me in the hospital, is downing a bottle of wine with over forty of my mother's various pills. I'm told that I flatlined for a few seconds and was brought back. A nurse cries later as she tells me this. I'm sad, too, but mostly because the student renting a room from my mother came back from France early and called an ambulance when she found me slowly passing out in the kitchen. Everyone tells me that I'm lucky to be alive.

I stay in the hospital for three weeks, trying to cut, trying to drown, as social workers scramble to figure out what to do with a suicidal thirteen-year-old who's adamant about not being placed into foster care. My mother is also rallying to keep me—despite the fact that just a couple of weeks ago she'd had a severe nervous breakdown and had locked herself in the bathroom and tried to kill herself as I pounded hysterically on the door. My stepfather, Robert, who moved out over a month ago and into his new girlfriend's house, is banned by the hospital staff from visiting me, partly due to the fact that he showed up drunk, partly due to the fact that he kept yelling that I was "just like your mother," and had to be escorted out. Given these facts, it's a small miracle and probably not a great testament to the wisdom of my assigned social worker that I'm discharged home to my mother. Life, unsurprisingly, doesn't get better.

As a small child, I'm fortunate enough to live with my great-grandmother, my maternal grandparents, and my mother deep in the heart of the countryside of Dorset. My mother shows no signs of the struggles that she'll later face when alcoholism will take control of her life and fling her (and me) around like a floppy rag doll. In fact, she doesn't even drink then. She is the quintessential good single mum: endlessly devoted; creative and permissive about my freedom to explore nature, art, play; fiercely protective; firm about my tantrums. We are close in a way that only a single mother and an only child can be. My grandmother, much to my chagrin years later when I discovered the photographic evidence, makes us matching outfits. A child of the late seventies, sadly these outfits consist of pinafore dresses and smocks with lots of flowers. At the time, though, I'm thrilled to be mimicking my young, pretty mother.

There is an "incident" when I am three years old. Something that is done to me in a park by older teenage boys. My mother tells me later that I won't speak afterward and just want to sleep for days. She has some friends pray for me and apparently I get better. My mother believes she has done the right thing, and the "incident" won't be mentioned again until my teenage years when I begin to have blurry, intrusive flashbacks.

Growing up, I pine a little for Robert, the man I believe to be my father, and struggle with the realization that I am the only person in my first-grade class who doesn't have contact with their father; even the few children whose parents are divorced still have a "weekend dad." I have no idea where mine is, what he's doing, if he thinks about me. Yet despite the father-shaped hole in my heart, I'm OK with it just being me and my mum. I know that we have financial struggles—for a time my mother cleans the house of the grandparents of a girl at my school. Even as a small girl, I am conscious of what this means. I visit their house one day when school is out and I'm struck green with envy. In comparison to our little flat, their home is palatial. They have a sunken bathtub! We rent rooms in a large Victorian house filled with students, my mother the oldest renter there. We share our bathroom with five other people, and later come to learn that our unstable landlord, who is also widely suspected as the murderer of my pet ducklings, has drilled a hole from his attic perch through our bathroom ceiling so that he can spy on us during bath time. I pine for our own bathroom, replete with a sunken bathtub, perhaps more than I do for a letter from my father.

Yet, amazingly, Robert, whom I've met only once for a few hours when I was three, reappears when I'm nine years old, literally knocking on the door and saying, "Hello, I'm your dad," by way of introduction. My mother, desperate to give me a stable family and perhaps desperate to believe that true love will conquer all—even a previous divorce from the man—marries him again six months after his unexpected entrance into our lives. It's hard to know what might've happened if he hadn't come back. Perhaps I would have dated older men as a way to deal with my father issues; perhaps my mother would have married someone else whom I would have resented; perhaps I would have grieved his absence but ultimately been OK. But he did come back, and they did remarry, and our lives were turned upside down. My mother comes back from their four-day honeymoon in Paris and tells me, her ten-year-old daughter, that she's just made the worst mistake of her life. Robert had gotten drunk and tried to choke her on the ferry back from France. I beg her to leave him, but she thinks maybe she should just try harder.

The incident in France is just the first of many. Within our first month as a family, Robert loses control one night, hits me, and drags me screaming by my hair up a long flight of stairs. My mother cries and begs him to stop. After that night, I keep my distance from him. Robert is an alcoholic who alternates between cold indifference and violent rage. His drinking leads to hitting, which leads to her drinking. The minister at the church where my mother has been a loyal member for years tells her she needs to "submit" as she walks around with a black eye. Our home is a battleground with me desperately trying to referee, standing on chairs and shouting at them to stop fighting, yelling at him to leave her alone, realizing that no one is listening, spending more and more time outside of the house.

Nobody notices. I feel invisible to everyone but the boys who are beginning to pay attention to me. My ideas about boys and sexuality are already distorted. By the time I take an overdose at thirteen, he's gone, she's a raging alcoholic, I'm no longer going to school, our home is up for foreclosure, and I've begun to try to take on the adult role of providing both financial and emotional support for my mother.

The suicide attempt won't change much. I'll see a psychiatrist once a week and my mother will drink herself unconscious daily. I'll continue working as a waitress and in a factory and will never return to school. I'll spend less and less time at home, eventually moving out totally, and will begin to have relationships with adult men that I'll think I'm ready for. I will live the life of an adult with the emotional maturity and decision-making skills of a teenager, which I am. The suicide attempt at thirteen will be just one of several over the next few years. I'll learn by example to deal with my feelings by using as many substances as possible to not feel anything. I discover that it's much easier to make money shoplifting and using dodgy credit cards than it is to waitress for eighteen hours a day. I'll get raped several times by the adult men that I hang out with, and treated horribly by the men I date, believing like my mother did that I just need to try harder. My doctor tells me that by the time I'm sixteen I'll be dead, in jail, pregnant, or some combination of the three. I am a flashing neon sign for danger, for abuse, for a tragic ending. A perfect conflation of risk factors, a statistic waiting to happen.

Most people assume that children sold for sex in the United States are generally poor, runaways, or homeless, and come from abusive or neglectful homes. The few statistics that exist on commercially sexually exploited and trafficked children and youth actually back up these assumptions. It is probably not surprising that research shows that over 90 percent of trafficked and exploited youth have experienced some form of abuse and neglect and that the majority are runaways or homeless. The most cited study was carried out by Richard Estes and Neil Weiner from the University of Pennsylvania and aptly titled "The Commercial Sexual Exploitation of Children in the U.S., Canada and Mexico." While Estes and Weiner stop short of quantifying how many children are actually exploited in the commercial sex industry, they do attempt to estimate how many children are likely to be at high risk based on a conflation of predicative risk factors such as sexual abuse, homelessness, and involvement in the foster care system. The authors place the number of children and youth at high risk for recruitment into the commercial sex industry at 325,000, and while there are some challenges in extrapolating "at risk" children into children who will end up sexually exploited, the Estes and Weiner study provides a sense of the magnitude of the problem and underscores the different risk factors that make children so vulnerable.

Yet to view this issue as simply one of individual risk, of dysfunctional families, of childhoods littered with abuse and neglect, ignores some larger socioeconomic causes. The vast majority of commercially sexually exploited/trafficked children and youth have experienced prior trauma and abuse, thereby making them extremely vulnerable to the seductive tactics of pimps and traffickers, but this hasn't occurred in a vacuum.

Commercially sexually exploited young women in the United States, like their foreign counterparts, often come from low socioeconomic backgrounds, making them at higher risk for recruitment than more affluent youth. When we think about children who are sexually exploited in other countries, we acknowledge the socioeconomic dynamics that contribute to their exploitation—the impact of poverty, of war, of a sex industry. Yet in our own country, the focus on individual pathologies fails to frame the issue appropriately. We ask questions such as, "Why doesn't she just leave?" and "Why would someone want to turn all their money over to a pimp?" instead of asking, "What is the impact of poverty on these children?" "How do race and class factor into the equation?" "Beyond their family backgrounds, what is the story of their neighborhoods, their communities, their cities?"

SUMMER 1997, NEW YORK CITY

I arrive at JFK Airport in the late afternoon and am picked up by my new boss, Susan, and her coworker, Val, the only two staff members at my new job, the Little Sister Project, a ministry for adult women in the sex industry. There are awkward introductions, but I'm a little too overwhelmed and excited to care. I'm in America! Everything is at once new and familiar, conditioned as I am to the idea of

the United States through television and the movies. We drive past
the World's Fair Observatory Towers in Queens and I immediately
recognize it as the alien spacecraft from *Men in Black*, which I'd just
seen a few days before! The cops look just like the ones on *NYPD
Blue*! The buildings are so tall! It's a blur of sights and sounds, big
and loud, and so many people. As the evening begins to turn dark,
Val says they have something to show me, and we pull up on a side
street in a place I learn is Brooklyn Heights. I have no idea what
to expect and Val and Susan are smug with their surprise. We walk
down the side street and turn the corner, and in front of me is the
most amazing view I've ever seen. The Empire State Building, the
World Trade Center, the Chrysler Building dominating the skyline,
a profile so familiar yet, in person, so breathtaking. The buildings
sparkle with hundreds of thousands of lights from office windows, all reflected in the East River and lighting up the sky above
it. I know immediately why they sing songs about this city, write
rhymes about it, boast about it. I fall in love at first sight. I know
that I am home.

A few hours later, after an Italian meal at the pier, we finally
make the drive across the Brooklyn Bridge into Manhattan and
head uptown via the FDR Drive. As we drive, I'm enthralled by the
buildings, the office towers, the projects, imagining all the stories
contained beneath each set of lights. When we turn off the FDR,
though, the buildings get smaller and duller. It's clear we've moved
past shiny, sparkling downtown Manhattan and have squarely
landed in the other Manhattan. Susan and Val warn me about the
neighborhood, telling me that you can't go out at night, that there's
a lot of crime and drugs. Given that I've spent most of my twenty-
two years engaged in, involved with, or participating in some form
of crime and/or drugs, this doesn't really perturb me too much. We
park at 116th Street and 1st Avenue, which I'm told is considered
Spanish Harlem, and enter a brown building with a brown door.
(It'll be some time before I learn that this doesn't actually constitute

a brownstone and for a while I tell everybody I live in one.) Susan tells me that she and Val share the second-floor apartment; I'll be living in the first-floor apartment, which also doubles as an office and a crisis shelter, though tonight there are no women staying with us.

Susan leads me into my new bedroom. The room is small and sparse. No decor to really speak of. A bed. Some linens. A dresser. A mirror. Not much else. I think of my nanny quarters in Germany. The best furnished nanny quarters on the base. My navy, white, and burgundy bedroom, courtesy of JCPenney, with my thick navy carpet and my white wicker furniture. I try not to look visibly crushed. Remind myself that this is where I'm meant to be, my calling, all that good stuff. Tell myself it'll look better in the daylight.

I'm exhausted. I've been awake for twenty-four hours and even the plain little twin bed is starting to look inviting. The three of us are crowded into my tiny room. I sit down on the bed to indicate my readiness to sleep. "Well, welcome again. We're glad to have you. Get some rest and we'll see you in the morning." Val is consistently chirpy.

Susan turns to leave, and then stops. "Oh, I almost forgot." She disappears into the dark hallway for a moment and then returns. "Here." She hands me a baseball bat and a can of Mace. I'm stunned.

"What's this for?"

"You know, just in case," she says brightly. "See you in the morning."

Once the door is closed, I sit on the bed and begin to cry. The beautiful skyline, the shiny buildings seem like a cruel facade behind which apparently lurks unforeseen danger at every corner.

I think of the folks in Germany, Americans themselves, who told me to purchase a gun. The woman from Texas at my church who, while she herself had never been to New York, "had friends" and told me, "They don't just rape you there—they gang-rape you." I think of all the warnings, the horror stories, the movie scenes, the TV shows. And I wonder what on earth have I just done.

It wouldn't take me long, probably till the next morning, when I went and explored my new neighborhood and met the Arab in the bodega, the old lady in the pet store, and the street vendor selling flavored ice, to find out that Val and Susan were just engaging in a bit of fearmongering. My little corner of Spanish Harlem doesn't feel that much different from half the neighborhoods I'd lived in most of my life, and I grow to love its rich energy. It's late summer when I arrive; the smell of warm garbage mixes with the smell of arroz con pollo and *pernil* from the restaurants and the *chimichurri* trucks that litter the neighborhood. Teenagers out of school crowd corners and babies and mothers sit out late on stoops, taking advantage of the evening's cooler air, and old and young men park lawn chairs in the middle of the sidewalks to play dominoes and chess. The daily chatter in Spanish, English, and mostly Nuyorican is punctuated by the soundtrack of salsa and merengue pounding from open windows and hip-hop blaring from car radios. The Mace and the bat remain stuffed in a drawer and I revel in the fact that, with my almost black hair and olive skin, for the first time in my life, I look like everyone around me.

Despite the relative ease that I feel wandering around, even at night, in my newfound community, it's clear that this is definitely not Europe. The crime, the poverty, the violence are worse. The population of all of England is around fifty million; New York City alone is home to eight million people. I'd seen, and experienced, my fair share of violence, but the weapon of choice in England, due to our restrictive gun laws, was a knife or a broken bottle, generally with the sole intent to maim the person's face. Even most of the police in England carried only nightsticks. In America, the prevalence of guns, both civilian and law enforcement, upped the ante. The week I arrive in New York, Abner Louima is attacked and brutalized by members of the New York City Police Department. A couple of months later a thirteen-year-old girl shoots a cabdriver in the face, relaunching the debates about super-predators and kids that kill. My natural and often unwise sense of invincibility is shaken a little as I read story after story in the news, see makeshift memorials with votive candles on corners throughout my neighborhood, and hear sirens so frequently that they begin to be just background noise.

Even the drug culture is different in America. I had had firsthand experience with crack cocaine, having been introduced to it by my "boyfriend." Yet crack in Europe in the early nineties was still perceived as just another drug, like speed or Ecstasy. Not only hadn't it reached epidemic status in Europe, in the early nineties crack was still considered something of a novelty, just a quicker way to do coke, yet I'd learned quickly that the addictive properties of crack were much more potent than anything else I'd ever tried. When I come to New York in 1997, it's at the end of the crack era, although the effects are still visible in the city, in the hollowed-out addicts striding up the block with the unmistakable gait of someone on a mission, in the disrepair of many communities, in the stories of the girls that I am meeting. I find that there is a common belief from people asking about my work, that sexually exploited girls *must* be drug addicted, and it is the addiction that fuels the exploitation. Yet even in the initial years, and in over a decade that has followed, I've found very few girls who are addicted to "hard" drugs and for whom the addiction came prior to the exploitation. To see not just community members but sometimes family members so strung out, so desperate, so scorned does not induce many young people to try a drug with such visibly horrifying effects, and with such a strong stigma attached. Girls weren't drug addicted, they were love addicted, and that, I'll learn, is far harder to treat.

As I do counseling and outreach in Rikers, on the streets, and in homeless shelters for the missionary project, I realize that the girls and young women in their early to late teens that I'm working with are indeed children of the crack era. Born in 1984, 1981, 1980, these are the children who've come of age throughout the 1980s and early 1990s as the crack hurricane tore through already struggling communities, ravaged mothers and their families, and left countless orphaned—literally and emotionally—children in its wake. These are the children, whether or not their parents were actually substance abusers, who watched their families rip apart, their neighborhoods disintegrate, who stepped over crack vials on the way to school, mourned the violent death of a brother, a cousin, a friend.

I realize, too, how much the crack epidemic disproportionately affected communities of color. One study on the effects of crack notes, "Between 1984 and 1994, the homicide rate for black males aged fourteen to seventeen more than doubled, and the homicide rate for black males aged eighteen to twenty-four increased nearly as much. During this period, the black community also experienced an increase in fetal death rates, low-birth-weight babies, weapons arrests, and the number of children in foster care." During this period, the AIDS crisis also began to hit communities. Children were left orphaned by a disease that no one understood and everyone feared. Children who were infected were often not adopted or taken in by extended family members, due to the pervasive stigma about how HIV was contracted, and they too began to flood the foster care system.

The impact of the crack epidemic and initial AIDS surge on family structures in New York City cannot be overestimated. In 1984, there were 16,230 children in foster care in New York City; by 1992, that number had swelled to over 49,000, overwhelming the already fractured system. These children were primarily black and Latino.

I think about my own parents' substance abuse and the devastating impact that it had on me, and then I listen to girls talk about relative after relative whose lives had been turned upside down. In the thirteen years that have passed since I first began to meet with sexually exploited girls, the ripple effects, not just in New York, but in urban areas throughout the country, still have a far-reaching impact that cannot be measured in decreased crime stats or fewer vials on the street. The streets have gotten cleaner and safer and New York is rated one of the safest big cities in America. The murder rate in 2007 is at 494, down from a high of 2,245 in 1990. Spanish Harlem is now called, unbelievably, SpaHa, and the South Bronx is SoBro, at least in the real estate pages of the *New York Times*. Brooklyn has become the borough of choice for hipsters and developers. In Harlem, 125th Street boasts two Starbucks, an H&M, and a Marshalls. Luxury condos are everywhere, there's a brand-new stadium for the Yankees, and yet there are still two New Yorks. Just as the gutted, abandoned buildings dotted throughout certain neighborhoods testify to the years when tourists were afraid to visit, and point to the poverty that still dominates many communities, the multigenerational impact of the crack epidemic continues to reverberate in the lives of abandoned and traumatized children.

While the crack epidemic has economically damaged many communities, the larger social and governmental policy decisions have been far more destructive. Of course many children who grow up in challenging economic situations thrive, but the reality is that far too many don't, and too many children's futures can be determined by zip code. Children in poor neighborhoods frequently receive a substandard education, are often exposed to lead paint in poorly constructed buildings, have higher rates of asthma, and live in communities where there are little to no recreational or green spaces and where entire neighborhoods have been abandoned and forgotten by those in power. Children born into poverty are at risk for many things, including being recruited into the commercial sex industry.

Nationally, over thirteen million children live below the poverty line. Over half a million children in New York City live in poverty, concentrated in some of the most economically depressed communities, where most of the tracks, unsurprisingly, are located: Hunts Point in the Bronx, East New York in Brooklyn, and Far Rockaway in Queens. Raising children, particularly girls, in areas where there's an existing sex industry, where johns are still driving around in the early mornings as children go to school, where pimps buy gifts for preteen girls with the intention of grooming and priming them, can be a constant struggle between the home that you try to create and the world outside your door.

For children separated from their families, the risk for commercial sexual exploitation increases. There are currently over 15,000 children in the foster care system in New York City, and a 2007 study shows that 75 percent of sexually exploited and trafficked children in NYC were in foster care at some point in their lives. When children who have witnessed or experienced abuse and neglect are removed from their families, they often bounce from placement to placement, perhaps experiencing fresh abuse from a new family. When you grow up three blocks away from a track, go to school in overcrowded, underresourced classrooms, and see violence in your community, it's hard to feel as though you have other options.

FALL 1989, ENGLAND

The van leaves at 5 a.m. to get us to the Estée Lauder factory for our 7 a.m. shift. It's still dark outside and it's too early for me to engage in the chatter of the other girls in the van. I sit smoking and staring out the window thinking how much I hate this job. Still, it's something, and it's helping pay the bills at home, stave off the foreclosure, and keep me stocked in cigarettes and weed, and those are the critical things right now. The social workers have stopped coming to visit, the school has stopped calling. No one seems to notice or care that I'm not in school or that I'm working full-time at fourteen. I'm working through the temp agency as a seventeen-year-old named Rose Johnson, after my great-aunt; the job before that was as Bailey Johnson, after the singer Pearl Bailey; the next place I think I'll be Cyd Johnson after Cyd Charisse. I can work for only a few months at each place before they start catching on that the National

Insurance number I gave them doesn't match with my name, which is also made up, and begin to ask too many questions for which I don't have any answers. I'm a few years off from being able to work legally so I've been bouncing from temp agency to temp agency, having figured out that they'll pay you through their own books for the first two months while they're waiting for your National Insurance card, which in my case will never arrive. One temp agency won't pay me for a month so I spend four weeks walking five miles one way, doing a twelve-hour shift, and walking five miles back.

Most of the girls that I hang out with are "Estée Lauder girls." It's a badge of honor to work at Estée Lauder as it's considered one of the more posh factories. It's also a lifer factory, with mostly women and a few men who have been there for fifteen, twenty years. In an industrial city like Portsmouth with unemployment rates, school drop-out rates, teenage pregnancy rates, and crime rates that are all higher than the national average, getting a secure job is a victory. The lifers look down on those of us who are temps, treating us with disdain. Girls who show real respect for the work fare better. I, on the other hand, make no secret of the fact that I believe I can do more than this. The women there make me sad. They all look so much older than they are, and whatever dreams they might have had have been drained out of them by the monotony of sitting next to a conveyor belt for years. The older women look at me with a mixture of scorn and regret.

I'm under no illusions, though, that I'll ever get hired on permanently. I'm forever in trouble. Talking too much. Getting up and leaving the line. Not being quick enough. I loathe the sit-down jobs that require real dexterity. I am, as my grandmother says, cack-handed, and therefore screwing the cap on hundreds of bottles of Red Hot nail polish in twenty minutes is beyond me. I prefer the end of the line, boxing and packing, loading up the pallets, working up a sweat. There I can move around and talk freely. The line manager calls me "Darky," as in "Darky, get this box," or "Tell the darky that she has lunch break now." I know I'd have a good case were I to sue them for racial discrimination, but I'm already working illegally and don't want to rock the boat. So I save my indignation and spend my shifts daydreaming about ways to get out.

Other than the "free" samples that somehow wind up in my pocket at the end of the day, and the factory discount store where I stock up on so much Beautiful and Youth Dew that I gift everyone I know with it for three Christmases in a row, I really hate Estée Lauder. I hate the potpourri factory next, although there I'm able to pick up some Christmas shoplifting orders; and then hate the aircraft parts factory; the IBM factory, where we have to wear coverups that look like biohazard suits; the tampon factory, where no one ever wants to admit they work; and the Johnson & Johnson factory, where I can never shake the smell of baby shampoo from my skin. As the months pass, I see myself becoming one of the women that I pity. Getting up, going to an awful, mind-numbing job, coming home, voluntarily numbing my mind with weed and alcohol, going to sleep, doing it all over again the next day.

I cannot share my friends' enthusiasm for this life, no matter how hard I try. I feel destined for something more, although having dropped out of school, I'm aware that my options are limited. The pressure to have a baby, at fourteen, already feels intense. The desire to create a family, to have someone who will love me, is overwhelming at times. All of my friends are older than me, although still mostly teenagers, and I'm one of the few that hasn't already had at least one child. Having a baby, getting a council flat, working and living and dying here, feels like the most obtainable goal.

When someone suggests that I should try modeling, I jump at the chance. I trek up to London to visit agencies and manage to get signed. All the other girls have their pushy stage mothers with them. I'm always alone and have a hard time being pushy, but still I manage to get a little work for some teen magazines that gives me a level of celebrity status in our town, and also gets me jumped by several groups of jealous girls. I will myself to grow the requisite five additional inches needed to sign with a better agency but I stay short. Still, I see modeling as my only ticket out of a town that can offer me nothing but the hopeless future I see in everyone around me. When photographers ask me to pose more "seductively," to slip my shirt off, to do some "artistic" nude shots for a calendar that I know will end up on some car mechanic's garage wall, I comply. Anything that'll get me out. Anything that will make me feel less invisible.

While there are clear systemic and social issues that leave children vulnerable, the recognition of this reality presents a constant challenge in advocating for exploited girls. In describing the poverty and the abuse that girls experience prior to their commercial sexual exploitation and trafficking, the response too often is that these girls inevitably aren't really going to have great lives anyway. I remember arguing fiercely one day with a lawyer who was representing a thirteen-year-old who'd been charged with a serious crime that her thirty-five-year-old "boyfriend" had committed. I wanted him to fight for her to be charged as a juvenile so that her record would eventually be sealed. Snorting with laughter, he said, "It's not as if she's going to be a brain surgeon, so does it really matter?" It appears that if you're already considered damaged goods, or doomed to a life of poverty, then being further victimized is not quite as bad.

For a time, one of the most widely referenced articles on commercial sexual exploitation in the United States was a 2003 *Newsweek* cover story titled "This Could Be Your Kid." The article's sensational claims of suburban "teen prostitutes" and otherwise supposedly normal girls who simply sold sex for designer clothes dismissed the real issues of commercial sexual exploitation, such as race, poverty, homelessness, abuse, ineffective city systems, and a public policy that blames the victims. The public reaction to this article, motivated by fear of so-called inner-city issues affecting their own children, was starkly portrayed by a "counselor" who was quoted in the article as saying, "People say, 'We're not from the ghetto.' The shame the parents feel is incredible." In follow-up media on this article, the unsubstantiated claim was made that 30 percent of prostituted youth were from middle- or upper-class backgrounds. This "fact" completely ignored the other 70 percent of youth from low-income backgrounds. It was as if this 70 percent didn't matter as much because their abuse was inevitable anyway.

All of this is not to say that only socioeconomically disadvantaged children are at risk. While there aren't clear national statistics on the socioeconomic backgrounds of children who are commercially sexually exploited, we do know that there are children who are recruited into the sex industry who don't fit the commonly understood profile of an "at-risk" child. These are children from middle-class backgrounds, children who haven't suffered extreme trauma or abuse, children who have been sheltered and cared for. Commercial sexual exploitation can happen to any young person. Every parent should be able to have a conversation with their child about the sex industry and how children are recruited. The Internet has opened up a whole world of information to children and yet it has also brought the threat of predatory strangers right into our homes. Global accessibility means that a teenager in Ohio can connect online with a teenager in Liverpool, yet it also means that a thirty-year-old man who trolls the chat rooms looking for children can instantly connect with a thirteen-year-old in his own community. Exploiters are utilizing the Internet more and more to search for vulnerable children and adolescents who can be used for both sexual and commercial purposes.

Children are vulnerable just by virtue of being children. Getting frustrated with your parents, thinking you're invincible, engaging in risky behavior, being interested in relationships, particularly with older men, and being enamored with money and consumer goods are all part of most American adolescents' experiences. In the heady mix of hormones, wanting to belong, confusing messages about love and sex, and a desire to be independent, it's easy to lure an otherwise well-adjusted fourteen-year-old girl into a meeting, into a car, into a bed. Pimps understand child psychology and adolescent development well enough to know the dynamics at play and can skillfully manipulate most children, regardless of socioeconomic background, prior abuse, or parenting, into a situation where they can be forced or coerced into being sold for sex.

Yet it may take longer to manipulate the well-adjusted fourteen-year-old, and in the process she'll be missed pretty quickly by her parents, who'll notify the police, who may put out an Amber Alert. There might be a story on the eleven-o'clock news about her disappearance, and once she's found, the perpetrator is likely to be prosecuted to the fullest extent of the law. But if you shift some of the variables in the case—make the child a child of color, a runaway, a child in the foster care system, a child no one's really going to miss, a child so starved of attention and affection that anything you provide will be welcomed, a child who'll be seen as a willing participant in her own exploitation—the story changes dramatically. There's no Amber Alert, no manhunt, no breaking news story, no *Nancy Grace* coverage, no police investigation, no prosecution. It's just another "teen prostitute," another one of the nameless, faceless, ignored, already damaged 70 percent.

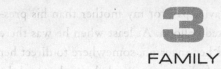

3

FAMILY

Rock-a-bye, baby, in the treetop,
When the wind blows, the cradle will rock;
When the bough breaks, the cradle will fall,
And down will come baby, cradle and all.

—*Traditional*

My mother sits on the big brown couch in our dark brown living room, staring straight ahead. When she'd first decorated, she'd been aiming for a Victorian theme, although now her mood, combined with the dark colors and heavy wooden furniture, just seems funereal. An empty bottle of wine sits on the table; if I had to guess, I'd say there were two more freshly finished empties stashed in the oven. My mother thinks I don't know about her hiding places, but it's a little difficult to ignore fourteen bottles of wine tumbling out when you're trying to cook some dinner, or the twelve cans of beer that appear mysteriously in place of the cleaning supplies under the kitchen sink. In recent weeks, or in the three weeks since Robert left, my mother's drinking has either dramatically escalated, or she's taken less pains to hide it; probably a little of both. She's trancelike most of the time, comatose sometimes. The violent-drunk stage won't come till later. I tiptoe around her and the huge elephant in the room that is her pain. At thirteen, I'm a little perplexed as to why she's so devastated. I'd thought she'd be relieved when he left. I am. I couldn't wait for him to go, and have been praying fervently at night for him to be gone, in a variety of ways, not all of them appropriate for prayer. Yet now that he's physically out of the house, his

absence seems to cast a heavier pall for my mother than his presence did. She's like a deflated balloon. At least when he was there
she had something to focus her anger on, somewhere to direct her
sadness. Now it seems these feelings are overwhelming her, and the
only place to unload them is on me. I feel like I'm drowning in her
grief. I try to leave the room before she notices me there.

"Where do you think he is now?"

I've got a pretty good guess, at a pub, but I just shrug and look
clueless.

She pats the seat next to her, so I reluctantly sit down.

"Do you think he's seeing someone else?"

Um, yeah, probably. "I dunno, Mum. Prob'ly not."

"I need to know. It'll help me feel like it's really over." If I was
older and wiser, I'd know that this is bullshit. But at thirteen, it
sounds logical.

"Can you go look for him? I need to ask him something."

This, however, does not sound logical. This sounds like a bad
idea. He'll be drunk. He's always drunk. If you could get a straight
and sober answer out of him, any answer, really, he'd probably still
be here and she'd be angry, uptight, sad, but a little less . . . still. It's
the stillness that's really bothering me. I'd prefer her to be throwing
shit, but all she does is sit, quietly, and drink. I did have plans for this
Christmas Eve, though: buy a bottle of Thunderbird, drink, walk
up and down Albert Road; linger outside the pubs (which I look old
enough to get into but, inconveniently, my best friend, Stephanie,
despite being three years older than me, doesn't); catch the attention
of some guys, probably older, probably coming out of a pub; flirt
with said guys; go to the kebab shop; eat; meet up with my sometime boyfriend, Ras, after his waiter shift; walk home; make out on
the couch; send Ras home. Not that much different from what happens on a regular Saturday night, really, but still, maybe something
cool will happen because it's Christmas Eve. Going on a mission for
my mother will probably screw up all these plans.

She's latched on to the idea, though, and keeps pestering me, or at least keeps looking pathetic and depressed until I agree. I decide to say, "I'm going to look for him," but then don't do it and stick to my regularly scheduled plans. Win-win.

Stephanie and I set off, Thunderbird drunk, up and down Albert Road. Christmas Eve, next to New Year's Eve, is the busiest night of the year. It's not as much fun as on a Saturday night. The streets are too crowded, the men are too drunk. We're about to walk into the Royal Albert when I walk straight into Robert. Not surprisingly, he's drunk; somewhat surprisingly, he's got a woman hanging on his arm with whom he's clearly engaged in some intimate conversation. Crap. I didn't really want to find him, didn't really want to be involved in this mess. He's too drunk to be embarrassed, although his girlfriend isn't. It gets a little awkward when he introduces me as his daughter but other than that, it's clear that he could not care less. To be fair, I don't care that much about him either. What I do care about and what I worry about the whole way home is how on earth I'm supposed to tell my mother that her husband has found himself someone else while she sits home and drinks and cries.

It doesn't go well.

The following day's Christmas dinner won't be eaten. It was shoplifted, as were most of the presents, which will be given a cursory glance then ignored. I knew we didn't have any money, that my stepfather had left us "high and dry," as my grandmother liked to say, so I'd resolved to bring some Christmas cheer of my own and engaged in my first of many shoplifting sprees to supply the need. It doesn't really matter, though. Nothing really lifts the mood at home, nothing really breaks the stillness except the sound of the liquor pouring into the glass.

The gloom of this Christmas will be replayed for several years. Me and my mother sitting quietly on the dark brown couch. She: sunk deep in depression; me: sinking right along with her. By the next year, I'll do whatever I can to not be at home for long. I'll try to stay at a boyfriend's, spend the day with his loud and raucous family, craving to feel included in someone else's home. People who know about my situation will feel sorry for me and will invite me over. I'll feel awkward but grateful and will always do the dishes, play with the kids, try to make myself a useful and thoughtful guest. Later, my mother will meet and marry a new man. It's probably not fun to have your teenage daughter around your new spouse and I'll be excluded from these Christmases. I won't want to spend them with her anyway but somehow I'll still feel jealous. Her happy holidays seem to be spent with someone else; on her sad ones, I'm expected to be there.

The silence of those Christmases, the sense that our family was irreparably broken, will stay with me. I grow to dread Christmas, and all that the holiday season represents. As I get older, I adopt my mother's trick of getting so drunk throughout the day that with any luck I would be semiconscious or dead asleep for the majority of the day and night, waking up only on Boxing Day. One year, when I'm living alone in a studio in Germany, I buy enough weed, alcohol, and cigarettes to last me three days, and proceed to get as wasted as I can so that I literally have no memory of the holiday, except for the buying of said substances and the recovery period several days later.

My mother eventually gets sober and much later I finally do, and we struggle as adults to work on our fractured relationship. Yet for many years, the holidays, Christmas, and even my birthday are just an inconvenient reminder of my family, my lack of family, a reminder of the type of family I always wanted. I come to love Thanksgiving, as it's not a holiday that England celebrates and so there are no painful childhood memories associated with it. I can create my own Thanksgiving memories and over time I'll figure out how to tolerate, if not embrace, Christmas without getting totally trashed. Coming to terms with my family, forgiving, and letting go take a little bit longer.

Growing up I believed that everyone had a pain quota, i.e., you could experience only a certain amount of pain and tragedy in your life before that quota was filled. In general, this meant suffering early in life was rewarded by a relatively pain-free and peaceful existence as an adult and enjoying a trouble-free childhood and adolescence meant that you were likely to get your pain quota later in life. As I looked at girls at my school whose lives seemed so neat, so foreign, so perfect, I comforted myself with the knowledge that my approved pain limit would soon be reached and that they'd experience their drama later. It seemed only fair and logical that everyone was meted out a level of hardship; some people's pain just came earlier in life, but I was confident that eventually it would come to an end.

When I first moved to the Bronx, a friend told me of a woman who lived nearby who had buried all five of her children. Two of her sons had perished in freak accidents in the same elevator shaft, never properly repaired, several years apart. A daughter had been murdered by a boyfriend, another son had died in a motorcycle accident, her last daughter had died of a drug overdose. I was stunned. I understood that burying a child had to be one of the most painful experiences in life, but burying five, one after the other, each time thinking your heart couldn't break anymore? It was so unfathomable; it seemed like an urban legend. How could one person possibly suffer that much? There was no moral to be learned, no great blessing at the end of it. She wasn't a bad person; there was no cosmic karma, just a string of mindless tragedies that seemed to directly contradict the biblical edict that the Lord wouldn't give you more than you could bear. My theory was shot to pieces. If there was a quota for pain and suffering, someone had forgotten to tell a grieving mother in the Bronx.

My pain-quota theory didn't work out too well either with

the young girls I was meeting in New York. There were moments where the litany of pain, abusive adults, and just downright awful luck seemed almost unbelievable. "So, you were there when your father stabbed your mother, and then you went to live with your aunt, but she was getting high and she fell asleep smoking and the apartment caught on fire, so then you went into the system and the brother in your first foster family abused you and then you ran away and the first night you were on the street you met a man, who then later became your pimp?"

As I heard more and more accounts like these, I learned that these weren't fantastical tales but the norm for girls whose entire lives had been punctuated with crisis, trauma, and abuse. Statistics, presented without the faces, the stories, the tears, couldn't even begin to measure the severity or frequency of the trauma these girls were experiencing. Girls who'd been sexually abused by every male in their family, girls who were orphaned by their parent's murder/suicide/death from AIDS who would then be abused in the system, girls who had only known the touch of an adult to be sexual or violent, girls for whom the concept of love, family, care, bore little resemblance to most people's definitions. Girls who had long ago exceeded whatever could be considered a reasonable quota for pain.

While my story was similar in some respects—violence, absent father, substance-abusing mother—I realized quickly that I'd been relatively lucky. For most of my early years, I had a mother who loved me immensely, who read to me every night, cuddled me a lot, and even baked cookies on occasion. It's just that for a period of years, the wrong men, alcohol, depression, and a few other setbacks impaired her ability to give me that love (or to bake, for that matter). However, those formative years helped lay a foundation and a memory of nurturing that would be instrumental in my own recovery process. Some of the girls I was meeting had never experienced that sense of safety or love. Ever. There were no good memories, no modeling of safe love, no time in their short lives that hadn't been chaotic, drama-filled, or painful. For other girls those memories of family and love were fleeting: Mommy brushing their hair before she started getting high, going to the park with Daddy before he got shot. Snapshots of happy times when they were either too young to understand what was really happening or in the days before some traumatic incident caused their world to fall apart. In listening to their stories, it was so clear how much the adults around them had failed them, how the family structures had cracked under the weight of a hundred external pressures, how the people that should've been the safest were often the ones who caused the most pain of all.

It's Christmas Eve and the GEMS drop-in center is relatively quiet. We've had our big party the day before and now there's just me and a couple of staff members working and a handful of girls hanging out and chatting. Sarah wanders into my office. "Raaaachel, Raaaachel . . ." The girls always seem compelled to call my name several times even if I'm right in front of them, just to make sure I'm listening. Although Sarah's often whiny, the way she's dragging out the syllables of my name sounds a little more whiny than usual. "Raaaachel, can you make my Christmas wish come true?" She looks at me expectantly, all big eyes and need.

I sigh, anticipating the request—iPod, cell phone, clothes, five dollars to get Chinese food—and mentally preparing my response, no to all of the above except for Chinese food and even then I wanted a receipt. It seemed like every day I'd leave the house with twenty dollars and come home with two and have purchased only a cup of tea and a bagel. I was constantly trying to figure out if you could somehow claim the daily random expenses of sixty teenage girls on your taxes. "Huh?" Sarah says expectantly.

"I don't know." I'd learned never to agree to anything without first knowing exactly when, where, how much. "What is it, hon?"

"Can you make me and my mom get along for Christmas?"

Just like that. A punch to the gut. All of a sudden I feel sad, and a little guilty for assuming that her wish would involve some material item. She half smiles, showing me that she knows I can't make this happen, but clearly wishing, wondering if maybe I could.

"I'm sorry, honey." I give her a hug. I've learned the hard way not to make promises about girls' families, not to build up unrealistic expectations. It's better to teach them how to be resilient, how to create a family from the people around them who are able to love them in a healthy way. Girls get their hearts broken more times by their families than by any guy, returning to the scene of their childhood abuse again and again, each time fresh disappointment opening up the old wounds. Constantly surprised by behavior they've seen all their lives.

I talk to her about the pressure of the holidays, how it's a really tough time but it's important to remember it's just one day, really, that's all it is. Given my own history with the holidays, I feel a little full of shit. I get it. It sucks to feel that everyone in the free world is enjoying the warmth of family while you're stuck with an alcoholic mother/an abusive father/alone in a group home/fill in the blank. The pressure to feel "normal," to buy into the media depictions of happy families around a yuletide log are stressful for most people who didn't grow up in Mayberry, but for girls for whom the concept of family is so distorted with abuse, neglect, and abandonment, this pressure can be lethal. The number of girls at GEMS who attempt suicide increases in the danger zone between Thanksgiving and Christmas. Sarah was recently one of them. I ask her about her plans and try to point out some minor bright points.

She interrupts me to ask, very seriously, "Why do you guys care when I'm stressed out?" *Stressed out* for Sarah is a euphemism for *Why do you care when I want to hurt myself?* Three weeks earlier, she had sent her counselor an e-mail in the middle of the night that said good-bye and that she'd realized that death was the final answer. The e-mail, not seen till the next morning, created a panic in the office as we didn't have her current address (most likely a hotel), and entailed three days of working with the cops to try to track her down. Given the frequency with which sexually exploited girls are kidnapped, I'd learned a long time ago that it's far harder to track down someone's Internet service provider address or trace someone's cell phone coordinates to an exact location than it looks on *Law & Order: Special Victims Unit*. However, we'd managed to finally determine her location and ascertain that she was probably still alive. Yet everyone involved, including the two detectives who worked diligently to find her, breathed a collective sigh of relief when Sarah strolled into the office several days later, seemingly having forgotten about her brush with death and looking genuinely perplexed as to why we were all making such a fuss. I try to explain all the reasons that we care whether she lives or dies, as that's what she's really asking. Because she deserves caring about, because we love her, because we want her to be safe and at peace. She twirls a piece of hair in her fingers and ponders this for a minute.

"It's just no one ever cared before."

Ah, the one-two punch, a fatal combination, especially on Christmas Eve. My head hurts.

I begin to try to address all the different things that are wrapped up in this statement, but Sarah's already thinking about something else. "Can I get a dollar for some soda, huh? Pleaaase." I give her two dollars, grateful for the reprieve. Finally a request that I can actually fulfill.

Five minutes later, Monica comes into my office to show me some poems she's written the night before. One she's modeled after the poem at the beginning of Antwone Fisher's memoir, *Finding Fish*, understandably a popular book with the girls given the author's history in the foster care system. Monica's poem reads in part:

You gave me a mother addicted to drugs
And didn't say, when I grow I must know how to love and be
  loved
You gave me sisters that keep their separate ways
You gave me a brother, who tries to rape me in my childhood
  days
You gave me no clear vision to see my way through strife
You gave me a father who couldn't guide me through life

I have to pause for a little while before I look up. Fuck, it's Christmas Eve. I came in only to answer some e-mails. Her poem, really a plaintive prayer to God, has no response. I've asked the same questions of God myself, about Monica, about Sarah, about the perpetual pain in the lives of the girls we serve. I tell her it's a great poem, fantastic, she's a great writer. I ask her if she wants to talk about what she's written; she shakes her head no, says she feels better having written it. I know that the holiday is weighing heavy on her, on all the girls, the fa-la-la-la-la of it all, the added reminder, if any were needed, that you don't feel normal. A reminder that in the family lottery drawing, you drew a short straw and there are no do-overs.

During the eighties, sociologists and clinicians identified the many ways in which gang culture replicated the family unit for children who found their support systems in the street. In the world of domestically trafficked girls, the same is true. The desire for a family is so strong and so overpowering for most children that it doesn't take much to create that illusion. Pimps play upon this desire by creating a pseudo–family structure of girls who are your "wives-in-law" headed up by a man you call Daddy. The lessons that girls have been taught, implicitly and explicitly, about family and relationship dynamics are all fuel for the exploiters' fire. The greater their need for attention and love, the easier it is to recruit them. The more unhealthy the patterns they've learned, the less a pimp needs to break them down, the less he needs to teach them. Growing up with an alcoholic or drug-addicted parent sets the stage for caretaking and codependency patterns that are helpful in making girls feel responsible for taking care of their pimp. Violence in the home trains children to believe that abuse and aggression are normal expressions of love. Abandonment and neglect can create all types of attachment disorders that can be used to keep girls from ever leaving their exploiters. For girls who've had nonexistent, fractured, or downright abusive relationships with their fathers or father figures, it's an easy draw. "My daddy," girls say with pride as they talk about the man who controls them.

I'm sitting in the office one evening talking to Tiana, a soft-spoken, guarded fifteen-year-old with long black hair and a slow smile. She's been referred to GEMS by her cousin, Maria, who's also been exploited. Maria is on the other side of it now, slowly healing and trying to find some normalcy. Tiana's still very much in the mix of things, currently living with her pimp, so I was surprised that she had come in to attend a couple of groups. I already know a lot about her family history from Maria and it's horrific. The level of violence that she's been exposed to and experienced would equal that of a child in a war zone. Witnessing her mother's murder at the age of six was just the beginning for Tiana. She was then sent to live with her aunt, Maria's mother, and like Maria she has fared badly. Her aunt's "care" is visible through curling iron burns and permanent scars from extension cords. It's not surprising either one of these cousins ran away.

"Maria's trippin. She worry too much. I'm good, I'm straight." Tiana's working overtime to convince me that she doesn't need any help. "My daddy takes good care of us." She gestures to her Baby Phat jacket and jeans as proof.

"How many girls are there?" I ask.

"There's five of us; all the other girls are older. I'm the baby."

"What's your daddy's name, hon?" I'm curious if I know anyone else who lives there.

She hesitates, thinking she probably shouldn't tell me, but unable to contain herself she proudly says, "Dollars."

I know him, or at least know of him. Dollars is the ex-pimp of Melissa, the first girl I'd worked with, the girl he beat unconscious on a regular basis. It's been about eight years since I last saw Melissa and yet he's still out there, preying on another vulnerable little girl. I figure he must be in his mid- to late forties by now. He'd recruited Melissa when she was fourteen; Tiana he'd gotten at fifteen.

"He can be a pretty violent guy, sweetie." This is an understatement.

"I know," she says, launching into a long and complicated story that ends with another girl being dragged out of the house naked and being run over several times by his moving SUV. "She's OK now, though." Probably seeing the concern on my face she says, "She shouldn't have been talking back." She looks to me to agree with this.

"Are you worried that something like that might happen to you?"

She shrugs. "Kind of."

"So have you thought about other options?" In fairness, she knows and I know that her options are limited and that there are no family members to take her. Like Maria, she'd have to go to a group home.

"But I like it there. We have a house and everything. And a dog. And we get to sit and eat dinner together every night. Like a family. It's nice. That's the best part."

It's hard to explain to Tiana that her feelings about this aren't indicative of what a great guy her "daddy" is but rather an indictment against how awful all the adults in her life have been. Imagine, I tell Tiana, that you've never seen a cow, never even seen a picture of one or had one described to you, and someone tells you that a horse is a cow. Of course you'll believe them. If you haven't had proper love and care, then a substitute will feel like the real thing, because you've got nothing to compare it to. For Tiana, whose entire fifteen years on the earth have been filled with physical violence, neglect, and horrific abuse, this analogy doesn't really make sense. Her "daddy" is the first person who's shown her any type of kindness, who's modeled what a "real" family looks like—even though after dinner he takes her and the other girls out and sells them on the street. Still, however distorted a facsimile of a loving family, it is as close as she's come, and I can see her swell with pride even as she says the word *family* out loud.

Despite the prevalent and often extreme levels of abuse and neglect, the girls literally crave a real relationship with their families, particularly their mothers. Even in the healthiest of families, conflict between adolescent daughters and their mothers is common. Navigating this intense relationship is a minefield of rolled eyes, reminders of lost youth on the one side, wanting to be nothing like her on the other—and that's in the good relationships. Young girls often idolize their mothers until one day they begin to resent them. They start seeing characteristics about them that disappoint them or embarrass them. They reject the choices their mothers have made and yet seem predestined to repeat many of the same mistakes. As a girl you reserve your harshest judgment for your mother; as a woman you see yourself, for better or for worse, in your daughter and you're alternately frightened and envious. Yet your mother is the one person who is "supposed" to love you and protect you, no matter what. For many sexually exploited girls, this relationship has been the one that has caused the most pain and left the deepest scars. It took me a long time to understand how impacted I'd been not just by my biological father's abandonment and my two stepfathers' abuse but by my mother and how difficult it had been to always come second in her life to a man, to a bottle.

WINTER 1990, ENGLAND

Like any Saturday night, the routine is pub first, club later. Tonight though, I'm not sure if I want to go out all night so after a few pints at the pub I come home. My mother and her boyfriend have broken up again for the eight millionth time this month and she'd been upset, and of course drinking, when I'd left earlier. I want to at least check on her. I know what she's capable of. My mother, however, is annoyed to see me come home at 11 p.m. and even more annoyed by the idea that I might stay home all night. "You should go out, you'll have fun. Go to Ritzy's." My mother knows that at fourteen I shouldn't be able to get into the nightclubs but given that I smoke weed, sniff speed, and pop Ecstasy tabs at home in front of her, we're long past the point where she's concerned about this. Some nights, embarrassingly for me, we bump into each other at the same clubs. My friends think she's cool. I don't.

"Nah, I'm OK. I'd rather watch telly tonight. It's just the same old people out every week anyway."

The truth is that I'm worried about her. She's drunk and slurring, but with the odd calmness that I've grown to associate with impending trouble. We debate back and forth as she insists that I go out. It's not exactly going to be a barrel of laughs sitting around the house with her, so eventually I agree. "You're fine though, right? Not gonna do anything?"

"I'm perfectly fine. I'm just going to go to bed soon anyway." I think she'll probably drunk-dial her boyfriend/ex-boyfriend a few times, but he's used to it by now. I wouldn't be surprised if they're back together by the time I come home. I give her a kiss and tell her to be safe. I'm used to the parental role now. It comes naturally.

By 4 a.m., I'm back home again. Tired from a night of dancing and drinking at Ritzy's. Happy because David Shaw, my latest crush, has finally paid attention to me and has come home with me for a cup of tea and a make-out session. The house is dark and quiet when we come in. Whispering and tipsy, we tiptoe into the kitchen and kiss for a few minutes in the dark until I put the kettle on for the obligatory cuppa. David puts the light on.

"What's this?" he asks, and I turn to see him picking up a piece of paper from the table. *I'm sorry, I just can't . . .* I snatch the note away and read the rest as my stomach drops and my hands go cold. "Fuck."

I drop the note and run upstairs to her bedroom, which is empty, check the bathroom, and my room. All empty. I have no idea where she is but I'm hoping that someone found her.

When I come back down to the kitchen, David's still there looking awkward. "It's OK. You can leave." I know he hadn't bargained for walking into a family suicide attempt. To his credit, he stays and we sit in the kitchen drinking tea while I try to call anyone who might know what has actually happened to my mother, if she's alive or dead. By daybreak, her boyfriend shows up and tells me that he'd come over to check on her and found her semiconscious. He was the one who called the ambulance.

He tells me they've pumped her stomach and that she's going to be all right. He tells me she took the overdose around 10 p.m. It's easy to do the math. While I was sitting on the couch trying to persuade her to let me stay home, the tablets were already beginning to course through her bloodstream. No wonder she'd been so adamant that I go out and have a good time. She wanted me gone so she could sit down and die. I look at David and think about what that would've meant had she succeeded. As she was dying, I would have been out dancing. I had almost been too busy kissing him to see her suicide note.

While my mother survived that episode and several other suicide attempts over the years, the impact of her virtual and often literal abandonment leaves me fearful and hypervigilant. Always looking out and waiting for signs that someone, anyone I care about, is leaving. Most of the girls I meet through GEMS over the years share some variation on this theme. Some have lost their mothers to AIDS, to overdoses either intentional or accidental, to murder, to illness brought on by drug addiction, to cancer detected far too late. For girls whose mothers have died, the abandonment is final; there's no chance for closure, for nurture, for a mother's touch. Regardless of how unhealthy the relationship was, their mother's death prevents them from ever "fixing" it.

One evening, Lisa, a new girl who has said very little to me in the few days she's been coming to the office, tells me that I look like her mother, who passed away a few years earlier. She stares at me for a long time, her yearning for her mother so raw and tangible. "I think if I could just touch your hair it would feel the same." The look of total longing on her face is hard to witness.

For those girls whose mothers are still alive, there is still hope, at least theoretically. However, this is rarely borne out by any historical evidence and is really just a childlike belief that one day things with Mommy will get better. *One day she'll treat me differently. One day we'll be a real family.* More often than not, the potential for change is outmatched by the potential for continual disappointment and rejection.

Over the years as I've worked with hundreds of girls and young women, I've often been outraged and angered by the behavior of so many of their mothers. Sometimes I've probably projected my own feelings about my mother onto theirs; sometimes I've just been horrified by the capacity for human cruelty. And yet as I've gotten older, reaching the age my own mother was when I was a teenager, I've wondered, if the situation were reversed, if life had turned out a little differently for me, how well would I have coped with raising a child alone? How much of my own pain and hurt would I have unwittingly passed down?

Even in a role as a mother figure to many girls, I've failed at times, made mistakes, or hurt them without ever meaning to. I've learned to have more patience with many of the mothers, grandmothers, and aunts that I know, understanding that many of them are simply overwhelmed and underresourced, are spending too much time working to pay the bills to pay attention to what's going on at home. For most of them, violence is generational and abuse is hereditary. Some mothers have heard the same words—*whore, slut, you'll never be anything, you're a piece of shit*—repeated from grandmother to mother to daughter. One afternoon at GEMS, I hear Aisha tell her two-year-old daughter that she'll break her fingers if she touches something again. I feel anger boiling up and tell her to come into my office. Immediately I start to launch into an angry diatribe about how you speak to children, but one look at Aisha's face and I remember the stories she's told me about her crack-addicted mother who abandoned her, the coke-addicted auntie who raised her. I can hear her aunt's voice telling me that Aisha was "loose" as a little kid and that she knows she "ain't shit," and I dial back my self-righteous lecture. I know that the result of this little chat will be that she probably won't yell at her daughter in the office anymore, but it will take a lot more than this or any other conversation, more than the court-mandated twelve-week parenting classes she's completed, to erase the lessons, the words, the reactions that have been drilled into her for the last eighteen years. I watch her daughter playing, a little guarded perhaps, and wonder how old she'll be before she starts resenting the fact that, like Aisha, she lives with Auntie, not her mommy; or how long it will be before she hates the way her mother talks to her, all the while yearning for her mother's undivided love and attention. I wonder what it will take to break the cycle.

Most of the mothers (or aunts and grandmothers who've taken their place) are dealing with their own struggles, bad memories, painful relationships, failed dreams, and disappointing jobs, but there are exceptions. There are mothers who have overcome addiction and reclaimed their children after being clean for a few years but are frustrated that their child hasn't "gotten over it," not understanding the depth of the damage that was done. There are the mothers who have walked away from abuse, struggled in the shelter system out of a desperate desire not to allow their children to witness violence. There are women who have gone from relative economic security to poverty because they chose to leave their abusers. There are mothers who are doing their best, struggling to work and make ends meet, who find themselves having to take a chance on makeshift day care, a neighbor, a friend of a friend. There are mothers who believe their child when she says she was abused, but are still reluctant to send her to counseling, out of a conviction that strangers shouldn't be in your business. There are mothers who try to do everything right once they find out their child has been molested, only to discover years later as adolescence hits, that their daughter is still scarred and broken despite the therapy appointments that were like a Band-Aid over an amputation.

And then there are the mothers who have settled, have stayed with the man, because he's a man, and you don't know when one might come along again, so you stay and you ignore it, whatever it is, the drinking, the late nights, the other women, the hitting; the line just keeps getting pushed back further and further, until one day your daughter tells you that he did something, and you just know she's lying, how could he, why would he, she's just a child, you're a woman, he doesn't need to, that's disgusting, of course she's lying, she's been acting a little fast, a little grown anyway, so you slap her in the face for telling such heinous lies, and when she doesn't say anything again you know she's learned her lesson about that kind of bullshit. After all, you didn't say anything when it was happening to you all those years ago.

Like all forms of child abuse, sexual abuse teaches powerful, life-changing lessons and with an estimated one in four girls being victims of sexual assault or sexual abuse before the age of eighteen, it's not surprising that sexual abuse often impacts families multi-generationally. Abuse that is passed down from grandma to mother to daughter, family secrets that are rarely shared. Girls and women bearing a silent burden.

Children who are victimized through sexual abuse often begin to develop deeply held tenets that shape their sense of self: *My worth is my sexuality. I'm dirty and shameful. I have no right to my own physical boundaries.* That shapes their ideas about the world around them: *No one will believe me. Telling the truth results in bad consequences. People can't be trusted.* It doesn't take long for children to begin to act in accordance with these belief systems.

For girls who have experienced incest, sexual abuse, or rape, the boundaries between love, sex, and pain become blurred. Secrets are normal, and shame is a constant. The lessons learned during sexual abuse are valuable ones for recruitment into the commercial sex industry. As Andrea Dworkin once said, "Incest is boot camp for prostitution." Numerous studies estimate that 70 to 90 percent of commercially sexually exploited youth and adult women in the sex industry were sexually abused prior to their recruitment. No other industry can boast of such a large correlation between early sexual abuse and future "employment."

Sexual abuse lays the groundwork. The pimp, the trafficker, doesn't need to do much training. It's already been done—by her father, her uncle, her mother's boyfriend, her teacher. She's well prepared for what's to come.

4
RECRUITMENT

Kaa was not a poison snake—in fact he rather despised the
poison snakes as cowards—but his strength lay in his hug, and
when he had once lapped his huge coils round anybody there
was no more to be said.

—*Rudyard Kipling,* The Jungle Book

There were many people on the Metro North train to Grand Central Terminal that day who stared at the young girl hunched in the corner seat. Perhaps it was the fact that she was wearing baggy pajama bottoms and slippers under her big overcoat, but despite this strange attire, no one approached her. Tiffany was aware of the stares but used her best tough-girl scowl to intercept any glances that might have turned from curiosity to concern. At twelve, Tiffany had perfected the art of warding nosy people away. She'd learned that nosy people took you away and put you in places where you didn't want to be: teachers who'd wondered about her absences, the stranger who'd called the cops when she saw the six-year-old girl in the park still waiting for her mother to come back way after dark, social workers who'd investigated her mother's drug use and decided that she was unfit, child welfare workers who asked too many questions and put her in an upstate group home. These lessons had taught her well, so Tiffany scowled. Everyone went back to reading their newspapers and taking naps. That day no nosy people asked that twelve-year-old girl in pajamas any questions and Tiffany rode the train in peace, away from the group home and back to the city.

When she arrived at Grand Central, she hopped the subway shuttle to the Port Authority terminal. Tiffany didn't really have a plan and she didn't have any money, but 42nd Street had always held a certain appeal for her, with its bright neon lights and constant bustle of people. It had that feeling of excitement, of opportunity, and Tiffany figured that she'd place herself smack in the middle and wait for opportunity to arise. It was early in the evening and a light rain had begun to fall. People hurried into the train station to escape the rain, yet Tiffany stayed outside, letting the rain wet her face, enjoying the feeling of freedom. She stayed outside the Port Authority as the rain fell harder, and just as she was beginning to doubt the wisdom of her decision to leave the relative warmth and safety of the group home, she finally caught someone's attention.

Tiffany was a striking child with skin the color of rich espresso and sharply accentuated cheekbones. Her body was still caught in a battle between childhood and adolescence. Tiffany had developed some breasts, but her gangly limbs and her physical awkwardness betrayed the body of a growing child. She was uncomfortable with her body and her appearance; she'd heard that she was "too dark," "too black" her whole life, and she carried that knowledge with her like a weight that she desperately wanted to put down. Attention from boys, or men, always helped ease that weight a little, so when the young man, dressed in neatly pressed jeans and a jersey, approached her and asked if she was OK, she smiled quickly and easily, grateful for the attention.

The boy, who said his name was Charming, seemed kind and friendly. He was more polite than the other boys Tiffany was used to, he talked to her like a person. He asked her if she'd like to get something to eat with him at a diner on 44th Street. Tiffany had not eaten anything since lunch, a ham sandwich and an apple, at the group home nearly eight hours earlier, and she nodded enthusiastically. The diner was run-of-the-mill as diners went, but a boy had never taken Tiffany out to eat before, so she viewed the red Formica tables and huge menus a little nervously. She was immediately self-conscious about her striped pajamas and furry slippers; the soft pink fur was now wet and bedraggled. But Charming made a joke about growing up in pj's and told her she still was the prettiest girl in the place, putting her at ease. Without even looking at the menu, Tiffany ordered her favorite meal in the world, buffalo wings, and munched hungrily on them. As she began to dry off in the warmth of the diner, and warmed under the kind and interested gaze of his eyes, Tiffany began to tell him that she'd run away from her group home and didn't really have anywhere to go. She surprised herself by telling him about her family, that her father was in jail and she wasn't sure where her mother was but that she was somewhere getting high. She told him how she'd been in foster care since she was nine and how she hated the constant upheaval, the moving from home to home, three times in three years. How she'd lost her virginity to a fifteen-year-old boy in a group home when she was nine, but then he broke her heart. How she wanted to be a lawyer and have three kids. Everything that she felt and thought, she told Charming as the night grew later and the other customers began to leave. The counselors at her group home were always frustrated that she didn't want to talk about her life, they said she kept things too much to herself, but it was because she didn't trust them. It was just a job to them, they didn't really care, they looked at the clock as she talked and rustled papers around their desk to signal it was time for her to leave, but Charming seemed different. He really did listen, didn't offer advice, just listened as it all came tumbling out of her mouth. When he finally did talk, his words were like music to Tiffany's ears, the words she'd always wanted to hear. He told her that she could live with him and he'd be her boyfriend, they'd be like a family, he'd protect her and make sure that she had everything she needed. Tiffany felt like it was fate: She'd run away and straight into the arms of a man who would care for her and love her. When he said, "Let's go home," she agreed, and in the back of the yellow cab that they took to his apartment, she smiled to herself and repeated silently over and over again, "I'm going home, I'm going home."

The first few weeks in her new home were the best time of Tiffany's twelve years. He took her shopping and bought her new sneakers, jeans, shirts, and even a pair of high heels and a sexy dress. Tiffany had never had so many nice things and for the first time she didn't have to hide new clothes from other girls in the group home who would surely steal them. She felt like a proper grown-up housewife; she cleaned and cooked and they had sex every night. Life in the group homes had taught her cooking skills, and Charming appreciated her lovingly prepared meals each night after he came home from a long day of hustling crack on the block. Life was perfect to Tiffany; she doodled their names everywhere, *Tiffany loves Charming* in big loopy letters with love hearts complete with arrows through them. She figured that he would marry her when she turned sixteen, in four years, so she practiced saying *Mr. and Mrs. Jackson* in the mirror.

Charming encouraged her to dress more grown-up and liked her to dance in underwear and high heels for him. At first she felt shy and awkward but he coached her gently, showing her how to shake her butt, undress in a sexy way, and when he was finally pleased with her performance, she felt so proud. One night, Charming came home and didn't want dinner; he seemed in a hurry. He told her that he wanted her to go to the club with him; he even picked out the sexy dress and high heels. He said it was a different type of club so they had to make a good impression. He gave Tiffany two glasses of Hennessy before they left the apartment, but Tiffany was buzzed enough on the feeling of going out with her man for the night to really feel the alcohol.

When Tiffany awoke slowly the next morning with a pounding headache, she had only a vague recollection of the night before, and as the thoughts of dancing, of men, of stripping flooded into her mind, they made her head hurt worse. Charming was on the side of the bed counting money happily. "Damn baby, that ass sure makes a lot of money." He looked so proud, Tiffany couldn't bear to tell him that she didn't want to do it again.

As Tiffany, now a tired sixteen-year-old, sits telling me how it all began, I can picture her, smiling at Charming, grateful for the attention. I can imagine the details, fill in some of the blanks, and while it's the first time that I'm hearing her specific story, it's all too easy to imagine because, save for a few details, it sounds pretty much like every other recruitment story I've ever heard.

Elizabeth tells me that she just knew her man loved her when he took her to a fancy restaurant. Where, honey? Red Lobster. After that, she thinks she owes him, so she does whatever he tells her to do.

Tanya's mother, an alcoholic, won't buy her the new Barbie. She hops a train into Manhattan to buy it herself at FAO Schwarz with her savings. Lost in Times Square, Tanya meets a man who says he'll help her. He takes her to the track that night. She's eleven years old.

Bethany's mother sells her for drugs on the street. When she starts junior high school she discovers that she's been sold to some of her own family members. Humiliated, she runs away and meets a guy who picks up where her mother left off.

Ashanti thinks that the cute guy she meets in a homeless shelter is her boyfriend. They decide to hunt for an apartment together, but are approached at gunpoint by three men who force them into a car. She thinks they're being robbed but then she realizes that he knows these guys and is part of the plan.

Shana's a quiet, studious, sheltered twelve-year-old when she meets a twenty-two-year-old who wants to be her boyfriend. She loses her virginity to him. He puts her out on the track. She says she's in love.

Alina watches her mother walk around the neighborhood offering her body in exchange for crack and then later watches her slowly dying from AIDS as the neighborhood shuns her. When she meets a pimp, it doesn't seem that bad by comparison.

Jessica is sixteen when she moves from North Carolina to live with an aunt who's just met a new man and doesn't want Jess there anymore. After she's kicked out, Jessica sleeps on the train for a few nights and eventually starts sleeping with men who feed her and let her stay over. It seems like a good idea to get a pimp for protection.

Maria is homeless due to her mother's schizophrenia and continual instability. She meets a guy who takes her in and sets her up in his mother's basement. He starts bringing guys in and forces her to strip for them. He's frustrated that she's too young at twelve to know how to dance "sexy" enough, so he teaches her.

It reminds me of a macabre version of the Choose Your Own Adventure books: A few options along the way will ultimately lead to one of not many outcomes. If you chose running away from your mom, skip to page 6, where you'll meet a pimp at the subway. If you chose running away from a group home, skip to page 7, where you'll meet a girl who'll introduce you to a pimp. If you're homeless and feel like you to have to trade sex in exchange for a place to sleep that night, jump ahead to page 15, where you'll be living with a guy who now sells you every night. There's no grand prize at the end of these stories, though, no reward. Just a few minor variations on the same theme—vulnerable meets predatory; abused child meets billion-dollar sex industry. Not hard to guess the ending.

Recruiting a vulnerable girl isn't hard either. As Lloyd Banks so aptly states in the remix of 50 Cent's platinum-selling song "P.I.M.P.," "I ain't gotta give 'em much, they happy with Mickey D's." Teenage girls, especially those who've already been abused, who are living in poverty, who come from fractured families, are relatively easy to lure and manipulate. In fact, despite 50 Cent's argument that the song is referring only to adult women being sold (presumably less disturbing), it's hard to picture an adult woman, unless she is literally homeless or starving, being "happy with Mickey D's."

Yet having worked with preteen and teenage girls for thirteen years, I know that nothing causes greater excitement than announcing a trip, especially in my car, to McDonald's. Like Elizabeth, who was wooed by her concept of fancy dining, teenage girls' culinary standards are relatively easy to meet. So are their standards for what qualifies as love, particularly for girls whose whole definition of love has been grossly distorted by the relationships they've seen growing up and the abuse that they've been told equals love. It doesn't take a lot: a good nose for sniffing out vulnerability, a little kindness, a bit of finesse, paying attention to the clues she gives away about her family, her living situation, her needs. Once he's got the hook in, a few meals, rides in his car, perhaps an outfit or getting her nails done can seal the deal. She thinks he cares. She wants to please him. It doesn't really matter how he introduces the topic, whether he gets her drunk and takes her to a strip club, cries broke and asks her to do it "just this one time," beats her into total submission, has his other girls encourage her that it won't be that bad, or spins the promises of a better future, money, security, being "wifey," the end result will be the same. He knows that once she crosses that line for the first time, it'll be hard to go back. It might take a day and cost nothing, it might take a few weeks and cost a few dollars, but ultimately the investment he puts in will be worth the return. Even if he strikes out with a few girls who are perhaps not quite as vulnerable as he first assumed, it doesn't really matter—there's always another girl right around the corner. In fact, pimping is really an economist's dream, a low-risk, low-investment, high-demand, high-income industry. Indeed, there are many pimps who are smart, shrewd, and calculating "businessmen," but this concept does beg the question of how shrewd you really need to be to lure a fifteen-year-old who has run away from abuse at home and is currently spending the night on a train.

Some of the girls, however, have been forced into the sex industry through kidnapping and violence, held at gunpoint, pushed into a car, kept in a locked room. Girls are then raped, often gang-raped initially, to break their will. The subsequent shock and traumatic response leave the girl feeling utterly helpless and totally subdued. The fear often keeps her from running away. The shame can keep her from reaching out for help. While it can be shocking for people to initially learn that American girls, ones who never, ever make the news, are kidnapped with increasing frequency, these are still, relatively, the cases that tend to engender the most public sympathy and interest from the criminal justice system. Their victimization seems obvious and fits into a tidier, more common understanding of human trafficking.

Yet for most of the girls, the force, the violence, the gun in her face don't come until later. Their pathway into the commercial sex industry is facilitated through seduction, promises, and the belief that the abuser is actually their boyfriend. Statistics show that the majority of commercially sexually exploited children are homeless, runaways, or the distastefully termed "throwaways." These girls and young women have a tougher time in the court of public opinion and in the real courts of the criminal and juvenile justice systems. It is presumed that somewhere along the line they "chose" this life, and this damns them to be seen as willing participants in their own abuse.

WINTER 1993, GERMANY

It's been three weeks and my money has dwindled down to about eight dollars. Eating for under a dollar a day may be possible in some countries but not in Germany. Nicotine, the good old appetite suppressant, has helped with the hunger pangs, but I barely can afford cigarettes now and I'm rationing them out to myself like a jailbird. Leaving England with girls I'd known for one evening on a one-way ticket, and believing that my ex-boyfriend would be so heartbroken that he'd send for me within a few weeks, doesn't seem to have been that great a plan. The girls are caught up in their own stuff, and have milked half of my money in the process. My ex informs me coldly by phone one night that yes, he was cheating and she's moved into my place and a one-way ticket really does work only one way. There are other unforeseen challenges. Not speaking German is proving a bit of a hindrance. Not being legally old enough to work, another roadblock. Bringing only enough money to last a couple of weeks? Strike three. I'm stuck. Stucker than I've ever been in my life. It's a tight jam when you're in London with no money and no way home, but if you live in Portsmouth, it's just three hours away. Stuck in Munich with no money and no way home is another story. Desperate times call for desperate measures.

It's late afternoon and I've applied for, begged for, cried for any type of employment at all the four million restaurants and bars in Munich. Having attempted to find work at all the major hotel bars and decent-looking restaurants, I'm down to crappy cafés and pay-by-the-hour motels. Rejection from places that look as if they'd be fortunate to get a visit from the health inspector let alone a guest is hard to swallow. I've gone full circle around the city on the U-Bahn and have ended up back at the Bahnhof, the main railroad terminal, where the streets are filled with clubs and bars. The streets are thriving during the day, although the glowing *Girls, Girls, Girls* signs are faded in the winter sunlight. The street seems less seedy, less threatening in the daylight, and as I stare at the *Girls* sign, a startling revelation hits me. I'm a girl. Although this may not be the most profound epiphany I've ever had, the Plan is beginning to formulate in my head, even as I walk toward the sign and into the entrance of the club. I'm moving too quickly to think it all the way through to a sensible conclusion, but the outline goes something like, *This is a strip club, girls dance in strip clubs, they pay girls to dance, I'm a girl,*

I can dance, I need money, they probably need girls, therefore I will dance to make money. Even as this genius hits me, the other side of my brain is protesting loudly, although apparently not loudly enough. *It's only for a couple of weeks, I've done nude modeling before, illegally of course given my age, and I've been a dancer in regular nightclubs, so combining the two shouldn't be that hard. It's not that bad, just a few weeks, go home and forget the whole thing.* I work so hard to convince myself that I'm sure my lips are moving. I walk down a long hallway, dark and painted red, and down a flight of stairs into a huge, empty club.

It takes an altered date of birth on my passport and about four minutes to get hired as a "hostess"—starting immediately, cash same day. It's too good to be true. Get paid to sit at a bar and drink? I already drink like a fish, or more accurately like my mother. This will be an easy job. My tired, hungry teenage mind wants to believe that drinking with the customers is really all there is to it. And with the first customer that's all I'll have to do. But by the end of my first shift, I want to scrub my skin off, even though I've earned more that night than any of those shitty cafés would've paid in two weeks. In a gesture of celebration that I don't really feel, and because I'm drunk, I use ten marks of my day's earnings to catch a cab home. Out of the club, in the cold air, the black line feels blurry. I feel like everyone's looking at me, everyone knows my dark and dirty secret, which I want to stay hidden behind the door of the club. Driving in the cab, I watch women on their way home from work, on their way to a date, and I feel like a voyeur into the normal world. I haven't crossed "The Line," but I've crossed a bunch that I thought I never would. Still, plenty of men have touched me when I didn't want them to; none of them has paid for the privilege. I figure I can keep some boundaries given that I'll be at the club only for a few weeks, three tops. Get enough money to pay the rent, buy a ticket home and never, ever, ever tell anyone what happened. That night, I buy food and pay the rent before I get evicted. The next day I pile on the makeup, give myself a whole different look, change my name, and go back to the club. The more distance I can keep between Rachel and this other person who just needs to survive right now, the better. But the Line keeps moving and the boundaries keep blurring and it'll be a long time before I see Rachel again.

In recovery, as an advocate and running GEMS, for a long time I'll feel guilty about the way I entered the sex industry. In a radio interview one day, an abrupt interviewer who keeps calling me an ex-prostitute objects to my correction and use of the term "commercially sexually exploited." "Well, you were older, so obviously you made a choice," she declares. I object again, but her accusatory and judgmental pronouncement stings. A few moments later when she calls my girls "ghetto girls," I let her know in no uncertain terms that I'll be terminating the interview, and hang up on her. I recognize that she's rude, obnoxious, and racist, but still, her earlier comments bother me. Obviously you make a choice. As I struggle with it that night, I concede that yes, I made a choice. No one put a gun to my head, unlike Samantha, who was snatched off the street as she walked home from school. I was seventeen, not twelve, thirteen, or fourteen like Maria, Crystal, Briana, Simone, Kei, Tionne, or thousands of other girls I meet, who are so young, so clearly children, so naive regardless of their supposed "street smarts" that it's unconscionable that anyone could ever suggest that they deserved this or wanted it. I wasn't lured by a pimp; in fact, I won't meet mine till several months later. No one forced me, coerced me, or even pressured me. I made a choice. I reflect on this over the years, and struggle with the implications of this choice and what this makes me: stupid, loose, greedy, lazy, sluttish; the list of words I've used to judge myself goes on and on. I listen to myself try to help girls to forgive themselves and alleviate their profound sense of shame. "Whatever you thought you had to do to survive or to stay alive, it's OK." It's easier, though, to see the girls' age and circumstances and recognize that they didn't have a choice than it is to see my own vulnerabilties and lack of choices. It's only as I get older that I'm able to extend to myself the same grace and compassion that I freely give to the girls. Only later can I give my scared teenage self a break and understand with compassion for myself how the "choices" I made were limited by my age and circumstances, and my lack of insight about how hard it would be to leave after just a couple of weeks.

The question of choice impacts the way that domestically trafficked girls are viewed and treated by our society. Many people believe that girls "choose" this life, and while it is true that most girls are not kidnapped into the sex industry, to frame their actions as choice is at best misleading. It is clear from the experiences of girls that, while they may have acted in response to individual, environmental, and societal factors, this may not necessarily be defined as a choice. The *American Heritage Dictionary* describes the act of choosing as "to select from a number of possible alternatives; decide on and pick out." Therefore in order for a choice to be a legitimate construct, you've got to believe that (a) you actually have possible alternatives, and (b) you have the capacity to weigh these alternatives against one another and decide on the best avenue. Commercially sexually exploited and trafficked girls have neither—their choices are limited by their age, their family, their circumstances, and their inability to weigh one bad situation against another, given their developmental and emotional immaturity. Therefore the issue of choice has to be framed in three ways: age and age-appropriate responsibility, the type of choice, and the context of the choice.

The age factor is perhaps the most obvious reason that discussions about true "choice" are erroneous and unhelpful to the debate. There's a reason that we have age limits and standards governing the "choices" that children and youth can make, from drinking to marrying to driving to leaving school, and it's because as a society we recognize that there's a difference between child/adolescent development and adult development.

This is also why the Trafficking Victims Protection Act of 2000 and its reauthorizations in 2003, 2005, and 2008 have all supported a definition of child sex trafficking where children under the age of eighteen found in the commercial sex trade are considered to be victims of trafficking without requiring that they experienced "force, fraud, or coercion" to keep them there. For victims of sex trafficking ages eighteen and over, the law requires the "force, fraud, or coercion" standard. In defining the crime of sex trafficking, Congress created certain protections for children. It's taken as a given that children and youth are operating from a different context, especially in light of age of consent laws.

Not only are choices these girls make shaped by external limitations decided by age, they're also dictated by the psychological and emotional limitations that are adolescent development. In hindsight, as adults looking back on our teenage selves, we can recognize our own impulsivity, risk taking, our need for peer approval, our rebellion against our parents, our limited understanding of consequences—in short, all the characteristics that define being a teenager. Very few adults would honestly want to revisit the naïveté, vulnerability, and often flat-out ignorance of adolescence. Many parents don't trust their own sixteen-year-old to drive their car, pick their own "good enough" friends, or stay home alone for the weekend without hosting a party. Yet interestingly, I've met lots and lots of adults who feel that a sixteen-year-old is completely mature enough to be considered fully capable of making the choice to be in the sex industry.

Given their age and psychological development, children and youth often make decisions that are not in their best interests, or that perhaps are unsafe. It's an unwise choice to meet a stranger in person whom you've met only on MySpace, not brilliant decision making to get into someone's car when you barely know them; nor is it a great idea to run away from home with six dollars in your pocket and nowhere to go. Yet none of these "choices" is the same thing as "choosing" to be in the commercial sex industry—even if they end up leading down that path. It can also be an unwise decision to go home with someone you've just met, particularly if you've been drinking, and yet making that decision in no way means that you "chose" to get raped.

The discussion about lack of choice based on age is not to suggest that teenage girls and young women are mindless, helpless, or totally without agency. One of the greatest joys of my work is getting to spend time every day with girls and young women who are smart, insightful, thoughtful, capable of real leadership, and have much to offer the world around them. Girls are capable of making choices—within a safe and healthy context, and with the safety nets of responsible, caring adults ensuring that those choices are age appropriate. Yet for most sexually exploited and trafficked girls, the safety nets aren't there, and they are left choosing the lesser of two evils. Children who are abused or neglected at home cannot simply "choose" to go get a job, earn some money, and move out into a safer or more pleasant environment. In the mind of a child or teenager, running away from a bad situation may seem like the most logical option, yet it's the context of the choice that's most important. It's a concept that seems clearer when applied to trafficking victims from other countries who are rarely presumed to have made "bad choices." Some of these women are cognizant of the fact that they will be working in a brothel when they reach the United States, but they are in no way prepared for the brutalities that they will face, the slavery which they'll endure, or the reality that they can't just leave once they've earned enough money—no matter what they were originally told. Still others may enter into a "marriage" only to find out that they will be a sex slave. These victims, many of whom are adults, have made choices. But their choices must be seen in context. Most of them have little to no other legitimate options.

Desperation and lack of options make for poor decision making, but provide ripe pickings for the traffickers. Their choices do not mean that they deserve to be trafficked, or want to be enslaved. In the same way, neither do the decisions that girls in the United States may make with the hopes of securing a better future, someone to love them, food and clothing, a sense of family, or a chance to escape their current abuse mean that they deserve, want, or choose the life that awaits them.

Nicole and I are working together on a writing exercise I've assigned about what she likes about herself. Not only is the entire concept tough for her to wrap her mind around, but she's struggling with the writing. I know that she feels limited by her literacy skills and sees herself as stupid and worthless, so the exercise feels like a good way to figure out where exactly she's at, skillwise, and to encourage her self-worth at the same time. It's not going well. She can come up with only two things she likes about herself, her hair and her feet, so I give her ideas: *You're kind, You're funny, You're a good friend.* She screws up her nose in disbelief at them all but with much prodding tries to write them down anyway. She writes slowly and carefully, putting a lot of thought into each word, and it quickly becomes clear that she has very little basic knowledge even of phonics and how letters combine to make different sounds. At nineteen, Nicole's literacy skills are equivalent to those of a first grader. It's obvious that she has a pronounced learning disability, and I'm angry that she was able to make it through to the sixth grade in the New York City public school system without anyone taking the time to help her build the most basic skills. I try to imagine how difficult it is for her to navigate a world surrounded by words that might as well be in Greek. I understand why she feels that being in the life is the only thing that she's capable of doing. It's hard to imagine a life of possibilities when she can't even read a book, fill out a job application, or decipher a street sign.

Many girls, even in this country, are growing up in a society that does not provide real and viable opportunities for the future. At the same time, they're living in a culture that increasingly teaches them that their worth and value are defined by their sexuality. Parallels can be found between girls in poverty in this country and girls in poverty internationally, as well as with girls growing up over one hundred years ago. In an article on the commercial sexual exploitation of girls and the abolitionist movement in Victorian England, author Deborah Gorham writes of a young woman who "allowed herself to be entrapped in a French brothel because life had given her little reason to believe that any genuinely satisfactory possibility existed for her. In a society that told a girl who had no possessions that her chastity, at least, was a 'precious possession,' some young girls might well have been led to believe that they might as well sell that possession to the highest bidder." If the word *chastity* were replaced by *sexuality* or *body*, then this paragraph could easily have been written about commercially sexually exploited and trafficked girls today in the United States.

With this in mind, the issue of choice must be carefully framed and understood in the context of the individual and cultural factors facing girls at risk. The sex industry may initially appear to provide a life of economic freedom, independence, and a secure future with someone who loves them, in contrast to the bleak futures that they may believe are their only alternatives. Selling sex may seem like a small price to pay, particularly for girls who have been abused and raped. Combine the power of media images of young women as sexual objects with the girls' familial and environmental situations and the trap is set. It is often not until the reality of the situation begins to sink in, when the situation becomes too toxic or when she finally accepts the reality that her boyfriend is actually a pimp, that a girl may choose to leave. At that point it is no longer a matter of choice, but rather a matter of escape.

PIMPS

"You know what? I think it just got a little easier out here for a pimp."
—Jon Stewart, Academy Awards, 2006

WINTER 1993, GERMANY

The guy who walks in toward the end of the afternoon shift is much younger than our usual lunchtime crew, but after a few instructive months of working in one of Munich's largest strip clubs, I've learned not to be surprised by anything. Bella, the bar manager and my boss, gives him a disapproving look. She's been working here for years and can sniff out money like a bloodhound on a fresh scent. To make matters worse, he looks "ethnic"—Turkish, Middle Eastern, perhaps Yugoslavian—which, according to Bella, means if he does have money, he'll be cheap with it and possibly rough with the girls. I've already heard Bella's lectures on the various sexual and financial proclivities of every race and ethnicity and know that her preference is for white businessmen in their forties or fifties, German or British, but not American ("too loud, too cheap"). Of course, her protests about us "girls" talking to the less desirable customers is disingenuous; she would have a fit if we actually didn't try to make some money or didn't quietly endure being roughed up. In this case, he's the only customer and with only thirty minutes left before the shift ends, she sighs dramatically but gives me the nod to proceed. I sidle up next to him at the bar, and start my usual spiel—broken *Deutsch* (with an Asiatic twist, as I'm learning the language from the Filipina bar girls), topped off with an English accent. *"Vilcommen. Vee gates? Miena namee est Carmen."*

He responds briefly, says his name is Fazil, and up close I see that he is probably early to midtwenties, and fairly handsome. He's dressed in the style popular with the eastern European guys: leather jacket, T-shirt, tight jeans, and a chain. He speaks a little English, as broken as my German, but it saves me from having to rack my brain for the remaining four sentences I know. Bella hovers, not particularly subtly, waiting for the champagne order. I know if he were German, or British, that she'd give it more time. He finally buys me a drink, although I hear Bella sigh loudly again, as it's the cheapest variety of champagne we serve. Either I'm already three sheets to the wind or it's been a busy shift, but I'm relieved to finally be talking to a guy who's close to my age and not one of the pervy older men who make up the majority of our clientele. At seventeen, anyone over thirty-five, particularly if they're wearing a suit, seems old to me. Twenty-four in a leather jacket? That's boyfriend material.

"I understand . . ." He motions to Bella and makes a drinking sign. "I buy you another drink outside—I give you the money if you want," he says.

I know the rules about dating outside of the club, but Bella has been annoying me all day and I feel like telling her to take her little racist attitude and shove it. I know that if we get caught, I'll get fined, but fuck it. I make a plan to meet Fazil around the corner after my shift ends.

We go to a bar, where he orders us some cognac. The champagne plus the cognac plus not having eaten anything all afternoon has the room spinning a little, although in a pleasant way. I don't understand much of what he's saying. The music's loud, his accent strong. But I don't care that much. He's cute, seems to like me, and I'm desperate to have a romantic, physical, *something* interaction with someone who isn't paying for my time. It feels like a date. He's talking about money, percentages, some other shit. Thirty, seventy.

You'd still get thirty, I hear him say. I try to snap back into focus. "What the fuck are you talking about?"

"Business. You and me. I manage you."

I'm a little too drunk to pick up right away what he's talking about. Why on earth would I want a manager? Sixty-five percent of my money now goes to the club. I already have a boss and she gets on my nerves. This doesn't seem like a good deal, drunk or not, but he's persistent. "OK, sixty, forty," he says.

It finally dawns on me: He doesn't want to date me, he wants to make money off of me. I already have enough people in my life doing that. I ask him to drive me home. The alcohol has made me groggy and I doze off in the car. When I come to, Fazil has stopped in a part of town that I'm not familiar with, but it's easy to figure out where we are by the number of women and girls in the street leaning into cars, the men lingering in doorways, and the dope fiends shooting up in the open. I try to shake myself awake. "What are you doing?"

"You going to work here for me. This is you." He points to a couple of girls, and says, *"Hure,"* the *Deutsch* word for *whore.* Believing as I do, and as Bella has taught me, that working in the club is really just being a hostess and that the taking-your-clothes-off-onstage part and the going-into-the-VIP-booths is just something you don't really think about or talk about, I'm horrified. What I do has nothing to do with what these women are doing, I tell myself. I know I don't want to "work" for him, and I say so. His demeanor immediately changes and he becomes rough and threatening. I realize that no one knows where I am and that I don't even know if the name he has given me is real. I'm crying but compliant and when he begins to drive me home, I'm relieved. When we get to my apartment building, he insists on coming up with me and forces me to show him where I live. He rapes me, telling me that it is only fair, as he has to try it first. Afterward he throws a gold necklace worth about twenty-five marks on me and laughingly tells me he'll be back to collect his money. I throw the necklace out the window when he leaves and lie awake all night, still not really understanding how things went so bad.

When I tell one of the older women at the club what happened, she explains that "Fazil" is a pimp looking for girls to sell. While I'm aware that pimps exist, I've never given them a lot of thought. Growing up, we would say *pimp* but not really have a clue what it meant. There was a guy in our town called Luther Cool, who was rumored to be a pimp. With a body like an upside-down triangle, all shoulders and pecs and chicken legs, and a perpetual uniform of huge, oversize sunglasses, a muscle shirt, and high-water sweatpants in every color, Luther Cool was just one of those odd characters that every town has and that every kid makes fun of. We didn't really understand the concept of pimping; we just knew he was sleazy and we snickered every time he walked by. It's this image of a pimp, a caricature, that more than anything is stuck in my head. Fazil didn't fit this image at all. I feel stupid and vow never to get caught up with anyone like him again. Fazil does come calling for his money, but I hide from him for weeks and eventually he seems to give up. One afternoon, I see him trying to recruit a teenage girl at the Bahnhof, and I turn and speed-walk in the opposite direction.

Just a few months later I'll meet JP. Ex–U.S. Army, currently unemployed but with so much potential. Strikingly handsome, with his huge doe eyes and high cheekbones, it will be love at first sight. Hearing his sexy baritone voice and strong southern accent, I want to melt every time he speaks. He's funny and smart and we click together from day one. I'll be so enraptured with him that I'm happy to give him anything and everything he wants, until of course it's no longer a choice. I'll love JP with all my heart and soul and feel sure that I never have and never will experience anything like this again. I'll think I could die for him—and I nearly do.

His growing addiction to crack and my addiction to him make for a volatile combination, but in my mind it's just the way love is supposed to be. We're Romeo and Juliet; I'm Billie Holiday, he's "My Man"; I'm Carmen, he's my jealous lover. The one thing I never see him as is my pimp. It isn't until much later that I remember the conversations that we'd had about his father being a pimp, that I'd been told to call him Daddy, that he had twisted some wire coat hangers together into a "pimp stick" to beat me, that I turned over all my money to him every night and got beaten. It's not until I start hearing the stories from other girls and women that I'm able to contextualize my experiences. At the time, he's just my boyfriend and I'm just a girl who dances in a club.

The average American adult probably imagines a pimp as a cross between a caricatured seventies Huggy Bear or a sleazy, leather-jacket-wearing, drug-dealing scumbag from an early *Law & Order* episode. Most teenagers, however, inundated as they are by glamorous, sexy, relatively benign images of pimps on television and music videos, have a very different view. The distorted glorification of pimp culture began in the seventies with the blaxploitation films and Iceberg Slim's pulp fiction. Today pimping has gone mainstream. It would be easy, as some do, to point to hip-hop culture as the primary culprit in this tidal wave of acceptance of pimps. Hip-hop clearly needs to take responsibility for its ongoing misogynistic images and lyrics, but rappers alone could not have achieved what has become a mass acceptance of pimp culture.

The tipping point came in 2003, when 50 Cent released his platinum-selling song "P.I.M.P.," in which he describes one of the girls working for him as having "stitches in her head." Several months later, Reebok rewarded him with a fifty-million-dollar sneaker-deal endorsement. A few years later, Vitaminwater did the same. Why wouldn't they? "Fiddy" proved unequivocally that no one was objecting to his blatant degradation of women and girls when "P.I.M.P" went platinum three times and reached the top ten in eighteen countries.

50 Cent isn't alone in his corporately sponsored pimping. Snoop Dogg (Calvin Broadus), who is infamous for bringing two women on dog leashes to the 2003 MTV Video Music Awards, was featured on the cover of the December 2006 issue of *Rolling Stone* in a Santa Claus red hat and a copy line reading *America's Most Lovable Pimp*. In the article, Snoop brags about his pimping, which he claims he took up during his successful rap career because it was a "childhood dream": "'Cause pimpin' aint a job, it's a sport. I had a bitch on every exit [in Los Angeles] from the 10 freeway to the 101 freeway 'cause bitches would recruit for me." Snoop's endorsement deals range from Orbit gum to Boost Mobile cell phones, and he was even featured in a General Motors commercial with former Chrysler CEO Lee Iacocca.

HBO has made a deal with the Hughes brothers, makers of the movie *American Pimp*, to produce a scripted series about pimps titled *Gentlemen of Leisure*. Ice-T, a self-described former pimp, now plays a sex-crimes detective on *Law & Order: Special Victims Unit* on NBC, despite still making yearly appearances at the Players Ball, a convention that awards real-life pimps with trophies for Player of the Year, Mack of the Year, and Number 1 International Pimp of the Year.

Examples of pimp references permeate every aspect of popular culture. Some argue that the meaning of the word has changed and now reflects something positive. The rapper Nelly had a short-lived scholarship fund called PIMP (Positive Intellectual Motivated Person), ostensibly to promote education but more likely to promote his energy drink Pimp Juice. The word *pimp* has become a verb, as in the name for the TV show *Pimp My Ride* and for a campaign by a Christian youth organization in Finland, called Pimp My Bible. Yet when MSNBC reporter David Shuster commented during Hillary

Clinton's campaign that it seemed as if Chelsea Clinton was being "pimped out," people were aghast and Shuster was suspended for two weeks by the network. The connotation of the word remains the same. It's society's attitude toward pimps and pimping that has changed.

As an award-show junkie, I was glued to my television for the 78th Academy Awards. I was always convinced, from a very young age, that I was going to be a famous actress, so I've had my acceptance speech prepared since I was five years old. Over the years, I've slowly come to terms with the fact that my dream of winning the best-actress Oscar would go unrealized. Still, I love the red carpet specials; the best- and worst-dressed competition; the drama of underdogs beating bookie favorites; and tearful, rambling actors onstage receiving the ultimate validation. That night, like every year, I curled up on the couch and prepared for an enchanted evening. I expected to be swept up in the glamour of the night, cheering for my favorites. And then the esteemed Academy honored "It's Hard out Here for a Pimp," which won the Oscar for Best Original Song, and I felt like I had been slapped in the face.

I watched the audience in their Badgley Mischka dresses and Armani suits clap vigorously for Three 6 Mafia and listened as presenters spouted on about the historic moment for hip-hop. Having seen the earlier musical performance of the song, I thought it was pretty clear to anyone watching that the song denigrated women and positioned pimps as hustlers just trying to "get by." Apparently the Academy had considered the word *bitch* to be too risqué for prime-time television, as it was replaced by *witch*, yet somehow they did not think that lyrics like *Wait I got a snow bunny, and a black girl too / You pay the right price and they'll both do you / That's the way the game goes, gotta keep it strictly pimpin / Gotta have my hustle tight, makin change off these women, yeah* were offensive. Admittedly this was the same venerable Academy that awarded Roman Polanski with an Oscar for Best Director, which he was unable to accept due to his still pending charges for raping a thirteen-year-old girl.

As I watched the audience and subsequent presenters embrace the moment, perhaps because they thought it was a great song, perhaps because they thought they were embracing "black culture," not understanding that these images did not represent or benefit it, or perhaps because to them, pimps were larger-than-life caricatures, driving Cadillacs and sporting diamond pinkie rings, I couldn't help but think of all the girls I've visited in hospitals, girls with lifelong scars, girls traumatized and broken, girls who've been brainwashed, girls who'd been beaten for not meeting their "quota." In my world, pimps are not managers, protectors, or "market facilitators," as one research study euphemistically called them, but leeches sucking the souls from beautiful, bright young girls, predators who scour the streets, the group homes, and junior high schools stalking their prey.

That night, furious at the Academy and the audience that was applauding, I imagined walking onto the stage, grabbing the mic, and giving them a reality check. As I fantasized, I struggled to think of an emblematic story but there were simply too many. How could I explain the violence, the devastation, the brainwashing with just one story? What could I say that would accurately convey the harm? Should I share the story of Jessica, who was fourteen when I met her in a detention center? Jessica is not entirely sure how her parents died. Recruited from a child welfare shelter by an adult man and his wife, she sleeps in their bed and they feed and clothe her. I first meet her when she's locked up on prostitution charges, struggling to figure out this relationship with the people she believes to be her adopted parents. The following week when I go to see her, she's shell-shocked. She'd taken an HIV test and it has come back positive. Jessica calls her pimp to say, "Daddy, I'm positive." He's nonchalant. "Of course you are; I've been positive for years."

Or would I talk about Sarah being beaten by a two-by-four, and like 50 Cent described, being left with "stitches in her head"—in her case over thirty. Or Naima, held down by her pimp and his friend while they used a home-tattoo kit to tattoo his name all over her body including on her hands and neck. Latavia, Tanya, Marie, Elizabeth, Jeanine, Markasia, all teenagers, all viciously beaten by pimps. Would I talk about Tiffany Mason, Christal Jones, or Hanna Montessori, all recruited by pimps, one in San Francisco, one in Vermont, and one in Los Angeles, and all later found murdered at the ages of fifteen and sixteen? These were of course just the girls who had made the paper, white girls who'd warranted a few lines. What about all the countless girls, especially those who were black and Latina, who had gone missing and were presumed dead? What would it take for pimps not to be seen as cool or sexy? For people to believe that they cause real harm?

SPRING 1994, GERMANY

JP is waiting for me after my shift outside the club. "How much?"

"It was OK." Stalling.

"How much, Raych?" JP refuses to call me by my working name, "Carmen."

"Six hundred." As I turn it over.

"*Six hundred?*" He's pissed. I knew he would be.

I consider giving up the two hundred that I've got stashed in my underwear, but realize that I'll just get in more trouble for trying to stash, and that money's for food this week. All of his/my money, he'll spend on crack in the next twenty-four hours. We've been eating corned beef hash and eggs for weeks now, as it's the cheapest food to buy, and we rarely have any money left over once he's gone on another binge.

I get the choking up and a smack on the side of the face, hard enough that it'll show tomorrow. I was expecting both, having walked out of a twelve-hour shift with only six hundred marks to show for it. There are people walking and driving by, but no one pays us any attention. After all, we're outside under the neon flashing light of a strip club.

JP disappears off into the night with my money to score. I know he'll be back soon; he always is. I walk a different route home and stop by the Turkish kebab shop. I haven't eaten anything in here for months since I got food poisoning, but the guys are cool and constantly worried about me and the never-ending new bruises that appear on my face and body daily. I give them my night's stash; they've been holding my money for a few weeks now after I ran out of places to hide it from JP in the house. It strikes me as sad that I feel safer with these relative strangers in a restaurant than I do at home. I don't have a lot of time to dwell on that, though, as I've got to get back home before JP starts wondering where I've been.

Demetrios, one of the cuter ones, tries to persuade me to stay, but he knows the deal. "Leave him, he no good," he calls after me. This much I do know.

I've already stayed out too long, as JP has beaten me home, but he's already too busy lighting up his rocks to care where I've been. He'll be calm for a little while now. It's when the high starts wearing off that I need to worry. I go into the bathroom to wash my makeup off, put a cool rag on my swollen face, and looking in the mirror, I wonder just as I do every night, how I got here: trapped with a man who'll beat me as soon as look at me, taking my clothes off onstage every night for a bunch of men who don't care about me. I'm so numb most of the time that I try not to even think about it, but I never imagined my life would be like this. I thought I'd be a lawyer or a journalist or a petite-size model or even a teenage mom living in Portsmouth. Working at a factory doesn't sound that bad anymore. I stare at the eyes reflecting back at me, the eyes my mother had recently called "dead," and I wonder if that's a premonition. I already feel like my life won't last much longer. I've made arrangements with some of the girls at work that if I don't come in for a few days, they should know that JP definitely did it, the spare keys are under the mat, here's my mum's address, get my stash money from the kebab shop to pay for shipping my body home. I've just turned nineteen, but I doubt I'll make it to twenty. This man will take my life. I'm not even scared anymore, just resigned to the fact.

"Raaaaayyyychh." He's yelling for me like we live in a mansion, not in a one-bedroom apartment. I switch the bathroom lights off and come into the living room, where he's bent intently over his crushed Heineken can scouring for any semblance of leftover rock from the piles of ash. In a little while, he'll be on his hands and knees searching the carpet and will invariably have tried to smoke several pieces of lint before the night is over. He looks up long enough to see my face, which is rapidly swelling and darkening. "Aww, shit baby. You know I didn't mean to hit you that hard. Daddy's sorry." His southern baritone makes everything sound so sincere.

"You just gotta try harder and make more money."

"I know." Too tired to argue.

"Come here, baby, I saved a little hit for you."

I put the can up to my lips and he lights the ashes for me. Within seconds the sickly sweet taste is in my mouth, my heart is speeding up, and for tonight dreams of ever leaving this man, this place, drift away with the smoke that rises up through our apartment and out into the street.

Just as there is no single profile of men who are batterers or child abusers, there is no single profile of pimps or traffickers. There are pimps who may have been abused themselves, whose fathers, brothers, uncles were pimps, who have grown up in the life, and who know nothing else. There are pimps who are mostly drug dealers but have one girlfriend whom they put out on the streets. While a few pimps have only one girl that they are selling, most pimps are committed to finding multiple girls. After all, half of the alleged glamour of pimping, much like the fantasy version of polygamy, comes from the macho ideal of having multiple women meeting your needs.

There are guerrilla pimps who are known for their violence and brutality. There are sneaker pimps, subway pimps, or *simps* as they're known, who are considered low-rent pimps at the bottom of the food chain. There are pimps who are sophisticated and savvy. There are pimps who are clearly sociopaths. Yet there are also pimps who probably wouldn't meet the clinical definition and who simply follow the cultural verity that we all do what we need to do to survive. As there are damaging racial stereotypes that have begun to be linked with pimping, it's critical to note that anyone who makes money off the commercial sexual exploitation of someone else is pimping them, be they a parent, a pornographer, or a member of an organized crime syndicate. Pimps can be male, female, or transgendered and come in all ages, races, and ethnicities, especially in different areas of the commercial sex industry such as escort agencies, brothels, and strip clubs. In a culture that has already done a good job at demonizing low-income young men of color, and that has increasingly conflated pimps with black men, it's important not to play into these stereotypes. Most people making money off the commercial sex industry are not men of color, yet that tends to be the first image people bring to mind when you mention the word *pimp*. Calling him a trafficker, on the other hand, tends to bring to mind a broad range of ethnicities and roles, from white American men who run child sex tourism agencies, to Korean massage parlor owners, to Mexican brothel managers, to eastern European men who traffic girls from Ukraine.

We know that in every country, pimps/traffickers tend to prey upon those that they have the most access to, girls and women from their own culture. So it is not surprising that since the vast majority of the girls I work with are girls of color, they have been under the control of street pimps who are men of color. Yet the faces of the men who own and operate strip clubs, brothels, escort agencies, and online "adult services," who are also exploiting and profiting from women and girls, are far more diverse. This reality must be acknowledged to avoid further demonization or a knee-jerk response to those in the sex industry who need to be held accountable.

In over a decade of listening to the stories and the tears of hundreds of girls who have experienced violence and exploitation at the hands of pimps, I've learned that pimp tactics of control and coercion rarely vary much from the script. Not only do pimps all seem to use the same tactics, but they also all seem to have graduated from the same mind-control training camp as cult leaders, hostage takers, terrorists, and dictators of small countries. While most of these groups may not have used the techniques of seduction and promises to initially lure their victims, pimps employ many of the same brainwashing and violence strategies to keep their victims under their control.

There is actually a framework for understanding this dynamic. It's a tool created by Amnesty International called Biderman's Chart of Coercion to explain the tactics used in controlling political prisoners and hostages. I showed it to a group of girls one night, wondering if they would agree with my assessment that it perfectly described pimp behavior. Clinical terms such as *monopolization of perception* or *enforcing trivial demands* sounded too removed from real-world application until we began to discuss them—"Oh, you mean like not letting you talk to anyone outside of the life," "Making you do dumb shit, little shit, just to see if you'll obey?" We drafted up our own adaptation of Biderman's list and the parallels were obvious. No wonder the tactics that were designed to work on hostages work so well on vulnerable girls and young women.

Like any subculture, American pimp culture has its own terminology and slang, all of which is about humiliation and degradation.

When a pimp uses the phrase *pimps up, hos down* he means that you
need to be in the street while he walks on the sidewalk. Being *out of
pocket* refers to showing disrespect for your pimp or another pimp
and can apply to infractions such as looking another pimp directly
in the eye, disagreeing with your pimp, or not making enough
money. Punishment for breaking the rules ranges from a beating
from your own pimp, being put into a *pimp circle*, where a group
of pimps harasses you and tries to force you to make eye contact
so they can beat you if you do. Your fine for breaking the rules is a
charge and you can be kidnapped by another pimp in order to make
back the money that you owe. There are myriad rules and codes — all
designed to break down individual will. In the beginning, you rarely
understand all the different rules, until of course you break one.

Pimps use the divide-and-conquer tactic that has been so popular historically to control girls and young women. One girl, the
bottom, is set up as the head girl, who may get certain privileges
or perhaps less abuse, until she does something wrong and is punished more severely because she is expected to "know better." The
head girl is generally the girl who makes the most money, although
it may be the girl who has children with the pimp, the one who's
been there the longest, or the one's who's the best "behaved," and
it can change accordingly. Like Holocaust victims who cooperated
with their abusers to stay "safer," and like house slaves versus field
slaves, the dynamic of one oppressed person set in a position of relative power over other oppressed people helps to ensure that there
is little solidarity and therefore less likelihood that there will be an
uprising against their oppressor. For trafficked girls their energy
is consumed between alternately competing with one another for
Daddy's attention and affection or trying to avoid being the one
getting beaten, even if it means snitching on or throwing another
girl under the bus. The rule is generally Peter pays for Paul, so it'll
be in Tanya's best interest to snitch if Melody tries to run away; otherwise they'll all be beaten. At the very least, Tanya will earn some

brownie points that will keep her in his good graces for a couple of days or might even get her some attention and affection.

While there are various historical comparisons to be made, the analogies to antebellum slavery are perhaps the most pertinent. One night, several GEMS girls and I were guests on a radio show when a pimp called in to disagree with our assertions that pimps were abusive. "The girls need protection. They wouldn't know what to do with their money, so I manage it for them. They're lazy. They like it. I'm giving them guidance because they're kinda dumb. I use violence only when I have to—it's more discipline than anything else. The only way they listen is if you're mean to them." Listening to him, I became aware that his justifications sounded strikingly similar to the paternalistic and condescending justifications of slave owners in the 1800s. Only today, our equivalent of slaves on the auction block is the ads on Craigslist, Backpage, and numerous other online sites, the street corners in certain neighborhoods, the stages of strip clubs. Four hundred years after slavery, pimps and traffickers are using the same lines, the same rationale, the same tactics as their predecessors in the antebellum South. Pimps thrive in America, a country where a modern-day slave system is too often justified and ignored.

In addition to their strategies of control and their paternalistic rationalizations, the other thing that pimps have in common, regardless of who they are, are the damaged lives they leave in their wake. To a girl who's been beaten because she didn't make her quota, or put out on the street after a rape and told, "There's nothing wrong with your mouth," it doesn't really make that much difference whether her pimp was a sociopath or not, if he had one girl or ten, if he ever felt bad about what he was doing, if he wished he could do something else with his life. The humiliation, the physical and emotional pain, the trauma, the nightmares all feel the same. The damage is done.

One night, by a set of bizarre and unfortunate circumstances, I am stuck in an ICU waiting room next to a man who, after a few minutes of pleasant conversation, I realize is the former pimp of one of my girls, Penny. The conversation quickly turns to his current girls, not a conversation I really want to have at 1 a.m. in the hospital. I tell him that perhaps it's not the time or the place to debate his pimping. He insists. And so begins a two-hour intense conversation in which he shares his upbringing, his father's pimping, his mother's being in the life, and his own entry into the game as a homeless seventeen-year-old. For me, it's both horrifying and fascinating to listen to his rationalizations. I'm angry just being around him, and yet sitting in the emergency room, I listen to a young man, twenty-four years old, who has experienced his own share of extreme trauma and abuse, who is smart and reasonably self-aware once he tries to stop justifying his actions and who is conscious that he's doing harm—even if over the years he's tried to make himself believe that "hos" are different. His experiences of growing up in violence, poverty, and neglect could be the story of one of the girls—except that he has become the perpetrator, not the victim. He talks about wanting to quit the game, about being addicted to it, about not knowing what else he would do. I tell him if the girls can leave, after the abuse that he and his cohorts put them through, he really has no excuse. I point to Penny, his ex, as an example. She is also the mother of his child and for most of their involvement, she was his only girl. It's clear, in a very distorted way, that his feelings for her go beyond the economic. I try to point out how much damage he's done to her, the conversation emotional and full of memories for me of sitting on the other end of the phone with Penny when she was screaming hysterically that he had a gun to her head or of going to get her in the middle of the night after he'd beaten her. In over two hours of intense conversation, it's only when I make the comparison to slavery and tell him that he put the mother of his child on the auction block and that he's no different from any of the white slaveholders that he's grown up loathing, that something registers. He's quiet for a long time and when he finally looks up he has tears in his eyes. On some level he is conscious of the damage he's done and continues to do but like the slaveholders, he is the one benefiting. He's not the one being sold, being scared, being hurt. His motivation to change is minimal, therefore fleeting. Before long I hear from Penny that he's pimping several more girls.

As an advocate and service provider, and as a survivor, I have many emotions about pimps, ranging from murderous thoughts to an understanding of the social conditions that can create this subculture. Yet the glorification of pimps and the minimization of their violent acts in American culture today make it difficult to have a nuanced and empathetic conversation about who pimps are, how they become pimps, and what we need to do to prevent this behavior. Any understanding we might have of the residual effects of slavery, the current effects of poverty, and the social messages that boys are receiving about what it means to be a man can't come at the expense of the victims. Right now, the pendulum has swung so far in favor of pimps that it's critical to bring it back to the reality of their crimes, the damage that they do, the callousness with which they treat girls' and women's lives. We don't have to demonize them. Stopping the glorification would be enough for now.

JOHNS

I will not cry, I will not think
I'll do my dance, I'll make them drink
When I make love, it won't be me
And if they hurt me, I'll just close my eyes
— *"The Movie in My Mind,"* Miss Saigon

WINTER 1994, GERMANY

It's five on a Tuesday, and the club is dead before the trickle of the after-work crowd. I'm curled up in my corner at the far end of the bar, wearing slippers and a big woolly cardigan to guard against the overactive air conditioner. Today I'm halfway through *Clockers*, immersed in Richard Price's richly drawn New York landscape, worried for Strike, wondering why Victor confessed, when my manager, Brigid, yells at me and interrupts my reverie. I'm always getting into trouble for reading so much at work. I'm allowed to read as long as there are no customers, but I'm often so caught up in whatever book I'm reading that there'll be people sitting at the bar drinking before I even notice anyone's there. I've always loved reading but now it's become something else. A way to escape into another world for a while. The night before, I'd had a vivid dream about Strike; today, while I'm working, I'll try to figure out what I think is going to happen next. Ina nods at me to go upstairs. She wants me to stand outside and try to attract some customers. I'm the only girl here for the day shift — two others called in sick and the rest won't be in till the evening — so I have no one to sic Brigid on. I'd rather read but there's no point in being here all day and all night if I'm not making any money.

Lately I've been pulling both shifts to meet JP's growing demands. Business has been quiet lately, but he doesn't believe me and always reminds me of nights when I've made triple the amount. Brigid and the club's owners, Ivan and Ina, are all riding us hard, complaining about how we're not making enough money, we're not aggressive enough, we're not getting enough VIPs. I'm tired of hearing the shit. I'm getting it from all sides, from everyone who's making money off me. I'm one of the best earners in the club, due to my age and English-speaking skills and my position as a house dancer. But I'd be the first to admit that I've been off lately. I'm too tired, too fed up with the hitting and the drama at home. As someone who takes her clothes off onstage, I have no way to hide what's happening. Ina told me recently when I came into work with bruises all over my body, again, that I needed to tell him to hit me only in the head from now on; otherwise I'll be suspended. I wanted to punch her in her face, but I just sucked my teeth and ignored her. I tell him to stop hitting me because of the bruises; he manages to figure out the head-hitting part on his own. I'm miserable and worn out, too, with all the drinking and lack of sleep, sick of the men, wanting to be left alone, not touched. Brigid raps on the bar with her knuckles and gestures upstairs again. I switch my furry slippers for a pair of black stilettos and shrug off my comfy cardigan, my blankie, to show my black minidress underneath. I only ever wear black at work, only ever wear clothes that are not my regular clothes but are part of my "uniform." It's just another way of separating, another futile attempt to be able to switch on and off.

I give Brigid a look. I've already had a few drinks courtesy of a couple of lunch-hour customers but I need a bit more if I'm going to step into my role. She rolls her eyes but pours me a triple shot of Hennessy anyway. I down it and then drag myself upstairs out of the artificial light of the basement club, which makes it feel like it's permanently midnight. It's daylight outside, people are getting off work, and here I stand in the doorway beckoning men. It reminds me of a scripture in Proverbs I learned as a child that says something about the harlot luring men from the window. Even then it had bothered me. Why was it all the lady's fault? Why didn't the men just not pay any attention? The Hennessy is kicking in now so I'm less bothered about scriptural ruminations; besides, thinking about the Bible just makes me feel guilty anyway. I pose in the doorway, keeping my mind on my money. A middle-aged couple walks past and the woman gives me the type of look reserved for child molesters and people who kill small kittens. It stings for a minute, but I'm used to it and have built up my defenses. I look her dead in the face and laugh, "You want something?" She looks away quickly as if meeting my eyes might turn her, Medusa-like, into the awful person I clearly am. I laugh again. I've already seen the look her husband was giving me. I'll lay money that he'll be visiting the club in the next few days. The ones who act like they are so disgusted always do.

The champagne is cheap but effective, though it's hard to stomach much of it without throwing up. Brigid knows my signal when I feel like I've had enough and will discreetly replace the champagne in my glass with seltzer and apple juice. Some customers are savvy about this trick and want to see you open the bottle of champagne in front of them. When that happens, there are other tricks: stuffing yourself with large amounts of dry bread before your shift begins in order to line your stomach and absorb as much alcohol as possible; forcing yourself to throw up halfway through the evening so that you can go the distance; and, riskiest of all, trying to pour as much of your drink into the plant pot in the VIP room while the customer is distracted. I never quite understand why some customers want to make sure you drink *all* of your alcohol and will get really angry if they think you're trying to pull a fast one. Everyone involved knows that the payment for the champagne is really about owning a girl for twenty minutes or an hour, depending on the size of the champagne bottle purchased. I don't get why the men are willing to

cause me a lifetime of liver problems by forcing me to drink something that neither one of us wants and that is simply their indirect
way of purchasing me.

The forced consumption of cheap alcohol is really about the customers wanting to feel as though they are on a date, not really buying sexual acts from teenagers or faded alcoholics in their forties.
Some johns have no desire to fake it, but most want the "romance,"
the flirtation, the process of seduction, despite the fact that we all
know how it's going to end. Hopefully, for me, it'll end with the
maximum amount of money for the minimum amount of contact,
although that's not always possible. Over the months, I've learned
to gauge what they are looking for. Some want the passive listening
type. As my German is still pretty shaky, this is my favorite since
I can just sit and make encouraging noises throughout a story that
I don't understand at all. I learn to read faces and voices so that I
don't smile and say, *"gut, gut"* if he is telling me how awful his day
was, or look sad and pained if he's asking to go to the champagne
room. Some want a story, so I create a few: "I'm half Filipina; I'm
leaving for Vegas soon to compete in the Gold G-String Awards."
None of them wants to believe that I have a current boyfriend, or
a pimp, so telling a story about an ex who broke my heart always
works. One of my favorites is the story of the husband who passed
away suddenly, leaving me destitute and penniless. I tell some of
these stories just to amuse myself, given how boring most of the
men are. I do my best to keep track of who I tell which story to,
but most of them know I am lying anyway and just need a narrative
upon which they can project their fantasies. There are the men who
want me to be their therapist and who spend hours sharing their
frustrations with work and relationships. Some even ask for advice.
The wisdom of asking a seventeen-year-old alcoholic who works in
a strip club for advice seems a little dubious to me, but I dispense
it anyway, practicing my best pop psychology learned from a few
self-help books and Oprah. Then there are the men who see them-

selves as rescuers, the "One" who will take me away from all of this and help me start again. Unfortunately their plans normally involve putting me up in an apartment where I would be at their sexual beck and call. Since most of what I know about the sex industry has come from *Pretty Woman*, I use Julia Roberts's line, "That's just geography," and feel wise and experienced that I don't fall for their offers of another life.

Other guys think of themselves as the "nice" ones. They are the ones who tell you that you don't deserve this life, that you should go back to school; that you're too smart, too pretty to be here. It sometimes seems as though they are seeing past the defenses, the alcohol-induced friendliness, the numbness, and are able to see Rachel, not "Carmen." In the beginning, I believe them, feel hopeful again, find myself believing that yes, I can do something else. But I'll learn quickly that in the end they're all the same, and that despite all their dream-weaving, they'll still want something from you. Strangely, it will bother me a little more with these guys. It's perhaps harder to rationalize that you could want to buy me if you actually see me as a smart, worthwhile person than if you don't see me as a person at all. Hard to accept that you would be able to see Rachel but then want to buy Carmen. After a while I'll learn not to be hurt by any of it, to stay numb, stay drunk, stay high. Focus on my books, my crossword puzzles; smile and ignore them; pretend they don't exist. I remind myself that there have been lots of times when I was touched but didn't want to be. Now at least I'm getting paid for the indignity of it all.

As a highly accomplished teenage shoplifter for many years, going into stores after I had quit shoplifting was a challenge for a long time. I was less interested in checking out the merchandise than in evaluating the security measures to assess how easy they would be to exploit. I would size up the exit, check out the locations of cameras, whether clothes had electronic tags or not, and how closely the sales assistants were paying attention. It was automatic and unbidden; years of viewing stores a certain way had trained my brain to see everything through a lens that most people didn't have.

For the first few years after I left the life, I experienced the same type of reaction toward the men I would encounter in my everyday life. Instinctively I would view the vast majority of men through the lens of my experiences with johns: *You're the type of john who shows pictures of his wife. You're the john who wants to be hurt. You're a cheap john.* Or, simply, *You are definitely a john* within the first few minutes, often seconds, of meeting or seeing a man. A midsize town in Germany wasn't the most diverse of places, so for me, most guys who were white, older, and wore suits were the most likely suspects as they had been my clientele.

I didn't realize how angry I was at these men until I came to New York and began working for the Little Sister Project. I was sent alone into all the downtown strip clubs and peep shows to give out flyers to women and girls. The flyers were ostensibly rallying against the new Giuliani policies on club locations, e.g., not near a school, but were mainly to get our contact information into the hands of women and girls who otherwise would not hear about our services. I was leered at and harassed within a few minutes of being inside these clubs and got propositioned at every one. I got riled up, forgetting that from the point of view of these customers, I was a young woman in a strip club, so of course I had to be working there. And that meant I could be talked to or treated any way they saw fit. I had forgotten how it felt to be robbed of personal space, to not have the right to speak up, to be seen solely as an object for purchasing, so at first I was silent and looked away. Three or four club stops later, a man's offhand comment to me sent me into a rage. I cursed him out, shaking and nearly crying. Why couldn't they see what they were doing? Why didn't they care? Why didn't someone stop them?

As much as I needed to process my experiences, it was hard to talk about them to people who'd never been in the life. I tried talking to a few friends but it was clear they didn't understand. In talking to a boyfriend about it, the conversation quickly turned awkward and I realized that no one, particularly not someone I was dating, wanted to hear me vent about all the men who'd purchased me. Only one man had made a profit off of me, but there were numerous men who'd bought me, and I felt my anger rise and rise. It began to occur to me that the exploitation of girls could not happen without these men.

John is in some way a fitting moniker for men who buy sex. Like *John Doe* and *Dear John*, the name is used as the generic catchall for the anonymous everyman who makes up the millions of men in America who buy sex from children. Those of us who have been exploited by the sex industry know that johns represent every walk of life, every age, every ethnicity, every socioeconomic class. Judges, mailmen, truck drivers, firemen, janitors, artists, clergy, cops, drug dealers, teachers. Handsome and rich, poor and unattractive, married, single, and widowed. Fathers, husbands, sons, brothers, uncles, neighbors.

Yet calling men who buy sex from children *johns* minimizes the harm they do. At the very least, they are statutory rapists and child abusers. That said, the reality is that most men who buy sex from trafficked and exploited girls aren't really pedophiles, as backward as that may sound. Most of these men aren't specifically attracted to children, and viewing men who purchase children and youth for sex as pedophiles leads to a sense that it is isolated behavior among men who are "sick" and "perverted." It allows us to overlook the fact that most of the men doing the buying are what we would consider "normal." Many of these men wouldn't dream of sexually abusing the girl next door but when it comes to a "prostitute," even a "teen prostitute," they figure it doesn't really matter. She's already out there. She kinda wants it anyway. She is working her way through college (even if she does appear to be in junior high). She needs to feed her kids. I'm actually helping her. There are a million rationalizations that men employ to deny the exploitation that they're a part of.

The buying of sex is so normalized that while we may frown upon those who get caught, there is an underlying belief that men have needs, and that sometimes those needs may be legitimately, if not legally, fulfilled by purchasing someone. While not all johns are looking to purchase a minor, there is a demonstrated link between the availability of the adult sex industry and the commercial sexual exploitation of children. A University of Pennsylvania study stated that "without equivocation . . . the presence of preexisting adult prostitution markets contributes measurably to the creation of secondary sexual markets in which children are sexually exploited." While many men would argue that they want someone who is of age, ultimately they want someone who looks clean and fresh, more likely to at least look disease-free. That desire generally translates into buying young girls. In research done by the Chicago Alliance Against Sexual Exploitation (CAASE), of 113 men who purchased sex, 76 percent of interviewees stated that the age of the woman was an important factor and 80 percent stated that they felt most men preferred young "prostitutes."

In a culture that continuously objectifies girls and women and that sexualizes and commodifies youth, it is little wonder that men prefer younger and younger girls when buying sex. When the Olsen twins came of age, there was a countdown clock on the Internet salaciously marking the minutes until they were "legal." Britney Spears's first video at seventeen, "Hit Me Baby One More Time," was memorable mostly for her schoolgirl outfit and her overtly sexual appearance. The cover of *FHM* magazine a few months later featured Britney clad in what appeared to be a slip, on a bed, looking incredibly young and childlike. The headline read, "My . . . hasn't she grown!"

There are hundreds of thousands of websites featuring legal "teen" or "barely legal" pornography and over twenty million searches a year for "teen sex" and "teen porn." Clearly the demand is there. While few men would argue that they are looking for a twelve-year-old, they might admit to looking for a seventeen- or eighteen-year-old, even if she looks fourteen. They rationalize that she didn't tell the truth about her age, so how are they supposed to know?

Former NFL star Lawrence Taylor probably didn't know that the girl he was purchasing for three hundred dollars was sixteen years old. It's impossible to know if he would've cared how old she was if he hadn't been caught. Reports claim he was "devastated" when he found out her age. Perhaps that's true. Perhaps he also had no idea that she was under the control of a pimp, had a black eye and bruised face when she came to his hotel room, and had a history of abuse and neglect. And yet men do know that the women and girls they're buying are exploited and harmed. In the CAASE research, 57 percent of men who bought sex believed that the majority of women in the sex industry had experienced childhood sexual abuse and 32 percent believed that most women entered the sex industry before the age of eighteen. Twenty percent thought that they had probably purchased someone who had been trafficked, either internationally or domestically, against her will. Forty percent had bought sex from a woman who he knew had a pimp or "manager." Forty-two percent believed that prostitution caused psychological and physical harm. So if men know that the sex industry is harmful to girls and women, why do they still participate in it? Many of the men in the study, and men I've talked to, cite peer pressure; being introduced to the sex industry by family, friends, even coworkers; the belief that women in the sex industry are "different" and therefore more acceptable to abuse. Most men cited the lack of consequences as a factor in their decision to purchase sex.

In most cases, though, men don't ask the questions that they really don't want to know the answers to. Easier to go along with the fantasy when she tells you her name is Extasy or Seduction, that she's eighteen, nineteen, twenty. When men are cruising the streets, scrolling through the ads online, ordering a girl from an escort agency, buying a lap dance, they don't want to really know how old she is or what her life is like. Most men would rather believe that she likes it, that she likes them, and that there's no real harm being done. Ultimately, however, most men in that situation just don't care.

Like almost every woman in New York, I've had my share of bad dates. The guy who took me to a nice restaurant only to discover at the end of the meal that he'd left his wallet at home. The guy who decided during lunch at his house that I'd be interested in his photo album of all his ex-girlfriends, including the pictures of them naked. The blind date who was clearly gay and kept asking me all night why everyone thought he was gay. Throw in a couple of unfortunate Match.com encounters and I've paid my dues in that often bizarre and frequently ridiculous world that is the singles scene in New York. While it can be discouraging to have gotten all dressed up for absolutely no worthwhile reason, these dates provide great fodder for girl talk over dinner. Like recovering addicts swapping worst-blackout stories, my friends and I compete to have the most outrageous, most horrifying tale of the ultimate date from hell.

Yet for the girls and young women we serve, a "bad date" means something else entirely. A bad date is a euphemism for being raped, being kidnapped, being held at gunpoint, or having a knife put to your throat. A bad date is when you get raped and are told by your pimp that you better get back out there. There are a few cops who take this type of violence against women and girls in the sex industry seriously, but for most cops, getting raped by a john just means that the girl didn't get paid.

Nikki tells me one night that she doesn't remember how many times she's been raped, but she thinks it's over twenty. Her experience isn't uncommon. When attention is paid to commercial sexual exploitation, law enforcement and public rhetoric focus their outrage on the pimps, rarely mentioning the johns, the buyers who fuel the industry. An assistant district attorney in New York tells me sincerely one day that "the johns are not the problem." To ignore the demand side of the issue makes no sense and trivializes the harm done by the buyers. Yet the girls and young women we serve don't make that distinction at all. If asked who's worse, pimps or johns, most would not be able to choose. They've experienced rapes, gang rapes, guns in their faces, beatings, sadistic acts, kidnappings—all at the hands of johns.

In 1992, Aileen Wuornos, erroneously dubbed "the first female serial killer" and later portrayed by Charlize Theron in the movie *Monster*, stood trial for the murder of Richard Mallory, a fifty-one-year-old john. She claimed it was in self-defense. While clearly Wuornos had severe psychological issues, likely due to her history of childhood sexual abuse and then later commercial sexual exploitation starting at age eleven, is it so difficult to imagine that perhaps Mallory, who had indeed served time for attempted rape, was actually trying to rape her?

Perhaps it was her own trauma that triggered her assumptions and her violent reactions, and that would then lead her to kill six more men over the course of the next year. Yet despite Wuornos's apparent mental health problems, her assumptions weren't totally off base. In studying the habits of serial killers who prey upon prostituted women and girls, it is clear how disposable these women and girls are seen to be. A Canadian commission found that women in the sex industry are 40 times more likely to be murdered than other women. Another study put the estimate as high as 130 times more likely to be murdered.

In 2003, Gary Ridgway, the notorious "Green River Killer," who for over two decades had preyed upon women in the sex industry, finally pled guilty to forty-eight counts of first-degree murder, although police suspected him of many more. Out of respect for the victims, we decided to honor them by putting their names and pictures up on a wall at GEMS. Next to their names were their ages and as I walked by the haunting display, I kept noticing the ages: Opal Mills, sixteen years old; Debra Estes, fifteen years old; Delores Williams, seventeen years old; Colleen Brockman, fifteen years old. In fact, twenty-seven of Ridgway's known victims were under the age of eighteen. This makes Gary Ridgway one of the most prolific child serial killers in the United States. Yet all of the media accounts of the victims called them women, not children. So why were they all portrayed as adult women? Ridgway himself seemed to have an answer in his allocution at his final hearing:

> I picked prostitutes as my victims because I hate most prostitutes and I did not want to pay them for sex. I also picked prostitutes as victims because they were easy to pick up without being noticed. I knew they would not be reported missing right away, and might never be reported missing. I picked prostitutes because I thought I could kill as many of them as I wanted without getting caught.

He was partially right. While his anger toward women and girls in the sex industry fueled his killing spree, picking "prostitutes" as victims was a strategic move. These women and girls were seen as less important, less like "real" victims, their murders less likely to be given the resources that other, more legitimate victims would receive. What he may also have realized was that just by virtue of being in the commercial sex industry, adulthood and maturity were imputed to these children. They were now seen as adult women, despite their ages, simply because they were also seen as "prostitutes."

I sit on the end of the bed. I'm not really sure what to say. I'd been warned that Sequoia's face would look bad, but hearing about her assault and then seeing the evidence all over her battered and fractured face is something else entirely. Her upper lip is split completely in two; her jaw is broken, her nose as well. Most of her teeth are gone. I hear my sharp intake of breath. What kind of person would do this to a child? She is sipping fluids through a straw.

I think of her, less than two years previously, at her youth leadership graduation, dressed up like a little girl at her first communion, replete with a white frilly dress and Shirley Temple curls. My social worker, Julie, and I had joked about how she looked like a tiny china doll. Now that doll has been mutilated, her delicate porcelain features smashed. Sequoia, always a petite child, is dwarfed in an adult-size hospital bed, surrounded by curtains with Shrek cartoons on them.

Somewhere out there, there's a man who beat a child nearly to death and left her by the side of the road. I wonder about this man, what he does for a living, if he's married or has a girlfriend, if he has children of his own. I wonder if anyone in his "real" life suspects what kind of man he is. I wonder when, not if, he'll do it again to another girl whom he views as disposable property. And I wonder if she, like Sequoia, will survive, and if anyone will notice if she doesn't.

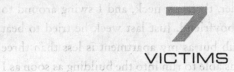

VICTIMS

The majority of rapes and sexual assaults perpetrated against women and girls in the United States between 1992 and 2000 were not reported to the police. Only 36 percent of rapes, 34 percent of attempted rapes, and 26 percent of sexual assaults were reported.

—*U.S. Department of Justice*

SUMMER 1993, GERMANY

I'm up at eight and out the door before nine, a minor miracle for me considering that I didn't get to sleep until 5 a.m. The money burning a hole in my pocket is propelling me to the electronics store. On the list today: a stereo, nice speakers, a TV, and probably a VCR. I worked my ass off for this three grand, so it's about time I treat myself. It'd be kind to say that my little rented room is sparse; right now it's a mattress on the floor and some boxes of clothes, lovingly decorated with a few empty beer bottles and an overflowing ashtray of cigarette butts and joint roaches. But I've been in Mainz a couple of months now and I feel like I'm ready to put down some roots. The club is OK, the money is good: 50 percent of the bar take plus whatever you earn in VIP. Actually, you're not supposed to make money for yourself in VIP, but early on in my dancing career, which was all of about eight months ago, I was taught by a much older and wiser woman that the real money came through your own private hustle. I caught on quickly. Hence the three thousand marks that I've been stashing for a couple of weeks—my "boot money," cleverly named because I hide it in my boots.

I'm excited about my little shopping trip. Too excited to notice anything as I leave my house and turn to lock the door behind me.

A hand grabs my shoulder, then my neck, and I swing around to see Mike, my recent ex-boyfriend. Just last week he tried to beat me up in front of the club but as my apartment is less than three hundred yards away, I was able to run into the building as soon as I saw him lurking. This morning he's obviously been waiting for me to leave the house and now he's grabbing me, asking me why I've been ignoring him, calling me a dirty whore. He's got me pinned against the wall, but I'm doing my best to get a few swings in. He's a slight man, but strong enough to punch me hard on my cheek. I try to kick him off me, but he's got me around the throat. I don't feel scared, just annoyed that he's got the audacity to ruin my carefully planned shopping spree. I kick as hard as I can and he relaxes his grip on my neck, just long enough to swing back and hit me in the head with full force. The blow knocks me off-balance and I see the ground rushing up to meet me. I close my eyes.

I awaken in the passenger seat of Mike's crappy little black Audi. He's muttering to himself and, in accordance with the no-speed-limit rules of the Autobahn, doing about 120 miles down the highway. I have no idea where we are or where we're going, although upon hearing me stir, Mike is happy to oblige me with this information.

"I'm taking you to Holland—Amsterdam, actually—and I'm going to sell you. I already have it all set up. I know a guy," he says. "It's what you deserve for doing what you did to me."

Still a little disoriented from his punches, or the concrete, or both, I can't really understand what's happening. Mike's talking about what a dirty, lying whore I am and seems to be vacillating between sounding mournful that we're not still together and ecstatically happy that his plan—to kidnap me? to sell me?—is actually working. As I stare at him, not sure how to respond, I see my purse sitting in his lap and I remember the three grand. "Can I have my purse?" He ignores me.

"Please?" Hating to grovel for my own stuff.

He laughs. "Sure." And throws it at me. I grab for it and open the inside pocket, already knowing how this is going to turn out. "If you're looking for your money, it's gone. I have it, and your passport."

"You stole my money?" Tears are coming now as I think about what I did to get that money and how carefully I saved it.

"You stole my heart."

"What? That doesn't even make sense! It's *my* money."

"It's *my* heart." He seems completely convinced by his own logic.

I tell him he's a piece of shit, which seems a bit mild under the circumstances, and turn my head to the window. I watch fields, trees, cows, and the few farmhouses that dot the scenery whiz by, and try to think rationally. We're going too fast for me to jump out and I have no idea how long he's planning on driving. I consider writing *help* or *hilfe* in lipstick on the window but there's about a million problems with that plan, none of which ever surfaces in the movies. I can't figure out how to escape and get my money and my passport. I worked too hard for that money to let him get it. Closed my eyes and gritted my teeth for it. Fuck no, he's not getting my money. I cry quietly out of the window, trying to ignore his verbal assaults from the driver's seat. Wondering if he really will take me to Amsterdam or if he'll think of some other way to punish me instead.

Another hour later and he pulls off the highway onto a dirt road. I'm guessing this isn't the way to Holland but stay quiet, trying not to provoke another onslaught. He's been quiet for a while, running out of steam and insults about eighty miles ago. Clearly his mind has been working overtime. The dirt road is becoming less of a road and more of a track until finally it peters out into grass and dirt. Mike continues to drive through nothing but fields for a while, stopping finally near the edge of a large river. We're in the middle of nowhere. I can't see anything but fields for miles to our right, a thick forest to our left, and the river in front. I know the Autobahn's somewhere behind us but at this point I'm not sure how far. If I can get away, though, I'll just run as fast as I can in that direction. Someone will eventually see me. Mike parks the car right on the river embankment. It's about a forty-foot drop down to the muddy water.

"Get out."

I stay seated, scared to move. The plan is becoming a little clearer.

"Get the fuck out of the car."

I get out, hearing the tone in his voice change. He no longer sounds merely angry, he's moved into pure rage. He comes around the car and grabs me.

"I've changed my mind. Fuck Amsterdam. That's too good for you."

He points to the river. "How far do you think you would travel before you washed up? I wonder how strong the current is today." He pulls me closer to the water's edge as I struggle to get free of his grip.

"Please. Please. Please don't do this."

"What? Hurt you? That's what you did to me. You hurt me, Rachel. So now I have to hurt you."

"Please, I'm sorry. I'm sorry. I didn't mean to hurt you. I didn't mean to. . . ." I'm crying hysterically now, begging for my life.

"I loved you. I fuckin loved you. I wanted to marry you."

He sounds as if he's about to cry and I seize on it. "I loved you too. We could still get married."

He loosens his grip a little.

"But I know you're fucking someone else. Who is it? Just tell me who it is and I'll let you go."

He's right. I have met someone else, a guy called JP, but I know if I confess, I'll be floating facedown in the river for the next few weeks until some old fisherman hooks me accidentally.

"There's no one, I swear."

He punches me dead in the mouth. "Every time you lie, that's what you'll get. Now, who is he?"

"There's no one." I brace myself for the blow, but it doesn't hurt any less.

I'm crying and bleeding and he's sweating and cursing an hour later, but I still haven't told him anything. Intermittently he'll stop and quiet down, pausing to smoke a cigarette and sit on the hood of the car, while I catch my breath from the blows and the crying.

The plan to kill me and dump me in the river seems to be fading. If I can just hang tight a little while longer.

I cry and beg as much as possible, and swear my undying love. Although he's entertaining the thought of forgiving me, he's having too much fun punishing me.

"Take off your shoes."

I comply and he snatches them and puts them in the car. "Now you can go home."

He gets into the car and drives off. Perplexed, I wait for a few minutes until I can no longer hear the engine and then start running as fast as I can in the direction of the highway. I can feel stones and twigs cutting into my feet. I feel as if I've run for miles when eventually I hear the engine getting closer and closer and he's back. He performs this charade, driving away, forcing me to run, coming back again several more times over the next hour until my feet are bloody and swollen. On the last round, I'm too tired to run and understand that it's futile anyway. I sit down on the grass and wait for him to come back. He sees me defeated and appears to relish the fact that he's beaten most of the fight out of me. "We learned that in the army: Take the shoes to disable the enemy." I figure I'll try one more time.

"But I'm not your enemy. I love you; let's be together." I'm pleading now.

Slowly he relents. He wants to believe me and so he does. I manage to convince him to drive us back to civilization where we can find a place to eat and relax. He agrees that it's been a long day. I'd like to argue that given the fact that I've been kidnapped, assaulted, and threatened with drowning, my day has been much longer, but I'm just relieved that we're turning back.

We pull into a small village, and Mike starts talking about where we will live after the wedding. I try to play along as much as I can but I'm plotting my escape. I've managed to get him to give back my passport but he's still holding on to the money. As soon as the car slows down, I jump out, stumbling and then running as fast as I can in the opposite direction. An elderly woman is walking by and I shout, *"Polezie—vo es Polezie?"* She points up the street, fortunately in the direction I'm already headed, and I run faster. Mike is trying to turn the car around to catch me but there's too much traffic and he's still trying to make a U-turn when I'm already halfway up the hill.

I run, out of breath and wheezing, into the precinct. I tell the officer at the front desk in English (as I don't know the words in German) that I was kidnapped and assaulted. He calls several other officers over. I describe Mike and his car and tell them he should still be in the area. There's some discussion among the officers that I don't understand and then a Sergeant Werner takes me into an interview room. He's tall and a little intimidating but I figure once I tell him what happened he'll warm up. I tell him the whole story, although my disheveled appearance, the bruises that are beginning to develop on my face and arms, and the torn soles of my feet pretty much explain everything. Sergeant Werner seems mildly interested, although he's clearly not the most empathetic of listeners. He asks questions and writes notes until we've been all the way through the event.

Another cop comes in to report that Mike has been brought into custody and is in the interview room next to mine. I tell Sergeant Werner to check Mike's pockets and that he'll find two thousand-mark bills, one five hundred, three hundreds, and four fifty-mark notes.

Sergeant Werner is gone for a while, and I can hear the low mur-

mur of men's voices in the next room. Then I hear them laughing, and moments later the cop reenters the room and casually asks me if Mike can have a cigarette. I can't believe what I'm hearing. "A fuckin cigarette? He just beat and threatened to kill me. Tell him to buy his own fuckin pack with the three thousand marks he just stole from me!" I'm yelling now, with tears streaming down my face, and yet the sergeant just stares at me as if I've just refused the most reasonable, logical request in the world. "Fuck this. I'm leaving. You're not gonna do shit."

I storm out of the interview room, still crying.

Werner runs after me and for a moment I think he's going to apologize, arrest Mike, and this whole bizarre scenario is going to be resolved the way it should be. Instead, he grabs my arm, tells me I can't leave, and demands my passport. I can't believe this is happening. I'm yelling and crying and trying to get away from him. "I didn't do anything, he's the one that did this to me." The cop is now blocking me from leaving as I try to walk down the stairs. I know that Mike can probably hear the whole thing and is enjoying every second. Fortunately, another cop—a woman, hears the commotion, too, and runs up the stairs. They are debating in German and I can understand only a few words, but it's clear that he's winning.

The female officer turns to me. She looks frustrated but is trying to calm me down. "Give him your passport or he'll arrest you."

The male cop looks smug.

With tears streaming from anger more than anything else, I turn over my passport, still confused as to why I'm being treated this way. She takes me downstairs to another interview room where I sit chain-smoking for what feels like hours, but is probably closer to forty-five minutes.

Sergeant Werner finally returns and hands me back my passport. The female officer is with him and offers an apology. Werner seems disappointed that he was unable to find any outstanding warrants and has no reason to arrest me.

"You can leave." He dismisses me with a wave.

"How am I supposed to get home?" We had driven for over two hours and I had no idea where I was.

"He will give you a ride."

I'm confused. "Who? Another officer?" I know I don't want to be trapped in a car with this guy for a couple of hours.

"Him." He points upstairs, and I suddenly realize that he is suggesting that I get back into the car with the same man who kidnapped and assaulted me that morning.

"What the fuck are you talking about?" Now I am about to get arrested.

"He says he will give you a ride. He is leaving now too."

"You're not arresting him? What about the assault? What about my money? Did you get it back?"

"He says it's his." Werner is already walking out the door, no longer interested in our conversation.

The female officer who has stayed puts her arm around me. In careful English and over my sobs, she explains what is going on. Yes, Mike is claiming the money is his. The bruises and cuts, the marks on my body and on my feet apparently come from the fact that I like rough sex, and that's what we were doing in the field. In fact, he was trying to break up with me but I didn't want to and that's why I came to the precinct. He's told them that I am a *"Hure,"* and that my place of employment is a strip club. With these "facts" on the table, my case has ceased to be a case.

The woman seems ashamed. "They do this to many girls," she says. "Girls . . . uh . . . rape." She mimes hitting. "Girls . . . they, ah . . . do not believe, um, when cabaret, das bordell, strip club." She struggles to explain, but she really doesn't need to. She gives me enough money to get on the train and writes Werner's name and badge number on a piece of paper with an address for what I assume is police headquarters. "Please. Write to them. Tell them what he did. He always do this." There are tears in her eyes and I cry as I hug her, thanking her over and over again. Of course, Mike is waiting for me when I get off the train. He's smug now and I don't argue with him. He won. I figure that the bruises will heal and I'll make back the three grand eventually.

Later when JP begins to hit me, night after night, I'll know better than to go to the cops for help. I never do write the letter of complaint about Werner. I don't believe it'll do any good. After all, I'm not exactly a credible complainant, an upstanding citizen. Girls like me, I realize, get what they deserve.

I was thirteen when the film *The Accused* premiered in England. Based on the real-life gang rape of Cheryl Araujo that occurred at Big Dan's bar in New Bedford, Massachusetts, in 1983, this film was one of the first Hollywood films to deal with rape in a direct manner. Jodie Foster plays the rape victim and in the end triumphs over the perpetrators of the crime and the system. In real life, however, the victim was vilified by her Portuguese community despite having been assaulted by six men on a pool table while a group of bystanders cheered them on. Candlelight vigils were held on behalf of the accused men and the victim was portrayed as a loose woman whose decision to go to a local bar alone late at night to buy a pack of cigarettes got her just what she deserved.

A few months later, as a victim of a date rape, I was told by the cops that given that I already worked in a bar, was on a date with a man in his twenties, and was generally considered to be "too grown" made for a difficult case. Despite the fact that the assault took my virginity and that the adult perpetrator had a record of sexual and physical violence, including putting a teenage girl in a coma, the case was dropped. Apparently I wasn't a great victim then either.

My experiences with cops, both growing up in England and in

Germany, left me distrustful and skeptical. When I came to New York and began working with law enforcement, I retained a lot of the perceptions that I'd carried for years. As I worked with cops, I'd hear the same complaints: The girls didn't want to talk to them, the girls were "resistant" to help, that perhaps they didn't really want any. Most law enforcement officers failed to understand the rationale behind the girls' responses to them. They sometimes understood why internationally trafficked victims who are undocumented and who've often experienced police corruption in other countries might be mistrustful of the police, but they expected girls from the United States to automatically trust and respect law enforcement. Yet many trafficked girls have grown up in communities that historically have feared and loathed the police, often with good reason. Communities of color and low-socioeconomic communities have rarely experienced police presence as a positive thing. Growing up in these communities, you learn that snitches get stitches and that cooperating with the cops is considered the lowest form of cowardice. In fact, cops are the ones you've seen regularly harassing your brother when he's late coming home, the ones who locked up your cousin last year, who took over an hour to come that time someone broke into your grandma's apartment. You learn not to trust them and often to fear them.

On the streets, it's even harder to tell the good and bad guys apart. Cops see men buying girls on the street and look the other way, cops taunt girls and call them names, and some of the johns are cops themselves. The overwhelming majority of girls I've worked with have reported being threatened with jail if they refused sex with a cop, and some girls who refused and were arrested were forced to have sex at the precinct anyway. Some cops would take money from the girls when they spotted them on the streets, knowing that they could never report it. In 2008, a New York City detective was arrested and charged with pimping a thirteen-year-old girl whom he had lured, drugged, and threatened with violence.

To be fair, these officers don't represent every police officer. Most cops are apathetic toward the girls, not abusive. Yet, like the johns who wouldn't dream of having sex with just "any" teenage girls, most of the cops who do use their power and position to abuse girls in the sex industry would never threaten a female drunk driver with arrest in exchange for sex. The fact that girls are "already out there" makes them less of a victim, less deserving of rights or boundaries.

Girls who are raped and assaulted by johns or pimps know that their abuse will not be taken seriously. The rape of a prostituted girl or woman is considered by many to be a contradiction in terms and the police normally believe that what girls claim to be rape is really just a question of not getting paid for their services. In fact, many cops literally call it "theft of services." How can someone be raped when they're already having sex anyway? What we've learned in the sexual violence movement over the years is that rape has little to do with sex, and everything to do with power. Being raped feels just as scary if you're a girl on the track who's been sold to seven men that same night as it does to a "regular" woman or girl. If you're considered sexually experienced, or even sexually active, the degrees of harm done by sexual assault are often measured out according to your level of "culpability." While this view isn't limited to girls in the sex industry and is also often imputed to victims of sexual violence who are considered promiscuous, women and girls in the sex industry are obviously seen as the least affected by sexual violence.

Working with the girls at GEMS over the years, I found that this theme continually emerged. In case after case, I saw that girls weren't being taken seriously, that their experiences of victimization were often disparaged at best and blatantly mocked at worst. In defending a sixteen-year-old rape victim, I was threatened with arrest. A cop told a girl he really couldn't see why she didn't just leave the man who had forcibly kidnapped her. A girl from Spain who got recruited in the United States and spoke very little English was told that because she hadn't used the word "force" in reporting her rape at the hospital, the police, who did not speak Spanish, could not charge the perpetrator. Another girl's body lay misidentified in a morgue for over a month while her family, having been brushed off by the police, frantically searched for her.

It's difficult to view yourself as a victim, no matter what happens to you, when your pimp, the men who buy you, and even those who are supposed to protect you see you as incapable of being victimized. Prostitution is viewed as a victimless crime, a statement that denies the humanity or victimhood of the women and girls involved. Women in the sex industry, and therefore trafficked and sexually exploited girls, are not believed to be capable of being hurt or raped. In fact, rather than being seen as victims, they're seen as willing participants in their own abuse and are often perceived as having "asked for it."

I meet Krystal in the hallway of the Brooklyn Supreme Court. She's late. Two police officers have driven her from a chain hotel upstate that the district attorney's office has paid for. She looks like she's barely slept, which I soon discover is an accurate assessment. Her hair is askew and despite my lectures on what to wear to court, she obviously just grabbed the nearest thing to her. Unfortunately, the outfit that she's picked is a denim mini-miniskirt, construction Timbs with no socks, and a tight-fitting, wrinkled T-shirt. I'm taking a wild guess that this is the outfit she wore till the wee hours. It's not exactly court attire and definitely not the outfit that we'd agreed on. Krystal's long, long legs make the skirt, which is short, look even shorter. I'm horrified. Today is a huge day; she's testifying in the trial of her ex-pimp and I'm already nervous about how she'll be perceived by the jury. I drag her into the bathroom, before anyone else in the court corridors sees her, and try not to yell at her about her fashion choices on one of the most important days of her life. She tells me she thinks she looks OK. I try to explain that there's OK for going to the bodega and OK for going to court, but we've already been down that road before and clearly it had little effect. I know she's nervous and I don't want to make it worse, but there's no way I'm letting her walk into court like that. I'm already worried about how well she'll do in her testimony: She's scared, and when she gets scared, she gets sullen. A pouting and sullen "former child prostitute" in a skirt short enough to be a belt is unlikely to win any supporters on the jury, and I'm guessing she won't impress the judge, either.

I size her up. "What?" she whines. Despite the fact she's got six inches on me in height, most of it in those legs, I know we're about the same size. When we were trying to get her out of New York for her safety, she'd stayed at my house for a few days and, as the girls liked to call it, "gone shopping" in my closet. I look at myself in the mirror. Damn, I was kind of feeling my outfit today. It's new and I look all pastel and preppy.

Ten minutes later, she walks into court wearing a mint green linen dress from H&M, low white heels, and a white cotton cardigan from JCPenney. I walk into court wearing a teeny-tiny denim skirt, Timbs with no socks, and a tight-fitting, wrinkled T-shirt. I hold my bag in front of my legs to try to hide how ridiculous I look, but it doesn't really help. The assistant district attorney, whom I'd seen earlier this morning, does a double take and raises his eyebrows. I shrug, whaddya-gonna-do style, but I'm fairly mortified and also extremely cold as my bare thighs hit the wooden bench. Mainly for Krystal's sake, but a tiny bit for mine, I pray that her testimony will be brief.

As it turns out, Krystal's preppy outfit doesn't even matter. She's rightfully nervous and is clearly thrown off by the sight of her pimp, Pretty Boy, in the courtroom. He knows it and stares intently at her the whole time, breaking eye contact only to scribble furiously on his pad after she answers a question. Adding to the intimidation are the glares of some of his family members, who take turns staring at her, at me, and at her case manager, the only people there for Krystal. I'd instructed her to look only at us, but her gaze seems inescapably pulled in his direction. Three years since the last time she saw him and he still wields control over her.

The direct examination from the ADA, who clearly hasn't prepped her properly, is terrible. As I'd predicted, fear has set off her defense mechanisms, which to people who don't know her and people who don't understand the effects of trauma, just appears to be sullenness and resistance. Krystal finally manages to look away from Pretty Boy but then just stares at her feet and barely mumbles into the microphone. She has to be directed over and over again by the judge to speak up, which begins to embarrass her, which in turn comes out as frustration. The mic is loud and the courtroom is quiet, so after the fifth time the judge rather sternly instructs her to speak into the mic clearly, her annoyed teeth-sucking is heard by all. We're off to a bad start.

The day doesn't get better. Krystal is confused by many of the questions and predictably reacts to confusion with frustration. At one point, the ADA asks her the same question in three different ways, as he's not satisfied with her answer. Krystal clearly thinks he's stupid, and to complement the teeth-sucking she now stamps her foot in frustration, visibly and audibly, in the witness stand. A couple of jurors snicker. The rest look at her with disdain. To verify that she was indeed "working" for the defendant and was arrested for prostitution multiple times, the ADA admits into evidence a Polaroid photo taken after one of the arrests and it's passed to the jury. Even from the court benches, we're sitting close enough to see the picture as it's passed from person to person: Krystal at fourteen, already tall and developed, in a skimpy bikini top and short shorts. The men on the jury are quite obviously leering, looking long and close at the picture as if it's a complicated diagram of blood-spatter patterns. The thoughts in their minds might as well be displayed across a ticker board. The women on the jury hold it like it's radio-active, looking scornfully at Krystal fidgeting on the witness stand. The picture has told a thousand words, all of them harsh judgments about the "type" of girl who would "choose" to do this. The fact that she's fourteen in the picture doesn't seem to register with any-one. The fact that an adult man is accused of beating her, brain-washing her, and selling her on the streets doesn't seem to provoke any empathy or sympathy. There's no smoking-gun picture of him brutalizing her with a baseball bat. There's just a girl in "provoca-tive" clothing, pouting at the camera, and charged with having sex for money. Any chance of being perceived as a victim has just dis-appeared. In the jury's minds she's been branded as a "bad" girl, "loose" girl, and "dirty" girl, and all the JCPenney white cardigans in the world won't make that go away.

While Krystal seems to have forgotten that the ADA is actually the one in the legal process who is on her side, I haven't. If direct is bad, cross is going to be awful. When it comes to the defense's turn, he paces like a wild animal about to attack his prey. He tries to make a couple of jokes to relax her defenses but she's not buying any of it; she knows where this is headed. When he finally pounces, it's actu-ally worse than I'd imagined. He's got her in tears within a few min-utes, angry and even more defensive that she'd been on direct, and contradicting herself with every other sentence. I feel physically sick and consider standing up and yelling something inappropriate with the hopes of causing a mistrial, just to end her misery. In the end, though, all I can do is sit there. An ineffectual advocate unable to defend her or protect her. It's horrifying to watch, made more so by the smug look on Pretty Boy's face. He's smelling an easy win.

Halfway into the afternoon, as Krystal stumbles, cries, and at several points completely refuses to answer, the judge calls a recess until the next day. As Krystal and I switch back clothes, I try half-heartedly to encourage her, but she doesn't want to hear it. She's shut down and I don't push it. She never asked for this. The cops and the DA wanted her to testify and yet she's the one being humiliated and intimidated in a public courtroom in front of the man she fears, and used to love, the most. I give her a hug and tell her I'm sorry this is happening and that it will be over soon. She wants it to be over today. She hates the lawyer, she hates the DA, she hates the judge, and did I see him staring at her, his family, too? She knows they're going to come after her. I tell her that she has a restraining order, yet feel disingenuous as the words come out of my mouth. What good is a restraining order against someone who really wants to hurt you? I offer to treat her to McDonald's. A Band-Aid on a boo-boo. The sort of thing you do for a six-year-old who fell off his bike and needed a stitch. Not a remedy for a teenage girl who's testifying in a hostile court against a murderous pimp.

She barely survives another excruciating day of cross-examination in which the defense attorney manages to confuse Krystal thoroughly about dates and times. I've told her that if she doesn't remember that it's better just to say that, but he's hammering her so hard, I doubt if she could even recite her date of birth properly at this point. It's agonizing to watch, particularly since it's obvious to everyone but exhausted, numb Krystal where's he going with his questioning. He's able to back her into a corner and have her swear up and down that on these days—yes, she is totally sure, yes, positive—she was threatened and assaulted by the defendant and forced to work on the streets. As he walks back to the defense table, he asks her one last time, for effect, if she's sure. Yes, she is. He waives a piece of paper triumphantly at the judge, "Well, Ms. Jenkins, it would've been hard for my client to do the things you said he did on the days that you were positive that he did them when he was incarcerated in Rikers Island jail at the time."

There's a glimpse of comprehension on her face when she realizes the trap that was set for her. Her whole body visibly crumples on the stand but the defense attorney continues pummeling her like a boxer up against the ropes, going in for the final kill until she no longer says anything, her chin pressed to her chest, eyes closed, willing herself to be somewhere else, anywhere else.

And then it's over. We get into the car and I drive away as quickly as possible. She's quiet. I want to scream and curse. Why didn't the ADA prep her better? Why didn't they call me or someone else as an expert witness to help the jury understand how trauma affects a victim's ability to testify in an open courtroom? Why can't she get witness protection now after everything she's risked?

She doesn't want to think about any of that ever again. Two days later when we get the phone call from the DA's office, she's not surprised. She didn't really expect to be believed anyway.

In her book *Sex Crimes*, former prosecutor Alice Vachss describes how victims of rape are perceived as either "good" victims or "bad": "In New York City, good victims have jobs (like stockbroker or accountant) or impeccable status (like a policeman's wife); are well-educated and articulate, and are, above all, presentable to a jury; attractive but not too attractive; demure but not pushovers. They should be upset, but in good taste—not so upset that they become hysterical."

Commercially sexually exploited girls don't have jobs or impeccable status. They sleep all day and get up at night, doing the same thing over and over again so they have a difficult time remembering specific dates and times. They have mixed feelings toward their pimps and feel guilty about testifying. They're often angry, rightfully so, and they each handle the trauma of testimony differently. Domestically trafficked girls who have learned that comfort is rare, that tears get them only more beatings, and that staying numb is the best way to survive, fare badly in the courtroom process. There is little understanding from justice officials and juries of differences in cultural responses and the varying effects of trauma. Girls are seen as either having a bad attitude or not being upset enough. If they are not *good* victims, in other words, they are not *real* victims. And this is true even when they are being framed as victims or witnesses. When they are the ones facing charges, the odds are skewed even further against them.

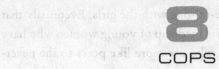

COPS

Larger social forces have stripped most of these young people
of any meaningful childhood. . . . In fundamental ways, they
have never gotten to be children and now they are being cast
as nonchildren. . . . These youths have not been afforded the
protection presumed to be part of childhood, and yet the
harshness of their lives frequently is disregarded or minimized,
even while their presumed responsibility and guilt worthiness
are used to justify punitive responses against them.
— M. A. Bortner and Linda M. Williams,
Youth in Prison: We the People of Unit Four

Horizon Juvenile Center is baby jail. Of course, you're not supposed to call it that, and in all fairness it is definitely a far cry from
New York's major jail facility, Rikers Island. But essentially it's
baby jail: juvenile detention for children, both boys and girls, under
the age of sixteen. While the facility itself is a marked improvement
over the old building that it replaced, it is still very much an insti-
tution designed not for therapy or rehabilitation, but to hold and
detain children. The doors are locked, there are Juvenile Justice officers monitoring the hallways, and the kids wear blue jumpsuits and
line up against the wall to count off by number before every "movement" to another locale. Both boys and girls are kept in the detention center, although they're in separate units. A handful of the girls
are in for serious crimes—assault, robbery, and, rarely, murder—
but most are in for minor crimes: petty larceny, minor drug charges,
and fighting, often the type of after-school fight that my friends
and I once had without any consequences, but that in a post-super-
predator world gets kids, especially kids of color, locked up with
alarming regularity.

For the first few years, I do outreach to the facility, conducting workshops and meeting one-on-one with the girls. Eventually that task is left to an outreach team made up of young women who have graduated from GEMS and who are more like peers to the never-ending stream of twelve-, thirteen-, and fourteen-year-old girls than I am, as I reach my late twenties and early thirties and become "old" in the girls' eyes. Today, at the request of her lawyer, I'm here to meet with a girl who's appearing in court on prostitution charges. She's been holding a lot of information back, information that could probably help her case, and her lawyer is hopeful that someone from GEMS will be able to break through and provide a treatment recommendation for the judge. I walk through the hallway and see girls in their shapeless jumpsuits lined up against the wall, counting down. "Four, five, six . . . Rodriguez, Rodriguez! Are you listening. Count!"

"Oh, my bad, miss. Uh, six? Wait, start over."

I'm struck, as always, by how young they all are. Swallowed by their massive jumpsuits, they look more likely to be playing double Dutch than to be in lockdown. I'm reminded of when I used to come to do outreach and would eat lunch in the cafeteria with the girls, a fact that staff seemed to be both disdainful of and perplexed by. On one of my first days there, we'd all been lined up with our trays at the lunch counter and the girls had all received a milk carton. One of the cafeteria workers nodded to me. "Gotta give 'em that, for their nutrition. They still growing."

And that pretty much sums up juvenile detention for me. Children who still require nutritional supplements are locked up.

It's with this in mind that I meet Keisha, a brown-skinned, heavyset girl, her frame more commonly referred to in the streets as *thick*. Keisha's thickness is evidently puppy fat and the childlike roundness of her face points clearly to her age, thirteen. We make small talk and then her lawyer and I try to impress upon her the importance of staying calm in court; on her last court appearance she had cursed out the court officer, who she says grabbed her arm too roughly. Keisha is uninterested in this discussion and would rather talk about a boy, Troy, she has met in detention. She talks about the kites, the little folded notes, that they send each other; about another girl who likes him and how she had to "check" the girl for her interest in her man. Keisha's been in the detention center for only two weeks and has had very little interaction with Troy, who is on another unit, but like most girls her age, it takes very little for a relationship to qualify as such. Especially in detention, where there is little to do to pass the time and kites may be the only mail that the teenager gets, relationships bloom, flourish, and die with breathtaking rapidity. A few stolen glances in the hallway, a message passed from his friend to her friend, and now Keisha draws love hearts all over her kites and signs them, *Your one and only true love, 4ever*. Keisha is excited about this new relationship, and after twenty-five minutes, it's clear she'll chatter about Troy all day without ever taking a breath if I don't interrupt. Keisha is reluctant to address the charges of prostitution that are facing her today, but I explain that although I know that she's probably tired of telling her story, I need to ask her questions so that I can talk to the judge. I already know the details of her arrest, but I need the background story and I have to help her decide if she wants to press charges against her pimp.

With a deep, dramatic sigh that only a teenage girl can utter, Keisha begins to tell me what happened the night of her arrest. After just a month on the track, she had caught a date with a middle-aged white man who to her looked the same as all her previous tricks. The man asked her if she would have sex with him, and as she had been trained, she asked him if he was a cop. Once he said no, she told him it would be fifty dollars. Once the verbal agreement for sex had been made, the man went on to request a hotel date. Keisha had not yet been on a hotel date and did not understand what she was expected to do. The man stated that he wanted to "Fuck the shit out of you." Still a little confused about the rules covering this type of arrangement, Keisha then asked to borrow the man's cell phone so that she could ask her pimp how much she was supposed to charge. Her pimp, who was standing just a few feet away from the car, yelled at her for her stupidity and told her to charge one hundred fifty dollars. Immediately after this exchange, the man in the car told Keisha she was under arrest and pulled out a pair of handcuffs. From the car, Keisha saw more cops pull up in another car and arrest her pimp. Keisha was particularly peeved that the officer had lied when she'd asked him if he was a cop. Conventional wisdom on the track teaches that a cop may be undercover but when asked directly if he is a cop, he is not allowed to lie. With the prevalence of movies and TV shows depicting undercover cops, it remains a mystery to me why so many girls believe this to be true.

Once at the precinct, Keisha says the officers yelled at her and told her she was dumb for having a pimp, and that then they asked her if she wanted to press charges against him. In their report, the officers felt that Keisha was "resistant" to their interrogations. In Keisha's words, "I told them, 'Fuck you.'" The following morning her pimp was released on twenty thousand dollars bail and now Keisha remains, four months later, in a juvenile detention center charged with an act of prostitution.

While the arrest of the pimp, and the fact that she called her pimp from a police officer's cell phone, made Keisha's story particularly unique, the process of proposition and then arrest wasn't. It is not unusual for cops to talk dirty to the girls they are arresting. Familiar, too, were the complaints from the police that Keisha was resistant to help: "She didn't want to talk to me." The absurdity of having an explicit sexual conversation with a girl who is being abused by adult men every day, then arresting her and expecting her to talk to or "snitch" on the man she loves to the same male officers who had treated her both as a sexual object and as a criminal, was startling.

The fact that Keisha's pimp had been released the next morning and was now free to have his friends make threatening phone calls to her auntie's house only reconfirmed her decision to stay silent. We discuss her concerns for her auntie's safety, given that her pimp lived in the same neighborhood, and talk for a while about possible placement options if the judge is open to it. Both her lawyer and I are realistic about the fact that she is probably going to be sitting in detention for at least the next few months, if not longer. Keisha is disappointed; she doesn't understand why she is the one in jail while her pimp is out, doesn't understand why she, who's been beaten and forced to make money for him, is being treated as the criminal. I don't have the answers for her. She is being criminalized for something that has been done to her. Punished for not talking to men who have shown her nothing but disdain. I figure in her situation I would be resistant, too.

"They just don't want help" was the comment I'd hear over and over again, and yet it wasn't clear what help was being offered to someone like Keisha. There was no indication that anyone had explored any placement options, like a residential treatment program, other than detention. Perhaps they believed that detention would "help," a misguided notion that I frequently heard used as a justification for incarcerating or detaining victims.

In some respects, though, Keisha was lucky to have been locked up as a juvenile, not as an adult. I've witnessed many girls under the age of sixteen processed through the criminal justice system and sent to an adult correctional facility like Rikers.

Not only do pimps train girls to lie about their ages, but cops often don't want to know if they are underage. Underage involves having to contact a parent, calling Children's Services, waiting hours for a social worker to show up, a paperwork hassle, a night ruined, chained to a desk with a defensive teenager. In New York City, if a girl is over sixteen, or at least says she is, then Rikers is standard fare. The girl is locked up at the precinct until the bus for the bookings comes, she sees a judge at some point and then likely spends a few days or weeks in Rikers, only to come right back out to the same street where once again, invariably, she'll be arrested. The cop's involvement is limited to processing her paperwork at the precinct, freeing him or her to go out and make more arrests. For cops working to meet unofficial, but widely sanctioned, arrest quotas that could be used to support or withhold overtime pay and other benefits, there is a financial incentive to make as many arrests as possible and a disincentive to investigate whether the kid in front of them with baby fat and braces is really nineteen.

While I knew some girls welcomed a few days in lockup as an opportunity to sleep and as a respite from the continual, exhausting demands on their bodies, that spoke more to how abused they were than to how "helpful" jail was. The cops knew that as soon as these jail stays were over, the girls would go right back. Pimps often picked their girls right up from where they were released. The Rikers bus dropped girls off in the early hours of the morning at Queens Plaza, a known track, with nothing but a subway token, right into the arms of welcoming pimps.

What I had found over the years was that even for girls who were identified as under sixteen years old, the longer stays in juvenile detention rarely resulted in their coming home and breaking free from their abusers. If anything, the forced separation sometimes just made the bonds stronger. In jail or detention, they were mocked and stigmatized, called names, and laughed at by both staff and other youth. Going back to where you felt accepted makes sense. During their jail time, unless they attended a GEMS group, nothing about their trafficking histories was addressed. It wasn't as if they were recovering in a therapeutic placement designed to address their post-traumatic stress disorder, their Stockholm syndrome, their prior abuse history, or their warped sense of self-worth. They were lined up against a wall in blue jumpsuits, counting off.

As I left Keisha that day, she was headed back to her bunk to write kite notes to Troy. I couldn't stop thinking about all her needs for intensive counseling, for nonjudgmental support, for love, for a family structure, all of which would go unmet while she was in detention. At least I knew she'd be getting her daily calcium intake.

I watched sexually exploited girl after girl arrested and charged with an act of prostitution and struggled with getting the cops, the courts, the families, even the girls themselves to believe that they were truly victims, when the law said that they were criminals. It was clear that there was a two-tiered response from the legal system. Under New York State law, children under the age of seventeen can't consent to sex and are defined as victims of statutory rape, yet when money was exchanged and the girl was considered a "prostitute," somehow she became mature enough to consent and to be charged with a crime. Even under the federal law, the Trafficking Victims Protection Act of 2000 (TVPA), children and youth under the age of eighteen who are bought and sold for sex, are defined as victims of "a severe form of trafficking," and there was no requirement to prove "fraud, force, or coercion." Yet regardless of their technical legal status as victims, in the real world, double standards were consistently applied. If an underage victim from Thailand, Ukraine, or anywhere else in the world was found at 2 a.m. in a brothel in Queens, she was eligible for the services provided and funded by the TVPA. She could be taken to a safe house, given counseling for her trauma, and treated, as she should be, as a victim. If the girl who was found at two in the morning is an American girl, especially a girl of color, she was arrested, charged with an act of prostitution, and taken to juvenile detention.

During my visits to the detention centers and Rikers Island jail, and in my work on the streets and at GEMS, it was hard not to see the obvious patterns. I saw face after face that was brown or black; girls of color disproportionately represented in both the criminal justice system and the commercial sex industry. It is clear that race and class make a difference in how much of a victim we believe you are. Many of these attitudes go back to slavery, when black women and girls were blamed for the sexual violence of their owners. As William Jelani Cobb, a professor at Spelman College, points out, "As long as black women could be understood to be sexually lascivious, it was impossible to view them as victims of sexual exploitation."

The difference in attitudes toward women and girls of color plays out inside the cop cars and the courtrooms and also in the way a case plays out in public. To get media attention, law enforcement and the justice system prioritize victims and hold news conferences that they know will get coverage. Understanding how to play the game includes understanding which cases no one cares about.

It's not exactly news anymore to point out the disparity in the media's coverage of victims, yet it is important to understand how this impacts domestically trafficked girls and young women. Chandra Levy, Natalee Holloway, and Laci Peterson are probably the best-known examples of how victims who are white, attractive, middle class, and with no "history" are given top priority by the national news media. This bias extends to children, too. Consider JonBenét Ramsey, Caylee Anthony, Haleigh Cummings, and Madeleine McCann, all white children. In a *Guardian* article about the disparity of coverage in missing persons cases, Martin Bright states, "There are certain rules in the missing persons game. Don't be a boy, don't be working class, don't be black. As for persistent runaways, children in care or teenagers with drug problems, forget it. . . ."

It's not just that the media's approach to victims is unfair and disparate. It is. But the real consequences come from the media's impact on how law enforcement resources are allocated, whose case is given priority, and the impact upon public perception. It makes a difference in whether your disappearance gets copters and dogs or flyers. It makes a difference in how you're treated by a jury of "your peers." It makes a difference in whether you or your family members are believed or taken seriously. In over a decade of working with thousands of girls, most of whom have been missing at some point, many of whom were literally kidnapped and held by force, I have never seen a GEMS case that has gotten an Amber Alert.

Few people outside of the Milwaukee area have heard of Alexis Patterson. On May 3, 2002, the seven-year-old girl disappeared without a trace. Just a few weeks later in Utah, another little girl disappeared, taken from her bedroom window. Her story would garner national, nonstop coverage, and there are few people in this country who are unfamiliar with Elizabeth Smart. The *Milwaukee Journal Sentinel* roundly criticized the national media for its bias and lack of coverage of the Patterson case, noting, "A Nexis search of major newspapers and magazines shows 67 stories about Patterson, almost all of them by the Associated Press and the *Milwaukee Journal Sentinel*. In the last week, there have been more than 400 stories about Smart." Even the *New York Times*, which had not covered the story on Alexis until it was criticized for its lack of response, noted in its only article on the case, "It would have been difficult this morning to argue against the parents' assertion that the Smart case had drawn far more news media attention than their daughter's. As the couple sat in their living room with their television tuned to MSNBC, two reports on the Smart case were shown within an hour, even as the ticker carried the message, 'Elizabeth Smart has been missing for three weeks.'" Alexis Patterson, like Diamond and Tionda Bradley, Teekah Lewis, Jahi Turner, and other missing children of color whom few people have heard about, has never been found.

Another stark example of the media bias is the divergent coverage of the murder of two adolescent girls, Tyisha McCoy and Brittney Gregory, in the New York City tristate area in 2004. While both girls had turbulent childhoods and both had been left by their substance-abusing mothers in the care of another family member, the accounts of their short lives and even their murders were treated very differently by the New York press. Tyisha, a thirteen-year-old black girl living in Harlem, was murdered by a man she had met on a teen chat line. Upon the discovery of a diary, headlines such as *Slain Teen's Sex Logs* abounded as she was described by newspapers as "wild" and "precocious." The *Daily News*, in classic victim-blaming prose, stated that "her precociousness may have contributed to her death."

Just a few weeks later, sixteen-year-old Brittney Gregory, who was white, was found murdered a few miles from her New Jersey home. Brittney, who was on her way to visit her boyfriend at the time, was spared the titillating headlines and dissection of her sexuality, and instead was described as "fun-loving," "sweet," and "caring" by the same newspaper. These public eulogies of two adolescent girls demonstrate the long-held public perception that black girls are "faster," looser, more precocious, and more promiscuous than their white counterparts, echoing the hypersexual Jezebel stereotype of the slavery era.

Domestically trafficked girls don't need their sexual histories to be imputed. It's there: in their records of arrests for prostitution, in the clothing that they are picked up wearing, in their case records marking them as chronic runaways. Throw in a lower-class background, a history with foster care or a single-parent home, and add to that being a girl of color, especially black, and you've hit a trifecta of sexuality, class, and race that will ensure that your credibility is doubted, that your victimization is disbelieved, and that you will be marked an unacceptable victim. In fact, it's much easier to see you as a criminal.

In 2004, a twelve-year-old girl, Nicolette, was charged with an act of prostitution. She decides to take her case to trial. She's assigned a Legal Aid attorney, Cait Mullen, who is a staunch advocate for commercially sexually exploited girls. Cait decides that as Nicolette is still five years away from being able to legally consent to sex, she can build a strong case in her defense, one that could set a precedent for the many preadolescent and adolescent girls who are being charged with prostitution. Cait and I talk excitedly about the groundbreaking case, believing that Nicolette will be treated, rightfully, as a victim.

Yet Nicolette, who ran away from a shelter at eleven to be with her pimp and is reluctant to testify against him, is not seen as a good victim. The *New York Times* stated, "The lanky and sour Nicolette did not cut a terribly sympathetic figure to some in court. There was also no evidence besides her word that any abuse she described had taken place." Yet the writer went on in the next paragraph to contradict her point: "No one argued, though, that she had suffered—either at the hands of her family or her pimp. A physical examination of Nicolette turned up burns from a hot iron and cigarettes as well as a recently broken rib."

The judge, like the writer, did not find Nicolette particularly sympathetic. So despite her age, the fact that she was under the control of an adult man, that she cannot legally consent to sex, and that there was overwhelmingly clear evidence of child abuse, the judge sentences Nicolette to a year in a juvenile detention center because she needs to learn "proper moral principles." While Cait and I are furious at the judge's decision, we know that he's well within his rights under the law. Cait files appeal after appeal until the appellate court sends back the decision: The court won't dismiss the case in the interests of justice; this is an issue to take up with the New York State legislature.

Cait and I, along with a small group of other advocates, realize that the only way to change things will be to change state law. It feels like a David versus Goliath battle, but there's no other way to redress the injustices that the girls face daily. The change needs to be systemic and it needs to be permanent. It's obvious to us that girls shouldn't be locked up for something that's been done to them, and we'll spend the next four and a half years trying to convince the legislature to agree. In the meantime, I hope and pray with each girl that they get a "good" cop, a supportive judge, an understanding prosecutor. There are too many girls like Nicolette who just don't get that lucky.

I'm dreaming that the phone is ringing. It takes another two minutes for me to realize that the phone is actually ringing about three inches from my head. It's Carol, an NYPD detective we work with regularly. The light on the cell phone tells me it's 2:45 a.m. I know this is probably not going to be good news.

"Yo." Carol's voice is booming and wired.

"Hey." I'm slurring and groggy.

"Guess who's fuckin sitting here with me?"

I sit up. Clearly it's someone I know. And if they're sitting with a cop in the middle of the night, there's a limited number of explanations for it.

"I have no idea." Although to be honest I have a whole lot of ideas; there are many possibilities for who it could be.

"Motherfuckin Nikki." Carol has never met a curse word she didn't like. Nikki has been through a string of previous arrests and has just turned sixteen. I'm lucid enough now to know that this means she's headed to Rikers. "Shit, Raych, you know I don't want to fuckin take the girl in."

I know she doesn't. Carol is one of the few cops who doesn't think that girls should go to jail for being sold.

"I'm supposed to fuckin book her, but if there was someone willing to act as a guardian?" She leaves the question in the air.

"Of course; meet me at my office?" I'm out of bed and throwing on sweats and sneakers.

"What's your ETA?"

"Huh? Oh, I can be there in fifteen."

I call Nikki's case manager, and we go through the same groggy-to-alert-in-five-seconds performance. She'll call Nikki's sister to see if she is willing to be the guardian.

By the time Carol and another detective, Ron, get there, I've already opened the office and have my ever-present cup of tea in my hand. Nikki trails in looking sheepish and then shocked to see me in my sweats and wild hair. I'm saddened, but not shocked, to see her wearing very little. She looks like a little girl playing a freakish type of dress-up in her mommy's clothes, and it's freezing outside. I go straight to the donation closet and rummage around until I find a huge sweatshirt and some leggings.

"Hey, hon." I give her a little squeeze on the shoulders; Nikki has never really been one for the hug.

"You look crazy."

"Um, yeah, thanks for that."

Carol laughs. "She's right. You look a fuckin mess, Raych; what happened? Got dressed in the dark?"

"Yeah, actually I did." I'm laughing. "Whatever, you don't look so hot yourself. What happened? Forty-eight-hour shift?"

"You fuckin know it."

Carol and I banter for a few more minutes while Nikki goes to get changed in the bathroom. It had taken me a while to get past some of my long-held prejudices about cops, but I've grown to appreciate Carol and her profane, no-bullshit, but deeply compassionate approach. She'd even brought candy and cuddly toys for the girls at Easter. Beneath all that hard-ass, cursing, quintessential New York City cop routine was a hard-ass, cursing, quintessential New York City cop who happened to really care about the girls. She knew, as I did, that yet another spell in jail was not going to address the needs of this sixteen-going-on-nine-year-old girl who had been on the streets since she was twelve. We wait for the case manager and Nikki's sister to arrive. I know that Nikki won't be able to stay with her sister for too long; if she could, she'd already be there. But at least it buys us time to figure out some options and hopefully get her some support and services. At the very least, Nikki has had an experience with a cop who treated her with dignity and respect, who saw her as a person and tried to get her some real help. I know that moments like this can have a real impact on girls. When compassion and belief in your potential comes from a cop, a judge, a prosecutor, an FBI agent, or some other unexpected source, it can feel so significant. Even if it doesn't make an impression on Nikki, it doesn't really matter. It was still the right thing to do.

Over the years, I'd work with Adam, Jimmy, Mike, and a handful of other cops who'd give me a broadened perspective on law enforcement, and as I traveled I found that most cities had their own Carol or Adam. In Dallas there was Byron; in Boston, Kelly; in Atlanta, Ernest; in Chicago, Tom. Cops who believed that girls are the victims, and pimps and johns the bad guys, and treated girls accordingly. These are the cops who visited girls on the weekends just to check in, who sat on the phone and listened to a girl vent, who came running when girls were in trouble, who scoured the streets night after night looking for a missing girl, who saw the girls as children no different from their own. These were cops that girls came to trust and count on, cops that they did talk to and often worked with to make a case against the pimps. These cops learned that there was a different way of doing their job and that it worked better. But these officers definitely weren't representative of the larger law enforcement community, and there weren't enough of them. The problem was systemic but the response was individual, based on a few caring people and their personal outrage at the selling and trafficking of children. Over the years, little has changed. There are undoubtedly good cops coming into the system, but there's still much of the same apathy and outright disdain for the girls that has, by and large, characterized law enforcement's response to this issue. In the minds of most cops, there are girls, probably foreign, who may be victims of trafficking. and then there girls who are "prostitutes," teen prostitutes perhaps, but prostitutes nonetheless.

It's well known in law enforcement circles that cops throughout the country have used the moniker *NHI* (no humans involved) to describe cases involving homeless people, addicts, drug dealers, and rapes and murders involving women and girls in the sex industry. At a training conference on the West Coast I mention this police jargon in my presentation, being careful to make it clear that I'm not suggesting any of the cops in the room would use that type of language. At the break, one of the cops comes up to me. "They call it the trash run," he says.

It takes me a minute to get what he's talking about. "Picking up the girls?"

"Yeah." He looks embarrassed.

I think about the girls I know and love. *Trash run*. And the cops wondered why girls didn't just ask for help.

9

STAYING

Sing me a pretty love song as I start to cry
Tell me you love me as you wipe the blood from my eye
Tell me why the only one who can wipe away my tears
Is the only one who's the source of all my fears

—*Me, age eighteen*

SUMMER 1994, GERMANY

The first blow to my head wakes me up. The alcohol and weed in my system tell me I'm dreaming, but the second blow wakes me fully conscious. As my eyes adjust to the dark, I feel another blow, close to my temple, and feel the weight of JP on top of me, punching furiously. I have no idea why I'm being hit while I'm sleeping. I'm doubtful there even is a why. There rarely is anymore. When I went to sleep, he was in the living room, smoking on his pipe, quiet and lost in his high. I don't remember an argument. The few explanations that are offered, or rather screamed at me, are less reasons than disjointed ramblings, crack-fueled imaginings of some perceived slight that I may or may not have committed. There's little time to understand what's happening, much less to protest or struggle before I'm being dragged by my neck, by my hair, into the living room and thrown across the floor. I'm already crying, disoriented, and confused. My head is throbbing and I think my lip is busted. I feel wet blood dripping down my face but I'm not sure if it's from my nose, mouth, or scalp.

The floor lamp is on and in this light I can see that the living room looks like we've been burgled by angry intruders. A chair is overturned, the table askew on its side, and broken glass litters the floor. The candleholder with its sixteen glasses, my first gift to him, has been smashed, tiny pieces of glass strewn everywhere. I'm not sure what provoked the rage toward the furniture that now seems solely directed at me, but JP's eyes are blazing, wild, and I think tonight might be the night that I've anticipated, the night that I will die. In one of his hands he holds a wide-blade kitchen knife. I can't help thinking it's my good chopping knife, and I'm strangely bothered that he's commandeered it. He sits on the couch, next to where I landed on the floor. He grabs my hair, pulls me onto my knees, and holds the knife at my throat. I look into his eyes once more and have no doubt that he is fully capable tonight of slitting my throat. I stay perfectly still and try not to cry; I know crying annoys him more.

"You're a fucking unloyal bitch."

I'm too scared to move, not sure if I should agree.

"I prize loyalty. You should know that. You can't fuckin play with me."

I try to shake my head, to show that no, I would never try to play you, but the knife is too close and I feel it graze my skin.

"I'm going to give you one more chance. Do you want it?"

My throat's so dry I can barely get the word *yes* out.

"OK, so repeat after me . . . I will not be unloyal."

For some reason, it sticks in my mind that the correct word is *disloyal* and that his word *unloyal* is actually not a word at all, but I have no doubt what announcing this fact will do.

"I will not be unloyal."

"Again."

"I will not be unloyal."

"Did I tell you to stop saying it? Keep fucking saying it."

"I will not be unloyal. I will not be unloyal. I will not be unloyal. I will not be unloyal. I will not be unloyal. I will not be unloyal. I will not be unloyal."

The time on the clock radio says 3:14 a.m. I wonder how long I will sit here on my knees trying not to move against the knife or fall on any of the broken glass on the floor. I pause in my mantra and feel the pressure of the knife again.

"Who told you to stop? Don't you dare fucking stop. Look into my eyes."

His eyes, the beautiful doe eyes that I first fell in love with, are now wild, pupils dilated, and yet still hard to look away from.

"I will not be unloyal. I will not be unloyal. I will not be unloyal. I will not be unloyal. I will not be unloyal."

My tears and the blood on my face feel dry and crusty and I've stopped shaking. I keep repeating the phrase over and over, watching JP's face relax as he hears me pledge allegiance over and over again. I try to think of other things but it's hard. I wonder why tonight I'm considered "unloyal" and what could've possibly happened between going to sleep and waking up to this. I wonder if it would be possible to kill him with the knife he now holds to my throat when he falls asleep. He must sense my thoughts, as the knife pushes in a little deeper and a new lecture begins on the perils and consequences of unloyalty.

"I will not be unloyal. I will not be unloyal." I'm believing it. His eyes remain centered on mine. I feel sucked in. Mesmerized. I think of the snake Kaa from the *Jungle Book* with his hypnotizing eyes. I can no more look away than run away.

By 6 a.m., outside light is beginning to enter the tightly closed curtains, but it feels like there is no other world than the one that exists between our locked eyes, between the knife at my throat and the man who holds it. "I will not be unloyal. I will not be unloyal. I will not be unloyal." Exhaustion is setting in. My legs feel dead; I want to shake out the pins and needles but I still don't move. Shock and fear have turned to a gradual sense of resignation. I will be here forever, proving my loyalty.

Sometime around 8:30 a.m., JP begins to show signs of tiredness. He leans back on the couch and takes the knife from my throat. I continue, "I will not be unloyal. I will not be unloyal." My words are slurring from exhaustion and my eyelids keep closing, but I cannot stop. I must convince him.

Finally he's satisfied. "I believe you. But remember what will happen if you betray me."

I nod, totally numb. "I love you," he says.

I cannot hear this, cannot comprehend this. I just nod again. He reaches out his hand and helps me up off the floor. Suddenly tender and quiet, he brushes my hair off my face. I wince at the touch, the bruises and welts on my face more painful now that the alcohol has worn off.

"I'm not sure why I did this." I think he's talking about me, but he gestures to the wrecked living room. He looks a little bewildered and then takes me by the hand and leads me to the bedroom. I let myself be led. We lie down side by side in the dark. Within moments, he's asleep, snoring. I lie awake, my body exhausted, my mind unable to sleep.

I will not be unloyal. I will not be unloyal, I think.

One of the first books I read after coming to New York was Dr. Judith Herman's *Trauma and Recovery*. As I read this expert take on the effects of trauma on prisoners of war, hostages, domestic violence, and sexual abuse victims, and how they might bond and identify with their abusers/captors, I began to recognize my own experiences. Dr. Herman wrote of concepts like Stockholm syndrome, battered woman's syndrome, post-traumatic stress disorder, terms I'd never heard of, yet that instinctively made sense in the context of my experiences. I read the book with a mixture of wonderment and horror, alternately crying and taking copious notes. Here I was on page 215, too scared to leave, too numb to fight back! Here I was on page 327, making excuses for my abuser, willing to defend him at all costs! I just knew the book was written for me, even if Herman never referenced girls in the sex industry. I read the book over and over, trying to make sense of everything that I'd experienced within this new framework. Perhaps it hadn't been all my fault.

"Why didn't you just leave?" In the first few years after I left the life, I was asked that frequently. Embedded in the question were unspoken accusations: How could you be so weak/stupid? Was it because you deserved/liked it? In the beginning, I would constantly ask myself the same question, the accusatory subtext included. In truth, I didn't know why I stayed and I hated myself for doing so. Yet as I began to work with strong, smart, brave girls who'd stayed with their abusers and who in spite of all the violence and exploitation continued to profess abject devotion—"But I love him"—I couldn't see them as weak or stupid. Instead I started to see a pattern. The girls I met—Melissa, Christine, Audrey, Tanya—were already bruised and vulnerable from the adults in their lives when they met the adult men who would seize on their vulnerability like sharks smelling blood in the water. The same tactics would be used over and over again—kindness, violence, kindness, a bit more violence. I watched helplessly as girls were jerked back from every attempt at independence by some invisible bungee cord, one end attached to the men they "loved," the other wrapped tightly around their necks.

Yet while I intuitively felt their struggle, I didn't really understand how to help them break free when I had struggled so much myself. How could I explain the girls' seemingly illogical behavior (and, of course, implicitly my own) to unsympathetic audiences, social workers, cops, judges, and family members? How could I help people actually *see* the invisible rope? In the social service community, we had slowly begun to recognize that there were all types of reasons—psychological, emotional, financial, practical— that kept adult women in domestic violence situations. Yet when it came to girls and young women in the life, it seemed hard for people to make the connection.

In 1973, Jan Erik Olsson walked into a small bank in Stockholm, Sweden, brandishing a gun, wounding a police officer, and taking three women and one man hostage. During negotiations, Olsson demanded money, a getaway vehicle, and that his friend Clark Olofsson, a man with a long criminal history, be brought to the bank. The police allowed Olofsson to join his friend and together they held the four hostages captive in a bank vault for six days. During their captivity, the hostages at times were attached to snare traps around their necks, likely to kill them in the event that the police attempted to storm the bank. The hostages grew increasingly afraid and hostile toward the authorities trying to win their release and even actively resisted various rescue attempts. Afterward they refused to testify against their captors, and several continued to stay in contact with the hostage takers, who were sent to prison. Their resistance to outside help and their loyalty toward their captors was puzzling, and psychologists began to study the phenomenon in this and other hostage situations. The expression of positive feelings toward the captor and negative feelings toward those on the outside trying to win their release became known as Stockholm syndrome.

In 2002, a fourteen-year-old girl from Utah, Elizabeth Smart, was kidnapped from her bedroom at gunpoint. Nine months later, after a police sketch of the suspect had been released, Elizabeth was seen with an older couple walking down the street in a nearby Utah suburb, and witnesses notified the police. When police confronted the trio and took Elizabeth aside, she repeatedly denied that she was Elizabeth Smart, stating that her name was Augustine Mitchell (taking the surname of her abductors). When she eventually admitted her identity, she showed concern for her abductors and frequently asked the police about their well-being. Elizabeth was returned safely to her family, and her father asked the press to respect his daughter's ordeal and not discuss any sexual abuse that she might have suffered.

In the subsequent media frenzy after her rescue, experts and pundits talked about her initial response to law enforcement and attributed her identity denial and loyalty to her abductors as "brainwashing," "Stockholm syndrome," and "mind control." While some of the explanations of brainwashing were a little simplistic, the media, the public, and law enforcement all readily accepted and understood that Elizabeth's unexpected response to her own rescue was a result of a serious trauma and psychological dependency. While some were initially surprised that Elizabeth had been, at various times throughout the nine months, only blocks away from her family's home and yet did not ever attempt to escape, and had been stopped by the police previously to her identification without ever disclosing who she was, no one ever doubted her legitimacy as a victim.

In 2007, Shawn Hornbeck, a boy who had been kidnapped four years earlier, was found still living with his captor. He'd been seen riding around the neighborhood on a bike and had seemingly been "free" to leave. Yet again, everyone immediately understood that he'd experienced a severe form of trauma and that while the door may have been open physically, in Shawn's mind he was no more free to leave than if he had been chained to a wall. Whatever happened to Elizabeth Smart and Shawn Hornbeck in those first few days, those first few terrifying weeks, was enough to convince them that they were unable to leave, that their best chance for survival was to comply and bond with the person who had the power to keep them alive.

Psychologist Dee Graham identified four factors that need to be present for Stockholm syndrome to occur: a perceived threat to survival and the belief that one's captor is willing to act on that threat, the captive's perception of small kindnesses from the captor within a context of terror, isolation from perspectives other than those of the captor, and a perceived inability to escape. The key consideration is the victim's perception. It doesn't matter if those on the outside believe that the victim had an opportunity to escape, that the threat wasn't really as great as the victim thought it was, or that the kindness shown was trivial and ludicrous in the face of the violence involved. All that matters is that the victim believes these things to be true. Bonding to their captor/abuser is simply a survival mechanism born out of great psychological fear and oppression.

There are no studies that suggest that it takes a "weak" personality to succumb to Stockholm syndrome or trauma bonding, but clearly children are more vulnerable and more easily convinced that their abuser has the power to carry out all and any threats. It is not surprising that they would bond more quickly than adults to their abusers. And yet while children like Shawn Hornbeck, Elizabeth Smart, and even those who have become adults during their captivity like Jaycee Lee Dugard and Natascha Kampusch are rightly seen as blameless victims, domestically trafficked girls under the control of a pimp are usually seen not as victims but as willing participants.

Yet many of these girls experience the same types of psychological conditions necessary for Stockholm syndrome to develop. Pimps make sure to isolate trafficked and exploited girls from perspectives other than their own. They often refer to families and friends as "the square world," and work hard to convince a girl that these people don't really care about her, don't love her the way he does, have never really been there for her. Traveling and being taken to cities where she knows no one and is on unfamiliar territory are also common. Everyone she meets is in some way connected to the life; her entire world becomes pimps, johns, and other victimized girls. Her wives-in-law are traumatized and bonded already, unable to offer a different perspective. Johns, by virtue of buying her, also reinforce the belief that this is who she is, what she deserves, that it's not worth running away because she has nothing to run home to. Even in rare interactions with social workers, emergency room personnel, passersby, rarely is she exposed to a different perspective or at least to one that could help her. Her pimp's already warned her that the "squares" are not to be trusted and will just judge her and make her feel worthless. After a while, the life, the game, becomes her only true reality. *Squares are stupid. Dumb girls give it away for free. It's normal to share your man with four other girls. Giving him your money is for the best, as you wouldn't be able to handle it anyway.*

Over the years I've heard girls at GEMS say that their pimps have called me "the poison pimp" because I try to poison the girls' minds against the truth. One girl who was court-mandated to GEMS as an alternative to incarceration tells me that her pimp has warned her that we will try to "brainwash" her and that she shouldn't believe anything we say. I ask her why she thinks he said that, and after a few minutes of deep thought, she says, "perhaps cos *he's* brainwashing me." For a moment, I think she's had a revelation, but if so, it's short-lived, as minutes later she's telling me how good he is to her, how much she deserves the beatings.

Of course, it takes more than simply isolation from other perspectives to develop the intense relationship with their abusers that clinicians call trauma bonds. Even if the grooming period is full of promises and "love," there comes a point where the pimp will begin to exert force and control in order to develop the strongest levels of loyalty and submission. In a book on rape, Drs. Lorenne Clark and Debra J. Lewis assert that "all unequal power relationships must, in the end, rely on the threat or reality of violence in order to maintain themselves." For commercially sexually exploited and trafficked girls, the perception of threats is almost always based on the reality of violence. Girls believe that their pimps will act on their threats to hurt, to maim, to kill, and with good reason. So many of these girls have experienced rape, had guns held to their head, heard their trafficker talk about other girls he's killed—enough violence, in other words, to ensure that girls are hesitant about running away. One girl I worked with, Marlene, went on a date to a bowling alley with a guy she'd met at the train station. Upon leaving the bowling alley, she was thrown into a van by her date and his accomplice and had her identification taken away. Her kidnappers knew that the address on her ID was her grandmother's and so they threatened to go to her family's house to kill them if she tried to escape. Marlene was taken to the basement of a house and shown a wooden pole with torn duct tape around it and then shown a vast array of weapons: swords, hunting knives, machetes, and nunchucks. She was told that this was where girls who were disobedient were brought. When Marlene was told that she had to work the streets, she complied. For several weeks, she worked hard to be obedient and trustworthy, although her pimp rarely let her out of his sight. When she overheard that she was to be sold to another pimp and taken out of state, she decided to try to escape. Because she'd been so submissive, doing everything she was told, her pimp finally left her alone for a few hours and she ran to the nearest phone and called her mother.

Her mother called us and we called the police, who went to pick her up. I drove out to meet her at the precinct. When I arrived, Marlene was being interrogated, accused of lying and being questioned as to why she hadn't tried to escape sooner. To me, Marlene had done everything she needed to do to stay alive, and had been smart and strategic about her survival. To the police officers, because she hadn't been chained up for her captivity and because she acknowledged complying with her abuser's orders to be sold for sex, there was no way she'd been kidnapped, no way she was really a victim. Marlene was able to provide an address and a name; her pimp had a record for assault and kidnapping, and yet the police refused to pick him up, citing lack of evidence. I spent a long and frustrating night arguing with two male officers who simply would not understand that Marlene's perception of threats to her survival was real and justified and that her actions were totally understandable. I was glad that these weren't the police officers who had found Elizabeth Smart.

In Marlene's case, her compliance with her captor kept her alive and reduced the occurrence of violence and harm. While she hadn't yet reached a stage of bonding with her abuser, the critical factors for Stockholm syndrome were certainly in place.

Angelina's been coming into the office for a few weeks now, referred by her social worker due to a yearlong stay in a juvenile detention center on a prostitution charge. Long and gangly, all limbs, with mild acne, at sixteen she's every bit an awkward adolescent. I'm the first person she meets on her arrival and we bond a little, although she's reserved and hesitant to talk much about her experiences. She does, however, read a newspaper story that hangs in the front of the office about my experiences in the life, and seems to appreciate this fact about me. While she's assigned to a caseworker, Angelina seems to gravitate toward me every time she comes in and slowly starts opening up, more and more, with each visit. I learn that she ran away at twelve although she's quick, too quick, to defend her family, and simply puts her running away down to "wanting to be grown." Something about the way she talks, particularly about her family, doesn't sit right with me, though. There's so much bubbling silently under the surface. Smart and thoughtful, Angelina strikes me as the kid who was trained a long time ago to keep secrets. Angelina, both book and street-smart, has been working on her GED since she came home. She has lots of questions for me—"Did you love your daddy?" "Where did you go to school?" "How did you leave him?" "What do you have to do at work every day?"—and seems to ponder the answers carefully, as if trying to decide what might work for her, where she might end up.

She sits quietly nearby, asking to help with whatever project I'm working on. One day, as she sits helping me file, she suddenly blurts out, "I miss him." I have no doubt who the "him" she's referring to is: her pimp, Suave, a thirty-five-year-old man who recruited her when she was twelve, less than a few hours after she first hit the street. Suave's currently in jail, although unfortunately not for what he did to Angelina.

"That's normal; it's normal to miss someone who was a big part of your life . . . even if it wasn't good. What do you miss?"

"Him tellin me to get my ass in the house. I miss him tellin me what to do. You know . . . what time to get up, what to wear, to go to work . . . stuff like that." She smiles just thinking about this. "I'd go back to him if I could," she says cheerfully. "He was like my father." The quiet surface begins to break. "I really love him."

Something about the way she says this, with true longing, breaks my heart. "What about the other things, though? The times he hurt you and the things you had to do."

"Oh, I know. He didn't mean all that stuff, though; sometimes I just made him mad." This leads to a discussion of "making people mad" as opposed to people taking responsibility for their own actions. I feel like I make some good points. She remains unconvinced. "I still want to go back, though."

I sigh, hopefully inwardly, although I can't be sure. She's still so stuck, physically free but emotionally tied; I know I can't push too hard. If I do, I become the bad guy as she defends her love, her man, her experiences and feelings for the last three years. I try a different tack. "Why don't we make a list . . . of the good things and the bad stuff? The things you miss and the stuff you don't. Maybe it'll help sort through some of these feelings." She looks skeptical. "I made one when I left my pimp and it kinda helped me think stuff through," I say. My own list-making process had, in fact, offered a startling realization that my version of love was perhaps a little distorted, to say the least. When I saw that on the plus side, I'd written *Put cocoa butter on my welts from the belt,* I knew something was wrong. Making the list hadn't changed my feelings for a long time, but it did change the way I thought about them.

I tear a sheet of paper from my notebook, and draw a line down the middle. I write *Things He Did That Made Me Feel Happy/ Loved* at the top of one column and *Things That Made Me Feel Sad/Cry* at the top of the other.

She goes to sit on the couch and I see her start scribbling. The writing stops after a couple of minutes and she sits quietly for a while, sucking on the end of the pen, thinking hard. I'm guessing she's working on the *Things He Did That Made Me Feel Sad/ Cry* side. I go back to my work and let her sit with her memories for a little while longer. After about forty minutes, she comes into my office. "I'm finished. Here." Thrusting the paper at me as if it's radioactive. I'm not surprised to see how short the *Things He Did That Made Me Feel Happy/Loved* column is, although I'm mildly surprised and secretly pleased that her list of negatives is so long; she's really put a lot of thought and energy into this. It is, as always, a jarringly unequal list of pros and cons: *He told me he was my daddy*, plus; *He hit me*, minus; *He takes me on trips*, plus; *He makes me have sex with other men*, minus; *He gave me an STD*, minus; *He beat me with an extension cord*, minus; *He said I was a dumb bitch*, minus, *He told me he loved me*, plus, plus, plus.

As we sit together going over the list, there's an item on the pro side that I don't understand. Her tiny printed handwriting reads *Cheetos.* "Huh, what's this, Angie?"

"You told me to think of the times when he loved me, so there was this one time, when he got mad at something I did, I can't remember what, and he hit me some. And I was crying and shit and so then he left and that made me cry more cos he left me when I was crying. But then he came back and he'd gone to the store and he bought me Cheetos and a chocolate Yoo-Hoo milk."

I look at her a little blankly.

"Cos they were my favorites. And he knew they were my favorites and he got them for me to make me feel better." She smiles at this memory and I can picture her drying her tears—"Thank you, Daddy"—oh, so grateful for $1.25 worth of junk food from the corner bodega. "That's the main time I knew that he really loved me." She must mistake the look of sadness probably creeping across my face as incomprehension, as she explains again, "Cos they were my favorite and that was mad thoughtful of him."

As we continue to go through the list—*Set me up to get raped, Left me in jail*—I'm thinking, how easy it is, how little it takes. A bag of Cheetos and chocolate Yoo-Hoo outweighed all the painful, awful, evil stuff he'd done. In the right circumstances, it didn't take much at all.

When someone has the power to take your life but doesn't, you feel grateful. It may not make logical sense but it does make psychological sense. Given that most people haven't experienced someone wielding the threat of death over their heads, it can be hard to understand just how intense that type of bond can feel. Yet even in cases where the threat is external and the people present are not the instigators, for example in a plane crash, a serious car accident, a natural disaster, a bond often develops between the survivors that is stronger than many other relationships. It's part of what makes combat vets, firefighters, or even police officers feel a bond to their fellow soldiers or partners that is indescribable to anyone outside of their worlds. Given the shared trauma that multiple girls under the control of one pimp may feel, there is the potential for the same type of bonds to develop between them; yet unlike the military or the police and fire departments, where loyalty to your comrades is strongly encouraged and supported, pimps work to create tension, jealousy, and betrayal between girls who are all suffering from the same threats. Bonding with the abuser, then, makes sense because after all, he's the one with the power to take your life, not the other girls.

The desire to perceive kindness when there is none, or to magnify small, inconsequential acts of basic human decency to proportions worthy of gratitude and love, can also be seen in other victims. Psychologist Bruno Bettelheim, in a controversial account of his concentration camp experiences during the Holocaust, notes that his fellow prisoners came to believe that the guards were showing kindness toward them even in the most mundane of acts such as wiping their feet before entering the barracks so that the prisoners would have less to clean up. In the *Interesting Narrative of the Life of Olaudah Equiano*, the former slave clearly developed a level of Stockholm syndrome toward his "master" Pascal and sought to find "kindness" even in the midst of his traumatic experiences as a slave. "I had sails to lie on, and plenty of good victuals to eat, and everybody on board used me very kindly, quite contrary to what I had seen from white people before."

Again, the critical factor is not whether the kindness is legitimate or valid, simply that the victim perceives it to be so. For Danielle, it's her cubic zirconia necklace; for Angelina, it's the chocolate Yoo-Hoos; for another girl it's the gift of a *Wizard of Oz* DVD, for another it's being allowed to sit in the *front* seat of the car. For some girls, the only kindness is the absence of violence, or at least the reduced levels of violence in comparison to what they knew he was capable of. I've heard girls say, "Well, he didn't beat me like he beat the other girls." Or, "He hit me with an open hand not a closed fist." The gratitude and the relief are palpable.

One night, I'm facilitating a focus group with the girls in our program for a city research study. One of the questions is: While you were in the life, do you remember an adult who tried to help you? While the conversation has been animated and raucous up till now, with girls weighing in excitedly on pimps, johns, and cops, the room goes silent. Finally, Jessica speaks. "This trick took me to a house and he brought a whole bunch of other guys, like maybe fifteen guys, and they all were raping me and I was crying and crying. And one guy wouldn't rape me and he helped me find my clothes. I guess he felt bad cos I was crying."

She was grateful. Not because he stopped the other guys from raping her, not because he called the cops, simply because he didn't participate in the rape of a fourteen-year-old. It was significant enough for her that he remained, in her mind, a good guy. A small perceived kindness in the midst of terror.

SUMMER 1994, GERMANY

I'm barely inside the apartment when JP locks the door behind me and grabs me by the throat. For some reason that I can't yet fathom, he's wearing surgical gloves. "I'm sorry, Raych." I'm struggling for air. "I love you, I really do." He kisses my face as I try to pull his hands off my throat. "Tonight's the night. I'm sorry." Now I know what's happening. He's going to kill me.

He's been threatening for weeks—stabbing me in my sleep, and sometimes when I'm awake, with hypodermic needles that he'd gotten from the drug clinic, pretending to be a heroin addict. An episode of *Matlock* where someone is killed by sending an air bubble to their heart gives him the idea. Last week, I'd been taking a bath and he started to drown me with the shower hose, sitting calmly on the side of the tub as I flailed and fought. It's become less of a threat and more of a promise. I've already made arrangements for my body to be shipped home and left a note at work with his name and birth date on it, making it clear that when I'm found dead it will be him who is responsible. My death, and his son's mother, who he feels has wronged him, have become his fixation. It's unclear what my crime is; according to him, it's just what has to happen. Sometimes the narrative ends with his suicide too, depending on his mood. He's even offered to do a suicide pact. I, of course, have to go first. I've been trying desperately to talk him out of it, but it always just feels like a stay of execution. Apparently I've run out of time.

He lets go of my neck and pulls me into the living room. I'm crying and begging for my life, professing my love, but he's resolute.

"You can choose. How do you want to die?" He says it like he's asking me what I want for dinner.

"What are my options?" I'm trying to stop crying and think clearly, despite all the champagne I've consumed.

He picks up the wooden leg from the coffee table that had broken in one of our fights a few nights earlier. "You can be beat to death with this or you can be strangled." Neither option appeals to me. I try to think rationally.

"Beat." I'm banking on this taking longer, making more noise and hopefully making him squeamish enough to give him second thoughts.

"OK." He doesn't seem too concerned. Now I'm second-guessing my choice.

"Can I sit down for a minute and have a cigarette?" I'm trying to stall.

"Go ahead, but I'm fixin to do this, Raych. You don't have long."

My mind is racing, trying to think of a way out of this but I can't. We have no phone in the apartment and the neighbors are used to the sounds of me screaming by now. They all find him charming. I remember that I have weed in my bag. There's no way he'll turn it down, he's an addict. The weed might mellow him out and could potentially put him to sleep.

"Can we smoke a blunt together? Please? It'll be easier for me."

"Yeah, roll it." He's pacing the apartment, still holding the table leg. "I wiped the apartment down. So they won't find no prints." He holds up his gloved hands. "And I stole these from the clinic that day." He seems to want me to be impressed by his ingenuity in planning the crime scene. I want to throw up but I'm scared that I'll lose my chance to get him smoking. It takes me longer than normal, but I finally get the blunt rolled and I take a few hits. I don't want to smoke too much and dull my own reactions although passing out right now might be the most painless option. He sits and finally puts down the wooden leg to smoke. I see him relax just a little. I wait till he's taken a few more pulls. "What about my family, Jay? They're gonna miss me."

"Yeah, I know. It's fucked-up." He looks sad for a minute. "It has to happen, though. You have to die. Ima be dead soon anyway. I love you, I really do. But you know it has to be like this, right?" I'm crying again. Unable to speak in the face of this logic.

"You can write your mom a letter if you want to say good-bye."

"Thank you, baby." A temporary reprieve. He gives me a pen and notebook he's been scribbling paranoid ramblings in. I write slowly. *Dear Mum, I'm sorry.* I don't know what else to write. I picture my mother reading the letter. "Can I look at some photos before . . . I go?" He gets up and hands me the photo album from the bookshelf. I was using it to stall, but as soon as I start looking at the pictures of me as a baby, me dressed up as Paddington Bear as a toddler, me smiling in elementary school, I'm sobbing. This is it. This is how my life will end. I pore over the pictures, committing each detail to memory. It takes me a few minutes to notice that JP has leaned back on the couch. He's still smoking and his eyelids are starting to look heavy. The weed might actually work. I start over at the beginning of the photo album, turning the pages as slowly as possible. He's drifting a little and paying me less attention now. Everything feels like it's moving in slow motion. He's trying hard to stay awake. I'm praying for him to fall asleep.

Finally, his head nods and his eyes are closed. I wait a little longer for his breathing to get heavier and then make a dash for the door. The lock and chain take too long to open and make too much noise and I hear him wake up. I've just got to get outside. The door's open and I'm in the hallway, just a few more steps to the stairs. He's coming. "*Hilfe*, help, help, please!" I'm screaming, praying that this time one of the neighbors will actually care. I reach the step and it's too late. My head jerks back as he grabs me by my hair. I twist hard and somehow I'm on the ground. Crawling. Scrambling to get away as he tightens his grip on my hair. "Help, please, please! Oh God, please!" I know the whole building has to have heard me. He lifts my head up and I see the concrete coming up to meet me. Each time he smacks my head into the floor it feels as if my brain is exploding. I see stars and all I can think of is a Tom and Jerry cartoon. *It's true, it's actually stars*, I'm thinking, as my head smashes into the ground again and again. And then it's over. He's dragging me back into the apartment. I blew my only chance to escape. He's yelling at me but I can barely focus, the room keeps spinning and fading in and out to black. I don't care anymore. There's no point in fighting this. I just want to go to sleep. Somehow he's brought me into the bedroom and is now on top of me. He's crying and kissing my face, saying he loves me, he's sorry, he loves me, he loves me, he loves me. His hands are around my neck and he's still kissing me. I don't even try to fight. He adjusts his hands to get a better grip on my neck and to be helpful, I lift my hair up.

"I'm ready," I say.

When I first wake up in the morning, I think it must've been a nightmare. But my head is throbbing and my throat and neck feel so sore and bruised I can barely swallow. I get up from the bed and see my reflection in the closet mirror. My face is swollen and discolored. I look closer and see that the red and purple marks are made up of tiny little lines. Hundreds of blood vessels have burst all over my face and neck. My eyes are bloody red. I'm not sure why I'm still alive.

I walk into the living room, where JP is lying on the couch smoking weed. He looks pained when he sees my face. "What happened?" I start to cry. Every inch of my head hurts.

"I don't know, Raych, it's weird. I don't know."

"You were going to kill me." I'm not sure if he's managed to forget that part already.

"I know. I tried. You were almost dead." He starts to cry. I sit on the loveseat, scared to get too close. "I was doing it, I mean, I was choking you." He holds up his hands as if they're still around my neck. "Your face was turning colors and your eyes looked like they was gonna come out. Your tongue was coming out too. You wasn't breathing. I figured I had about thirty more seconds left, if that." He makes a tightening motion. I cannot move. Listening to him describe my near death. "And then, I don't know, I can't explain it." He looks spooked. "It was like something came and pulled my hands away. It was crazy. And it was enough, just those few seconds when my hands came off, for you to get a breath again. And then I couldn't do it again. I just came in here and let you be."

I don't know what to say. He could've killed me but he didn't. He nearly killed me but he didn't. I know I have to leave him. He will kill me one day. But I stay still on the loveseat. He reaches out and strokes my hand. "You want some orange juice, Raych?"

"Yes. Thank you," I say.

10

LEAVING

*Came to believe that a Power greater than ourselves
could restore us to sanity.*

—*Step 2,* "The Big Book," Alcoholics Anonymous

FALL 1994, GERMANY

I can barely see with the tears and mucus running down my face. I know that it's not worth it, I know that I'm tired, that I don't want to go through this anymore. The situation with JP is out of control; either I'll kill him or he'll kill me, although the odds are squarely in his favor. The copious amounts of alcohol I've consumed help calm my nerves. I know it's the best decision. I feel bad for my mum but figure she'll get over it eventually. Besides, she wasn't thinking about my feelings all the times she tried to take her life, so it's hard to feel that bad. Mind made up, I wrap the cord to my bathrobe around my neck and tie it tightly, and walk out to the balcony. It's raining hard but I figure that getting wet is, at this stage, the least of my problems. I'm relieved it will all be over soon. The rain and the darkness make it difficult to see the drop from the balcony, but I know it's about ten feet. JP had forced me to make the jump one night when his crack-induced paranoia had him convinced that the cops were about to break down the door at any moment. Of course they didn't, but I cut my knee open and sprained my foot. Tonight, though, I'm not worried about the drop. I have no intention of ever hitting the ground. I climb over the railing where there's a little ledge and tie the other end of the belt around it. I say a quick prayer, "God, please forgive me," take a deep breath, and jump into the blackness.

It's hard to tell how much time elapses, but I come to while it's still dark. I wait for a heavenly light, a tunnel, something, but nothing appears. For a few moments, I'm perplexed. Am I in heaven or hell? I wonder if there really is a purgatory, or perhaps everyone's wrong and in the end there's just a nothingness. As I still try to make sense of the afterlife, it slowly dawns on me as I regain consciousness that I'm lying in about three inches of water and that not only am I not in heaven, hell, or any combination of the two, but I'm still quite alive. I cannot fuckin believe it. My plan failed. I failed. I'm about to cry when suddenly the absurdity of the situation hits me. I'm lying flat on my back on the second-floor roof in a puddle at 4 a.m. in the pitch-dark, and in the middle of a rainstorm. I feel ridiculous and I can't help but laugh, albeit a little hysterically as it has been a rough night. As I lie there, soaking wet, rain mingling with tears of both sadness and now full-out laughter, it occurs to me that despite all my best efforts to end my life, I'm still here. No matter how many near-death experiences I've had in the last few years, I'm still here. Maybe there is someone somewhere protecting me, someone who sees more of a future for me than I see for myself. I think God has saved my life. Suddenly I'm grateful. As I feel the rain on my face, I realize I don't want to die anymore. Finally, sore and knowing I'll be bruised all over tomorrow, I get up. The only way off the roof is to knock on my downstairs neighbor's bedroom window and climb through into his apartment and back up the stairs to mine. I hadn't taken the key with me, not thinking I'd need it, but I remember that there's still a spare key under the doormat. I'm way past the stage of feeling mortified, so I knock on my neighbor's window until he wakes up. He's a little startled to see my face peering in, but he lets me climb in without any questions. I try to mumble something about needing to get something off the roof, but trail off halfway through hearing how silly I sound. I figure while

I'm there I might as well ask for a cigarette. Staring at me standing there soaking wet in the middle of his bedroom, he gives me four. It's not until I get upstairs to my own apartment that I realize that the bathrobe cord is still tied tightly around my neck.

That night I have an epiphany that will change my whole life. At the time I don't realize it. At the time, I've probably never used the word *epiphany* in a sentence. But the thought that maybe I have a greater purpose leads me to a small nondenominational American church the following Sunday, and that sets me on a path that will result in my walking away from the life two months later and never going back. This inexplicable belief in God's love for me at a critical moment sustains me over the next few months, and ultimately over the next decade. It doesn't make leaving easy, but it does make me leave. It is perhaps an atypical exit, although as I've come to learn from many girls that while recruitment generally follows the same script, leaving the life looks very different for each individual girl. There is, however, to borrow language from the substance-abuse community, always a sense of hitting bottom. A feeling of being sick and tired of being sick and tired. For some girls, it's the indignity of a brutal beating that forces them to finally escape. For others it may be a change in the status quo—a new girl comes into the house, a wife-in-law gets pregnant—that shifts the dynamic and helps them to see that all their labor is in vain. Jail may interrupt the cycle, with a pimp's arrest taking him out of the picture and giving her a chance to think clearly. Even sitting in jail waiting for him to bail her out and realizing that despite all the money that she's made him, his refusing to come and put a mere five hundred bucks down to get her out of Rikers might be the final straw. Some girls may even view an unexpected pregnancy as a sign, an opportunity to start afresh with a new life, a chance to give their baby something they never had.

Regardless of the circumstances, what makes the most difference in whether a girl leaves or not when that door opens up is if she believes that she has options, resources, somewhere to go, and the support she'll need once she's out. Without that glimmer of hope, whether it comes in the form of family, a program like GEMS, or a church community like the one that helped me, it's unlikely that she'll leave. And then the door will close just as quickly as it opened, leaving her feeling trapped once more. And this time even more convinced that this is the life that she's destined to lead. Hope and the belief in other options is why I founded GEMS and what we've tried hard over the years to impart to every girl who's walked through the door. "Here's my number, you can call anytime" is the mantra. Sometimes they don't call for months; sometimes they never call; sometimes they call frequently when they are almost but not quite ready to leave. But we take each call seriously, even from the girls who return to the life over and over again. You never know when someone's "hit bottom," but you just hope she has that critical phone number on hand when she does.

"Yo, Raych, wake up, wake up. Raych."

My boyfriend, Jason, is shaking me. "*What?*" I'm aggravated; we'd been out late, and I'd just fallen asleep.

He points to the phone in his hand. "I think it's an emergency."

The voice on the phone is crying and frantic. "Yo, Rachel, I cannot take this no more, I'm done, yo. Please come get me. Please. I gotta go, Rachel, I gotta go."

"It's OK. Try to calm down a little, OK." The girl is speaking a mile a minute and it takes me a minute to figure out who it is. So many girls have my home number and any one of them could be frantic in the wee hours of the morning. I check the caller ID but it's a 718 number. She's probably calling from a pay phone. I take a guess. "Patricia?"

"Yeah, hurry. Please. I can't go home. I can't go back again ever. I wanna leave. Please. He's gonna kill me. Rachel?"

"I'm here; it's gonna be OK. Try to breathe. Are you safe right now? Where are you? Where is he?" I'm trying to piece the situation together in my groggy mind.

"I'm on Ditmars and Thirty-first, but he's not here."

"OK, you know that gas station on Astoria? I think it's a Shell."

"Yeah."

"Go inside there and wait for me. I'll be about twenty minutes, all right? Just hang on."

"Just hurry, please." She's pleading.

"I'm hurrying, hon. I'll be there." I'm already throwing on my sweats and hunting for a left sneaker. As usual, my bedroom has clothes strewn everywhere so the sneaker takes a while to locate.

"She OK?" Jason already knows the drill. We've been together long enough for him to have witnessed the crisis calls, the late night runs, the never-ending needs of a hundred teenage girls. While he isn't a fan of girls calling me to see what I'm watching on TV, and in fairness, neither am I, he gets the emergency part. He follows me to the bathroom as I splash water on my face.

"You want me to drive you?"

"Nah, I got it." I'm still trying to make my eyes open properly.

"You got your keys? Driver's license? Money?" I'm notorious for leaving the house without any combination of all three.

"Yep, yep, yep."

"OK, be safe. Drive carefully. Call me when you get down there."

"I don't know what time I'll be. . . ."

"Yeah, I know. Just call me."

He walks me to the door, kisses me on the forehead, and goes into the living room to finish playing his Madden NFL game. Just another GEMS crisis night.

As I drive to the Triborough Bridge to cross into Queens, the rain that has been coming down lightly all evening suddenly worsens, and within minutes I'm driving in a downpour, wipers turned up to the max, fog lights on, gripping the wheel tightly with both hands. I think about that day I first met Patricia about six months earlier. She was court-ordered to come to the program after several arrests for prostitution. She was shy, initially, and reluctant to commit to the program, but a choice between GEMS and Rikers wasn't a hard one to make. I liked her immediately and learned quickly that her shyness masked an extremely talkative and lively personality. After a few sessions, she began to connect to the staff and the other girls, and before long everybody had developed a soft spot for her. Patricia completed her five sessions but stayed in touch, calling me and her counselor and still coming by GEMS sporadically to check in. Lately she had been vacillating between a real desire to leave and an ingrained loyalty/love/fear of her pimp, Lucky, whom she'd been with for several years. She believed that Lucky had murdered another girl who had tried to escape. Lucky had recently been locked up on some random charges, and we'd all hoped and prayed that this would present the opportunity Patricia needed to make the decision to leave. Instead, his cousin took over the family pimping business, and out of guilt and fear, Patricia gave him most of her money every night and put the rest in Lucky's commissary. Despite my fervent prayers, Lucky managed to get out on bail and picked up right where he'd left off. Patricia had said that her pimp had been increasingly violent since he came home, and her calls and visits noticeably dropped off. This man had his hooks into her mind and soul, and I wondered what had precipitated tonight's decision.

I can see Patricia as I pull up to the gas station. She's shaking, and while I think initially it's because she's gotten soaking wet waiting for me, as I turn the heat up and she dries off, I realize that the rain has nothing to do with her tremors. Patricia, who starts talking as soon as she's in the car, is close to hysterical, chattering about a gun and his threats tonight to beat her down when she returns home. She's an odd mixture of emotionally exhausted and exhilarated. She rants, her Puerto Rican heritage colorfully expressed by a variety of English and Spanish expletives, some of which I know, others of which I can guess the meaning of. "I hate him, I fuckin hate him, can you believe this bullshit? After everything I've done for him? *Maricon!* He's got the fuckin balls to tell me he's gonna beat *my* ass? I should beat *his* ass! He's a piece of shit. He's a lowlife. He ain't shit. He thinks all those other girls are gonna be there for me if he gets locked up again? Hell no. I been there for him and he's gonna kick me like a dog last night? Just straight kicking me for no reason. *Hijodeputa.* I swear to God, I can't take it no more. I'm out here risking my life every night and you just wanna beat on me every time I come home? That don't make no sense. I don't know why. . . ."

Her rapid-fire monologue is halted by sudden sobs. I let her cry it out for a little while, but she's too angry to cry for long. She starts venting again, all the years of suppressed feelings about her abuse pouring out. But she's heady with the drama, almost euphoric after making her decision. I mostly listen, stopping once at Kennedy's for chicken wings and French fries as she hasn't eaten all day.

It doesn't take us long to get to the GEMS apartment where she'll be staying. She's calmed down now, worn herself out with her tears and yelling. Total exhaustion sets in and I know she'll probably sleep half the day. In the beginning, most of the girls are seriously sleep-deprived after all the long nights when they've been forced to stay outside on the track, sometimes for days at a time until they have brought in the necessary quota. I get her a care package with toiletries, pajamas, and some sweats, and talk for a while about the rules at the apartment—the phone cannot be used to call him; the address has to stay confidential; safety first. I explain to her, as I explain to all girls who are leaving their pimps, that she may want to call him and may even miss him and that this is a normal part of the process. Tonight she doubts what I'm saying; this will be a conversation that we'll need to have again and again. Patricia is adamant that it's over, that she doesn't ever want to hear his voice again, that she'd rather set herself on fire than go back. I know that she believes this now. There's a determination in her voice that makes me believe that this is real. I have to believe this is real every single time, with every single girl; otherwise I couldn't do this work. Yet life is rarely that simple, and traumatic relationships that are characterized by brainwashing and submission rarely end this cleanly. I believe that like me, she's had an epiphany in the wee hours of a miserable, rainy night. I also know that knowing you don't want something anymore is very different from actually being done, free and clear. I very much doubt that she will never speak to him again, but I hope and pray that by the time she does, she'll have had enough time away to think a little more clearly, to experience what life could be without constant violence and oppression, to have enjoyed her emancipation enough that she ultimately makes the decision to truly stay free. It's our job to provide an alternative, a safe environment where she will be surrounded by people who love and value her, as opposed to the life of pain and virtual captivity that she's gotten used to. If we're lucky, we'll have a few weeks with Patricia as the anger sustains her and keeps her away from him and from the life. I'm hoping it will be enough time. I know, but Patricia doesn't yet, that it's when the anger subsides that the hard part begins.

Leaving is difficult. Yet there's often an initial euphoria normally fueled by anger, relief, a desire to "show him," and a new heady sense of freedom after having been a slave to someone else's every whim. Girls are relieved to finally be able to get some rest. They tend to eat everything in sight, are excited to be able to hang out like "normal" young women. They start to believe that things can get better and begin to excitedly make plans for the future, going to school, getting a job, finding a "square" boyfriend. Unfortunately, most girls expect these things to have happened by day four.

Slowly the day-to-dayness of mundane reality begins to sink in. Your new life isn't quite what you thought it would be when you ran away at 3 a.m. one night. Your family doesn't accept you back with open arms. In fact, your family's still crazy and you remember why you ran away from them in the first place. It turns out that since you haven't been to school since the sixth grade, you've got a lot of work to do until you're ready to take your GED. Then it turns out that you can't even register for school until you get your ID, which takes forever because your mother was from Jamaica or Kansas or Georgia and your birth certificate needs to be mailed from another country or state. Living in a group home with a bunch of other teenage girls is frustrating, and someone keeps stealing your shirts. Even though you get to keep your money now, it's hard to make ends meet. Jobs are hard to find, impossible if you're fifteen, close to impossible if you don't have a GED. Boys are unreliable, inconsistent, only after one thing. Not only are you frustrated with your lack of progress, but you feel bored and depressed. It's the same shit every day: get up, go to program/school/look for a job, go to groups, come home, eat, go to bed. It feels like something is missing. You begin to believe it must be him, the life, or a combination of the two. Suddenly the initial euphoria is gone and you just feel sad and numb all the time. You don't remember feeling like this when you were with him. You have nightmares and sometimes flashbacks. You wonder if you're going crazy and if you'll ever know what normal feels like.

THANKSGIVING 1994, GERMANY

I wake up screaming, tears streaming down my face, clutching my nose, trying to wipe blood away. But there's nothing there. It takes a few seconds for me to realize that there is no broken nose this time, no bleeding to stem. I try to breathe, to calm down, still shaking from the nightmare that felt so real. It's been like this for weeks. JP is gone, and I've been out of the life for almost a month, yet it's hard to shake these moments that come by night and sometimes by day. The daytime ones are easier; I do my best to control them. But I feel powerless over the nightmares. No matter what I read, how much I pray before I go to bed, they come unbidden and unwelcome. In these dreams I experience terrifying moments of total paralysis where it feels like I'm awake but I can't move, I can't scream, I can't breathe, and there is often the sense of an evil presence in the room, or sometimes on top of me, crushing my chest. I know I'm about to be killed at any moment and I am helpless to resist. I wake from these encounters in a cold sweat, shaking, unable to go back to sleep.

While I was with JP, I sometimes would dream about a situation that we had just experienced, or more accurately that he had just put me through, and in my dream I would manipulate the ending so that it all came out the way I wanted it to. He would stop right before hitting me and apologize; the night would end with us going to bed calmly, not with me crying alone under the covers. These happy-ending dreams are now occurring constantly along with the violent nightmares, leaving me totally stressed and confused about my feelings the next day.

When I first get out, I become a nanny for a single mother in the military. Miraculously, she agrees to hire me, although I've neglected to tell her much about my past—only that I'd been in a bad relationship. I spend my days alone doing my best to take care of a thirteen-month-old child, despite the fact that I'm desperate for someone to take care of *me*. It's a job that barely pays in a month what I could make in a few hours at the club, but at least room and board are provided. Taking care of a small child is draining enough, but with all the nightmares, I'm getting a fractured night of sleep at best. I'm now getting up at the same time as I used to come home, and the sudden change to my body clock is jarring.

I'm tired most days and on edge. I have daily nosebleeds and regular headaches, both of which the doctors had warned me would happen due to the damage done to my nose and head and the facial fractures caused by the constant punching. My body aches all the time. I cry without warning. In church I cry from the moment I walk in, until the moment I leave. I feel as if I'm in a fog most of the time. I'm easily startled and quick to react to anyone invading my personal space. Another nanny in the building is joking around one day and goes to put her hands on my neck. Without thinking, I punch her in the mouth.

My entire knowledge of trauma comes from having seen *The Burning Bed* and *The Accused*. I understand that I'm reacting to what I've been through, but I have no way of knowing if the intensity of what I'm experiencing is normal, what I'm supposed to do with my feelings, if and when this might end. Normal is a concept that I'm still figuring out. I feel exposed, like there's a huge neon sign flashing above my head alerting people to the fact that I am somehow deficient, tainted, not quite right. Although no one in my new life as a nanny, or at church, really knows much other than that I was a dancer, I'm sure they can tell that I'm damaged goods.

To reaffirm that, a woman at the church unhelpfully informs me that I have a "spirit of seduction." I'm not sure what this is, how I get rid of it, or what I'm supposed to do with this information. I'm crushed and spend the next year avoiding all eye contact with any men at church, petrified that I'll accidentally seduce them. It'll be a long time before I consider that perhaps the men might bear responsibility for their interests and actions. I learn quickly, though, that what I consider appropriate attire for church and what other people consider appropriate are two different things. I dig out a skirt suit that I'd purchased for some occasion and wear it happily one Sunday, glad to have a suit like the other women. When four separate women come up to me with "lap skirts" to cover my legs, I'm mortified. Apparently skirts need to be longer than your jacket. Who knew?

Yet it's not like I have a lot of options. I've gone from having a closet full of some really nice clothes to being embarrassed by my wardrobe. It's November and yet I own two pairs of summer leggings, a few T-shirts, a pair of sneakers, some sandals, a skirt suit that is now unwearable, and three odd shoes without mates. I'm starting over again with less than a suitcase of clothes, the rest having been stolen by a crackhead I stayed with while I was homeless. My boss tells me in a way that she probably thinks is tactful, but that still makes me cry, that my sneakers smell. I already know this but I don't own another pair. When she hands me some clothes that clearly haven't seen better days since the 1970s, I want to die with shame.

I try hard to conform to this new life, this regimented schedule, to suppress all the feelings that want to bubble over and threaten my newfound freedom. Everyone thinks I should be grateful that I've been given a "second chance." Of course, I fuck it up, over a married guy in the apartment building. I don't even like him that much in the beginning, but he's quiet and kind and totally besotted with me. He pesters me daily, follows me to the laundry room, declares his undying love constantly. In the end I'm too numb, too tired to resist. My standards at this point aren't high. The fact that he doesn't hit me is about all I require.

As I worked with girls over the years, read articles, and studied trauma and trauma responses, I began to construct a different framework for my experiences. I realized that I suffered from posttraumatic stress disorder (PTSD) and began to understand that my experiences were normal given what I'd just gone through. It was a pattern that I saw time after time with the girls who came into GEMS, the vast majority of whom have symptoms of PTSD. A study done by Dr. Melissa Farley of 475 people in the commercial sex industry in five different countries found that 67 percent of them met the criteria for PTSD, a figure that rivals that of combat veterans. Traumatic responses can look different for different people. Some girls are numb, so accustomed to pushing down feelings and ignoring their own needs that it's hard for them to feel anything at all. Others are consumed with anger that's built up over time, a rage that's directed at no one and everyone. Some girls struggle with trauma reenactment, a compulsion to re-create the same situations over and over, continually putting themselves in danger, trying to have a different outcome this time. Other girls crave some level of danger just to feel "alive." It's the emotional equivalent of going from living in Technicolor to living in black-and-white. Girls whose nights were filled with fighting and violence, a level of danger every time they got into a car or went into a hotel room, who dodged and ran from the police, who never knew what to expect at any moment, now struggle with the relative safety and the danger-free, "excitement"-free, existence that the "square" world affords them. In dangerous and traumatic situations, our bodies are in a fight-or-flight response, physiologically. Once the immediate danger has passed, we can begin to truly feel all the pain and trauma that our minds and bodies have suppressed in order to function. For commercially sexually exploited girls who've experienced constant trauma, constant danger, their bodies and minds have been in a continual high alert with little respite to process the experiences they've had to suppress. It's not until things calm down that their feelings surface, and it can be overwhelming, especially if you're not expecting them or don't understand why they're happening to you.

Just as women who escape domestic violence may experience greater depression once the relationship has ended than they did during the relationship, almost everyone who leaves the life experiences a phase of depression ranging from mild to severe to debilitating. This delayed response to the trauma can be confusing, as the victim may feel as if she was actually better off before. *If I'm this miserable now, perhaps going back wouldn't be as bad.* Feelings of depression become linked with feelings of missing him. *If I'm this sad, it must be because I can't be happy without him.* In most abusive relationships, there is at least respite from the sadness when the relationship feels good, when he's being nonviolent. In the context of an abusive relationship, these moments feel all the more rare and precious. In the early stages of leaving, though, there's little relief from the grief and cumulative pain.

The emotional aspects of the transition are just a part of the recovery process. Unless girls are lucky enough to have all their needs comfortably met, they are burdened by having to figure out housing, employment, and basic sustenance issues even as they are trying to process all their pain. Just as some domestic violence victims know that leaving the abuser will mean a drastic change in finances and lifestyle, girls understand that in leaving the life they may have to leave everything they own behind and may initially be "worse off." Victims of commercial sexual exploitation and trafficking are not profiting handsomely from their abuse, but there may be some indirect "benefits." They usually don't have to deal with issues of shelter and food, although food may be withheld as a "punishment." Many girls will be allowed, if not required, to get their hair and nails done. Most pimps provide clothing that ranges from a fur coat (rare) to jeans and sneakers (common). But when girls decide to escape, they're not allowed to take anything with them. Starting from scratch is frightening, and struggling in the first few months to feed and clothe yourself can exacerbate any existing depression.

Also problematic is that law enforcement, service providers, hospital staff, and family members have such a lack of understanding of the impact of trauma on these girls that they tend to believe they are inherently damaged and irreparable. Girls are labeled "resistant" and "difficult" even by people within the antitrafficking field, and there's a lot of frustration when they return to their abusers.

"Rescuing" trafficking victims may sound like a fantastic idea, but talk to any service provider who works with these children and youth, whether in India, Cambodia, Ukraine, Atlanta, or Brooklyn, and you'll hear that the reality is a little more complex. Victims rarely rush gratefully into your open arms; they're not immediately compliant with shelter regulations; they don't trust the people trying to help them. They're tired and traumatized and hurting and lonely and depressed and scared and to them, missing the life is as normal as breathing. Healing is a messy, complicated process that's rarely linear. Girls need intense amounts of support, love, and patience. Without someone around to understand and explain that their feelings are a "normal reaction to an abnormal situation," without practical resources such as food, shelter, and clothing, without constant reassurance that leaving was the right thing to do and that it's going to get better eventually, and without counseling or even psychiatric care for depression and PTSD, and the support of people who truly "get" it, girls struggle, and the alternative seems more and more attractive every day. Sometimes even with services, support, love, and patience in place, it's just not enough to break the trauma bonds the first time around, or the second, or the third. But this doesn't mean we should stop trying, or that girls don't want help.

11
RELAPSE

Someday I know he's coming to call me
He's going to handle me and hold me
So, it's going to be like dying, Porgy
When he calls me
But when he comes I know
I'll have to go

—*"I Loves You, Porgy,"* Porgy and Bess

Omnipotent, omniscient, omnipresent. Even though it takes me years to actually be able to say omniscient properly—I'll call it omniscience—I know exactly what it means, both the dictionary definition, "having complete or unlimited knowledge, awareness, or understanding," and how it plays out in my real life. I know that he knows everything about me, past, present, and future. I know that he is all of the "omnis," he's all-powerful, all-knowing, and no matter where I go he's there. Even when I run away, he finds me, and either punishes me or cajoles me into "forgiving" him. He feels like a part of my skin, he's in my bloodstream. When he tells me that even if I get married, have children, and am gone for ten years, he'll find me, I believe him. When he says that I'll have no choice but to go with him, that I'll always belong to him, that I was born to be his, I believe him.

No one knows what I've gone through like he does, largely due to the fact that he was there, putting me through it. During my first few months in the United States, almost three years since we'd last been together, as memories are stirred and trauma is revisited, he'll be the only one I want to talk to. The only one who'll understand.

I call him, ostensibly for closure but truthfully because despite all my progress, there is a part of me that is still glued to him. We talk into the wee hours and slowly I get sucked back into believing that we can be together, until one night when he asks me to wire him some money and I refuse. His reaction, angry, violent, threatening, is so familiar that even on the phone with him thousands of miles away in another state, I get on the floor and cover my head with my hands. I change my number the next morning.

Years later, when I find myself in his home state of Texas, just a few hours' drive from his hometown, I'm tempted to look him up. I realize that like me, he's aged, yet I'm curious to see this man, now in his forties, even though in some of my most vivid memories he remains young and handsome. He rarely appears in my dreams anymore, and when I'm awake I have trouble picturing his face. It seems strange that while I can see his clothes, his sneakers, his tattoo, his haircut, and his hands, in my mind's eye I can't see the face of this man who wielded such power over me. I wonder if he's even still alive and am strangely disturbed by the thought of him dying— the only other person who'll ever really know what happened between us, the person who changed me forever, who set me on a whole different life course. We have no acquaintances in common anymore, so no one would call to tell me. He'd just be gone and I wouldn't know, and for some reason I find this upsetting. Perhaps after years of believing that he would always somehow, somewhere be in my life, that he would never really let me go, I recognize that he isn't and never will be again. This bothers me enough that I look in the phone book for his number and write it down. But the years and the distance, the therapy and the healing, God, and all my hard work, keep me sane. I stay away.

Many girls, however, don't have the option of just ignoring their former pimp. He's there around the corner, lurking outside their grandmother's house, threatening their family, sending other people to grab them off the street. The threat is real, his hold secure. Even the pimps who don't actively pursue girls once they've left have created a strong enough psychological hold that girls find themselves inexplicably calling their pimps despite their fervent desire to stay away. Sometimes it's the very fact that he appears to have moved on and replaced her with a new girl that keeps them going back. *Maybe I wasn't as special to him as I thought.* It can be hard to accept that the man they've sacrificed everything for isn't breaking a sweat that they aren't there, that it really was about the economics of the game. The frightening reality that it was all a lie begins to intrude, and the enormity of that realization can be too much. *Perhaps he never loved me.* For so many girls, it's easier to go back and reconstruct the carefully built walls of denial than face the fact that they were manipulated, used, played. That all those nights they were scared, the rapes and the beatings and the arrests, were simply to line someone's pockets. It's not surprising that a girl in this situation, feeling ashamed and betrayed, foolish and sickened, will try to think of the good times, and search for a sign that maybe there really was some love there. *That night when he said he loved me and took me to a hotel by myself and didn't make me work, or when he took me shopping, wasn't that proof?* Within a few weeks or months, those are the parts that seem more real and the beatings, the lies, the reasons why she left get hazier and more distant. Calling him just once, going around his neighborhood just to see how he's doing, doesn't seem like such a terrible idea. *Maybe he's even changed.*

Very few bad relationships are *all* bad. The same man who used to both physically and emotionally abuse me was the same man who would give me a pedicure and carefully paint my toenails, the same man who would make me the most elaborate breakfasts in bed, clean the house, make me laugh harder than anyone else could. If there had been nothing good, I wouldn't have stayed. Even most girls' relationships with pimps, while defined as they are by economic gain and forms of slavery, have elements that are "normal." Incidences of violence are juxtaposed with the day-to-day realities of everyday life: cooking, eating, sleeping, watching television. Even being put out on the track becomes so normalized, so numbing, that it's hard for most girls to view this as abuse. It's just what you're expected to do, another part of a regular day. Viewing pimps as one-dimensional monsters isn't that helpful in terms of understanding the girls' experiences. While the acts that pimps have committed are heinous and deserving of full punishment under the law, overlooking the humanness that the girls surely see only makes it harder to understand why they stay or, especially, why they go back. We understand that women in domestic violence relationships don't necessarily want the relationship to end. They just want the abuse to stop. It's what keeps the cycle going, the belief that this time it will be different, that he'll change, that you can get the good parts back, without any of the bad parts intruding this time.

Despite pimps' claims that "pimpin ain't easy," it actually is. There's little reason for them to stop or to change, to choose one girl to "square up" with and start a normal nine-to-five life. Unfortunately, this is the part of the equation that the girls don't see. Their desire to be "that" girl, the one he really loves and who will make him leave the life, overwhelms all logic. Girls who go back to their pimp aren't going back because they "miss" the life, they're going back believing, just like anyone else going back to an unhealthy situation, that things will really be different this time.

Girls relapse because the pain is no longer tangible. Human beings have a remarkable ability to forget pain. We all remember feeling sad, or hurt, or in physical pain, but we don't *feel* it anymore; it's a cerebral memory, not a physical one. This great defense mechanism probably accounts for the survival of the human race. It's what enables a woman to go through the pain of childbirth again. It's what enables us to date again after a soul-crushing divorce, to trust people after horrific betrayals. It's also what allows us to pick up that one cigarette or drink after months or years of a hard-won freedom from addiction. It's what enables us to go back to the person who has broken our hearts and who, inevitably, will do so again.

One of my favorite examples of our ability to forget pain comes from the Old Testament story of the Israelites after they escaped from slavery in Egypt and were led by Moses to the Promised Land. Most of the girls at GEMS are semifamiliar with it, either due to some knowledge of the Bible or from the animated movie *The Prince of Egypt*. I tell the girls how excited and grateful the Israelites were when they first escaped, thanks to God's parting of the Red Sea. But the Promised Land's a bit farther off than they thought, and so they've got to spend time in the desert first. It's cool at first, but after a while the Israelites are eating nothing but manna. While they don't miss being slaves, they miss the good food back in Egypt and forget how bad it really was, how hard it was to leave, how frightened they were, how it took many miracles before Pharaoh would let them go.

It's easy to miss the food, whatever that represents to you, when the manna sucks. Especially when you're fourteen or even eighteen years old. For adolescents who generally have not yet developed a sense of the future, right now feels like forever. The ability to endure a bad situation and imagine an alternative future is something that most adults develop over time. It's only after your third or fourth serious heartbreak that you begin to realize that the world probably won't end and that your heart will continue to beat, despite your fervent wishes to the contrary. "This too shall pass" was not said by a teenager. Combine normal human behavior with short-term adolescent thinking, add in the complexities of Stockholm syndrome or trauma bonds, with the persistence of a skilled manipulator, and it's not that surprising that girls struggle so much with returning to the life.

Jasmine has been coming to GEMS for almost a year. Initially mandated by the courts, she's infamous for sitting down with her court advocate on her first day at the program around 9:30 in the morning, and talking straightthroughwithoutstopping until 5 that evening. We joked that we could see her case managers' eyes glazing over and that she nearly passed out from lack of hydration and food, but it was clearly a significant moment for Jasmine. She's progressed in leaps and bounds since that night, returning to school, working part-time in the office. I know she's still struggling with some family issues, but so is pretty much everyone else. Jasmine has real leadership qualities, is compassionate to the other girls, already has begun to serve as an informal peer counselor to some of the newer girls, and is working hard toward getting hired as an official outreach worker. One evening after my weekly group, she starts telling me about her ex-pimp and her face lights up, just a little. He was her first love, at fifteen, and the intensity of the experience is still fresh almost a year later. Nothing can really compete with those heightened feelings of love and fear and belonging, and being owned. Certainly not the day-to-day challenges of being lonely, of feeling unloved, of meeting boys who are ambivalent in their desires. Pimps are never ambivalent. They always want you. Maybe not for the right reasons, but still they want you. And I know that if he calls, she'll go running. I pray he doesn't.

Of course, a few months later he calls. He's home from jail and wants to see her. Tonight. She calls me. What do I think? Should she go? Despite the desire to scream "hell no!" at the top of my lungs, I know she's already made up her mind. She tells me she knows that she won't "do anything," that she'll never go back to the life, that seeing him will help her move on. I use every analogy I can think of—moth to the flame, invisible bungee cord, alcoholic walking into a bar—to persuade her to perhaps do the "closure" thing just over the phone, but it's too late. She's already deciding what to wear.

We've agreed that she'll call me when she gets there, call me if she gets upset, call me when she's leaving. For the first hour, she calls every ten minutes. She calls from outside the diner where they're meeting, calls me when she sees him walking up the street, calls me when he goes to the bathroom. On each call, I can hear her voice changing, the hypnosis of his presence taking effect. In the beginning, she tells me that it's going well, that he says he's sorry. I don't believe him. Within an hour, she calls me to tell me that he wants her to go "work" that night. I'd thought it would take a couple of days at least to introduce this idea; clearly he's hearing what I'm hearing in her voice. Jasmine tells me that she said no, and I tell her to get out of there, run. Immediately. There's nothing else to say; he hasn't changed and she's never going to get the kind of closure she wants. She agrees. I wait for the call that tells me that she's getting on the train home, but it doesn't come. I call and call her phone but it's going straight to voice mail. I feel physically sick knowing that once she's crossed the line, it will be a long road back. I drive downtown.

It's 3 a.m., and the lights of 42nd Street are still flickering. Crackheads and dope fiends roam the streets in search of another hit, young dealers appear from the shadows ready to oblige, and middle-aged men skulk nervously out of the peep shows. Cars pull up slowly alongside the curb, looking for a girl or a woman from whom they can buy sex. On some of the side streets, 45th and 46th between 8th Avenue and 9th, young girls and older women blatantly jostle for the attention of these cruising cars. On 42nd Street, by the Port Authority Bus Terminal, girls are more discreet, trying not to attract the attention of passing cops.

I'm walking in circles up and down 43rd, 44th, back down 8th, over again to 42nd, and back up Broadway, not sure what I'll do once I see her, but I hope seeing me will pull her back from the fuguelike state she's already slipped into. I know that feeling well. It's like you're hypnotized into walking off a cliff. Your eyes can see the sheer drop, you can fully imagine the pain of being splattered against the rocks below, one side of your brain is screaming at you to stop and yet your feet keep landing on the ground, one in front of the other, closer and closer to the precipice. People on either side are yelling—*You don't have to do this, you can turn around*—and you hesitate. But then you look into his eyes. He doesn't have to say anything, he just beckons. As if pulled by an invisible force, you take one step, then another, then another.

I later learn that Jasmine's former pimp had taken her straight from the diner to the East Side, as there were too many cops around 42nd Street. While I'm walking around, feeling like the codependent wife of an alcoholic about to fall off the wagon, Jasmine is being sold for the first time in almost eighteen months. Less than three hours after she first saw him again.

I drive home in tears, frustrated, sad, and annoyed at myself for thinking that I could change things. I know Jasmine believes that this time she can make this work, that he'll change in the end as long as she does what he wants. I know that she feels powerless to do anything else. But when reality kicks in and the fugue wears off, it will only be worse. She'll realize how far she's regressed but be too ashamed to reach back out. The memories of everyone who was so proud of her will make her feel sick inside. The worse she feels about herself, the more she'll cling to him. After all, she's risked everything for this and now feels that she's got to stick it out.

It takes three hours for him to lure her back in, but it'll be another two years before Jasmine, tired and traumatized, slowly begins to take steps back. For Sara, it takes four years. For Amanda, eight years. Eboni, Tiffany, Donna, Peaches. . . . we're still waiting for them to come back.

After years of watching girls relapse and struggling with my own feelings of not having "done enough," I eventually discovered the Stages of Change model, a framework often used in the treatment of eating disorders, substance abuse, and alcohol addiction. A critical part of this model, designed as a wheel to emphasize the ever-evolving and fluid nature of recovery, is that one of the phases is relapse.

To use the language of addiction in the context of children who've been bought and sold is not to suggest that commercial sexual exploitation or trafficking is an addiction. We should no more accuse a domestic violence victim of returning to her abuser because she's "addicted to the violence" than we should misconstrue girls' struggles to stay free as their "liking it." Yet it's important to understand that their relapse and the recovery process bear some similarities to the recovery process of addiction.

Understanding triggers, staying away from "people, places, things," and taking it one day at a time, all intrinsic to the language of recovery from addiction, are also important components of the recovery process for girls who have experienced the trauma of being trafficked. Girls have to be equipped with skills and tools to support them through the challenging process of leaving and have to feel empowered enough to remain free from their trafficker. They have to understand that it's normal to miss the life and to still have feelings for their trafficker but not to act on those feelings. Having conflicted emotions doesn't mean you *should* go back, it just means you've been conditioned to feel this way. And they have to be equipped with strategies for dealing with the feelings when they arise.

Long-term healing requires that these girls understand that what they have experienced is not their fault. So many of these girls, their family members, the social workers, and law enforcement officials believe their exploitation was their choice. This perspective keeps them stuck. If I believe that I am inherently dirty, loose, or bad, then there is no hope for me and I might as well go back to my trafficker anyway. If I can begin to understand all the factors that made me vulnerable—the impact of race, class, and gender; the role played by my dysfunctional family; the power of the billion-dollar sex industry; the recruitment tactics of my pimp; my limited options as a teenager—then I can begin to shift the blame to the perpetrators instead of carrying it myself.

At some point girls have to be able to move past a sense of being perpetual victims and having no control over what happens to them. They need to feel empowered, utilize safety strategies, recognize unhealthy and manipulative relationships before they even begin, understand what might make them vulnerable, and take steps to mitigate that, whether it's cutting certain people out of their lives or becoming economically independent. Most of all, they need to finally understand what makes for a healthy, intimate relationship, an understanding that has been distorted over the years and which, if not corrected, puts them at risk for victimization over and over again.

UNLEARNING

He beats me too, what can I do,
Oh my man,
I love him so
—*Billie Holiday, "My Man"*

WINTER 1995, GERMANY

I've been out of the life for a couple of months and am slowly trying to pick up the fragmented pieces of my life. I've been attending a
small nondenominational church that sits off the American air force
base where I live, doing my best to pretend to fit in with the "square"
world without betraying my dirtiness, the huge scarlet letter that I'm
sure is visible to all. People know I was a "dancer" but that's all I'm
willing to reveal at this stage. While there are definitely some people
at church who are giving off a judgmental vibe, there are also some
kind women who seem to sense in me a desire for acceptance, for
love, for safety. Since I cry from the moment church begins till the
end of the service, including sniffling through the announcements
about Sunday School and the "Can the owner of the Dodge Caravan
that's blocking the entrance please move their car?" it's probably not
that difficult to spot the huge gaping wounds, but nonetheless I'm
grateful for their support and their attempts to engage me in conversation. Sonia, a pretty woman with a dry sense of humor that I
immediately gravitate toward, invites me over for an afternoon with
her air force sergeant husband, David, and their two young children.
I'm nervous about being around a man, worried that I'll give off the
wrong vibe accidentally, worried that he'll be a creep, but I like Sonia

and want her to like me, too, so I go. I think they sense that I haven't had much "normal" in my life, so they keep the visit low-key. We sit around watching *The Little Mermaid* with their kids. Despite my nerves, I feel myself relaxing and marveling at the picture-perfect tableau of family life: a pretty wife and a handsome husband who seem to genuinely like each other; two beautiful, well-adjusted kids; nice furniture; American accents. I feel like I'm spending a day with the Cosbys. I decide I want to be Sonia when I grow up. Toward the end of the afternoon, my entire worldview is shaken when David asks for a cup of tea. Sonia and I go into the kitchen, start chitchatting while she prepares some snacks for the kids, and we come back out sans tea. "Where's my tea?" David asks, and I steel myself, preparing for the scene that's about to come.

Sonia, who has sat down, begins to rise. "Oh, I'm sorry, I forgot, honey." Any moment now. I'm waiting for the explosion.

"It's OK, babe, I'll make it myself, don't worry about it," says David, and with that he smiles, rubs her shoulder, and trots off to the kitchen to make it himself.

I'm stunned. Sonia is acting like everything is normal, but I'm having a hard time figuring this out. What just happened? What happened to the explosion, the anger, the disgust with her forgetfulness? I try to hold it, knowing somewhere in my head that my question is about to sound marginally crazy, but I need an answer.

"Why he didn't hit you?" I whisper, worried David will hear.

"Huh?" Sonia is confused.

"I mean"—frustrated that she's not getting the obvious—"why didn't you get in trouble over the tea, why didn't he yell at you or something?"

Sonia looks like she wants to laugh, but when she realizes that I'm serious, she looks horrified.

"Oh, sweetie. That's not how we do things in this house. Ever. That's not how people should ever treat each other." Now she just looks sad.

"Oh, OK." I feel bad that I've upset her and realize that I've betrayed exactly what I've been trying so hard to hide. I'm embarrassed.

David comes back in with a tea for himself and one for me and one for her. This is just too much. He must be the nicest man on the planet. I'm completely thrown off.

Sonia, guessing that we probably need to discuss this whole "Why doesn't he hit you?" thing a little more, tells him we're going into the kitchen for some girl talk. We spend the rest of the afternoon talking about love and abuse and how they're not the same thing. While I think I probably know this intellectually, at nineteen it's the first time that I've ever really begun to believe it. Putting this realization into practice will take a few more years.

Most women have been in a relationship that they know is no good for them. Your friends and family know it is no good for you, but you're too besotted to see straight. It may take a few attempts, some late-night crying sessions, some serious talking to from your girl-friends, but eventually you're able to leave and look back with a mixture of regret and disbelief that you put up with that person for so long. The relationship may not have been physically abusive, but bad relationships can fall anywhere on a continuum, from the guy who doesn't call when he says he will to the guy who has a wandering eye to the guy who cheats with your college roommate. At the far end of this continuum are the men (or women) who are emotionally or physically abusive. Your boundaries or tolerance for an unhealthy relationship often depends on what you're used to, what the deal breakers are for you, where that invisible line falls. Some girls and women have a higher tolerance for pain, mostly because they've experienced it in various forms growing up. Some women have no idea what to expect from a relationship because they never saw a healthy one modeled. Many children grow up watching violence play out in their families, setting the stage for later dating and relational patterns. Sadly, this is even more common than we like to admit, as one in four women in this country will experience physical violence from a partner at some point in their lives.

Chris Brown's attack on Rihanna was perhaps the most public example of dating violence for young women. Yet instead of the incident provoking a thoughtful national dialogue, it showed how entrenched attitudes still are about where the responsibility for violence lies. I was horrified by the response on many of the message boards, blogs, and even by some of the celebrities who initially tried to downplay Chris Brown's culpability. Message after message not believing her, blaming her, excusing Brown's actions along the lines of "she must've done *something* to deserve it." A survey carried out by the Boston Public Heath Commission a few weeks after the attack found that almost half of the two hundred teenagers interviewed thought Rihanna was responsible for her alleged beating at the hands of Chris Brown. Only 51 percent thought Brown was responsible for the incident, and 52 percent said both individuals were to blame for the incident, despite knowing at the time that Rihanna had been beaten badly enough to require hospital treatment. Forty-four percent of the teenagers thought that physical fighting was a normal part of a relationship.

Clearly, then, it's not just girls who've experienced trafficking and commercial sexual exploitation who believe that violence is normal. Even now, thirty-plus years into the domestic violence movement, too many girls and young women are still taught to accept gender-based violence.

It is well known that Chris Brown grew up witnessing domestic violence. While on some level he knows it's wrong, on many levels it just feels normal. So too is it normal for girls who have witnessed domestic violence or experienced physical abuse from their family members or "caregivers." In addition to any exposure to unhealthy family dynamics, girls, especially girls of color, are growing up in a culture that glorifies violence and frequently implicitly and explicitly devalues and sexualizes them. Domestic violence is also often framed as a result of uncontrollable passion, leading girls to believe that men who don't hit are apathetic and uncaring. It's not surprising that so many teenage girls accept violence as a part of their relationships—violence as a demonstration of love.

It's a Tuesday afternoon at the office and I'm talking to Tyria, who lives in our housing program, about her inability to keep curfew. She's turning around and around on a swivel chair while I talk to her. It's clearly not a conversation that she's thrilled to be having. For our girls, curfew is a constant challenge; they are used to coming home in the early hours of the morning and sleeping all day. They're also teenagers who need space to be teenagers, to mess up, to break the rules. And yet we still try to maintain order and boundaries for the whole house, all the while recognizing and addressing the trauma that has led our girls to be there in the first place. Even though keeping curfew is not high on Tyria's to-do list, it is a priority on ours.

"So, what's going on with you right now? Not doing so great with this curfew thing, huh?"

Tyria mumbles that she has a hard time following the rules, which I adamantly agree with. I give her the standard response about the importance of rules in the house, but feel as though there's something else going on for her around this issue.

"Why do you think you're having such a hard time with the rules? You're doing pretty well in other areas; you're doing great in school." By great, I mean that she's actually attended class for ten consecutive days. Baby steps.

Tyria shrugs. "I dunno. It's like y'all too soft."

"Really?" I'm surprised to hear this; earlier she'd been complaining about how strict the rules were. "You were upset though that we'd placed you on an earlier curfew, right, so I'm not sure that I totally understand what you're asking for."

"Y'all should hit me. If you just hit me, I'd listen and follow the rules and stuff," she says.

I feel tired and sad, looking at this little girl twisting back and forth and fidgeting around in a rolling chair, a child who's asking to be hit—who believes that this is how she'll learn to "act right."

"Ty, honey, we don't do that and we won't ever do that. Not just because it's against the law, but because we don't want to. Ever. We believe that you shouldn't be hit, that you should be protected. That's why you're at GEMS, to be safe and not hurt."

She looks skeptical.

"Why do you think it would help for you to be hit?"

"Because I'm hardheaded and when I get hit, then afterward I listen. I need it sometimes; I act better then."

"Did someone tell you that?"

"Yeah, my ex." At GEMS, you don't really need to add the word *pimp* onto *ex*; it's a given. "He said I needed it to act right. He didn't do it all the time, just when I was wildin out and needed it, but afterward I did what I was supposed to. It's just discipline. It's not bad."

I picture her subdued and compliant after a beating. Of course she did what she was told. You don't have that much fight in you after a beating. It's the calm after the storm. If anything, you try harder, act sweeter, and feel more attached than ever. This behavior would of course prove his theory that she "needed" to get hit. I'd heard the same line myself many times.

I ask her about the times she "acted up" and what she thought she'd done to deserve it. She cites the heinous crimes of being mean to one of her wives-in-law, getting jealous, not making enough money, forgetting to do something he'd asked her to do.

Tyria's a bright, no-nonsense girl, so I figure we'll use some logic to take each incident apart and try to explore the notion of what "deserving" it really means.

"So, let me get this straight, you're in love with him, right?"

She nods vigorously.

"And he's sleeping with another girl and you get jealous? That's pretty normal, though, right? I know I'd be mad jealous. I might even say something slick. You've got the right to feel jealous, he's hurting your feelings. But then you're the one that gets beaten up?"

She catches on quickly and starts smiling. "OK, so it wasn't that bad what I did, but still. . . ." She's not sure how to justify this one.

"OK, how about the money thing. . . . He's selling you, you're the one that's out there in danger, having to put in all the grind, while he's in his car chillin, and he's mad at you for not making enough money?" I mimic him posted up in his car, doing nothing.

Tyria's laughing now. She knows it sounds a little off. It just *feels* so logical. "OK, OK, so I didn't do a lot of bad things but it did make me act better." Her need for "discipline" has been drummed into her so hard that even though a part of her brain knows that she probably shouldn't get beaten up, in her heart she remains otherwise convinced. We talk for a while about abuse and love, about hitting and deserving and the concept of healthy, safe consequences for her behavior at the house. I can see it sinking in just a little on the surface, but still barely penetrating her core beliefs. Somehow we get to the subject of how she met her pimp and she mentions in an offhand way that she met him the night she ran away from home, trying to escape her mother's violent rages and extension cord beatings. Apparently her mother also believed she "needed" to get beaten in order to behave. It's not really surprising that Tyria wants us to hit her. That's her baseline for normal. Boundaries, respect, unconditional love are not. Neither is it surprising to me, although still upsetting, that a few weeks after this conversation, Tyria goes back to what feels normal, where she understands the rules and consequences and knows exactly what to expect.

In the language of sociology, a subculture comes replete with rules and norms, a common language and social mores. This is true for the culture of domestic trafficking. Pimps use mind control and domination to teach girls the norms and mores of "the game," building on the core values and beliefs that have been ingrained in them since childhood. Many people often think that sexually exploited girls want freedom, but even if that's true for a few, what they find is a level of control and structure in their new lives that is far greater than anything they ever experienced at home. It's precisely the freedom from that control that can be incredibly frightening for girls in the beginning of their recovery. If a pimp feels like an anchor, then leaving feels like being cut adrift in a world where the rules aren't always clear and the consequences don't always make sense. Just as ex–cult members need deprogramming after leaving an abusive cult, there's a lot of unlearning to do once girls escape the commercial sex industry. Their attitudes and core beliefs have to be reframed. Their boundaries are so blurred and distorted that even once girls get the basic concept that violence is not OK under any circumstances, it can still be a struggle for them to develop healthy boundaries in intimate relationships and in friendships. Commercially sexually exploited girls are used to giving and giving and giving—taking care of their pimps, taking care of their johns' "needs"—an ingrained pattern that often goes back to childhood when they took care of family members, whether it was younger siblings or parents. Most girls struggle with codependency in and out of the life, and it can take a while to stop being the caretaker. Even their relationship with money is distorted. Money, love, and sex have all become entangled, and girls often have a tough time setting limits on giving money to needy family members, and especially needy boyfriends, even when they're barely making ends meet themselves. For girls who're used to seeing but not keeping large amounts of money, it's hard to adjust to getting paid biweekly and making less in a week than she made, for him, in one night. Trafficked girls, and girls who've grown up in poverty, haven't had much opportunity to think about the future, let alone plan for it financially. It can be very tough for them to save money. When I first started making a salary, I was so convinced that I was going to lose it soon anyway that I frittered and gave it away like it was tap water. Helping girls develop a healthier relationship with money, seeing it as something neutral and showing them that people can make money doing something they actually enjoy, is an important step in helping them unlearn old patterns.

When your self-identity has been tied up in how much money you can make and how many men want "you," it can feel scary to not have any of those things left to define you. So many girls have told me, "I don't think I'm good at anything else," and within their words, I hear their fear that this is their destiny, what they were made for. *Once a ho, always a ho*, and *Can't turn a ho into a housewife* are phrases that stick in your brain. When you've been told the same thing for years by your family and every adult man you've ever met, and society's attitude confirms it, why wouldn't you believe that this is who you are and all you'll ever be? Undoing these lies is like unraveling a twisted ball of yarn; each distorted belief leads to another.

My weekly group, brilliantly titled "Rachel's Group," is one of my favorite parts of the week. Our theme tonight is "struggling with relapse," a recurring topic among others such as "how to deal with my feelings about Mom when she's still using/going back to the man who abused me/bringing up my past and throwing it in my face/not acknowledging how she hurt me," and frequently "should I/how do I tell this new boy I'm dating that I've been sexually exploited?" As always, we have girls in the group who are at various levels of recovery, and the conversation quickly gets intense as Isabel, the oldest member of the group at twenty-one, begins to share her frustrations about "missing the streets." Isabel is tall and slim with a permanent pout and a mountain of curly braids cascading from her head. She'd been mandated to GEMS by the courts several months ago, successfully completed her required amount of "days," and then disappeared. She returned a month later but didn't seem to want to engage with anyone. She'd sit on the couch, pull a book out from her purse, and begin reading. Attempts to interact with her were generally met with a sullen look and a bothered sigh. Requests to participate were turned down with a vigorous shake of her braids and sometimes simply by her getting up and leaving. Still, she kept coming back, almost every day. I'd thought that Isabel was mandated again, so reluctant did she look to be here, yet I've just found that she's actually been coming—and glaring—voluntarily.

In the last couple of weeks, she's slowly begun to warm up, hesitantly entering into brief and cursory conversation, smiling slightly and being asked to be called by her real name, Isabel, not her alias Rebecca. This is a major victory and a sign that's she's beginning to feel a little more comfortable. Tonight she begins to talk openly for the first time.

"It's hard, Rachel, it's like I know it's messed up but I feel kind of lost and lonely. I almost went back last week but I decided not to."

"That's a really big step, Isabel; how did you manage to not go back?"

"I dunno. I just thought that maybe bad things would happen and that I might not make it back out again, so I went to sleep instead and when I woke up I felt a little better."

"That's great."

"Not much, though," she cautions, as if I think she's gotten over the hump. "It's still really hard, every day."

Other girls in the group uh-huh and nod vigorously in agreement with Isabel's assessment. Nee-Nee, a chubby-faced thirteen-year-old, finally speaks.

"I feel like this is the only thing I'm good at."

The group sits quietly for a minute, absorbing the impact of the statement and nodding in agreement. Nee-Nee follows her heartbreaking statement with a rambling and unrelated story about some girls who tried to steal her clothes at the group home. I can feel the group itching to get away from the uncomfortable realities that Isabel and Nee-Nee have just brought up and realize that at any moment the group could turn into a vigorous and heated discussion about "them girls who steal clothes," as everyone in the room has shared this experience, too. I quickly write PROS and CONS in big letters on either side of the chart paper on the wall. When in doubt, make a list, is my general philosophy. "Does everyone understand what pros and cons are?"

A few girls look blank. Michelle, a fifteen-year-old who's been quiet up till now, says, "The good and bad things of something. Helps you make a decision."

"Yup, that's exactly it. So we're going to write down all the good things about being in the life and all the bad things and then we'll discuss the lists."

"I think the cons list is gonna be longer. Right, Rachel?"

I smile. "Let's see what happens. . . ."

The girls have endless stories about the brutality of their pimps and johns but manage to find humor in much of it. It's one of the benefits of a survivors-only group; everyone understands the pain. They jump in excitedly to each others' stories, "Word? That's the same thing that happened to me except he dragged me out by the hair!" Ebonie dramatically reenacts the hair-pulling incident to gales of laughter. "Nah, son, lemme me tell you . . ." another girl interrupts. "My daddy chased me down the street and I was wearing these heels that were mad high and I kept falling over." More reenactments, more hysterical laughter. All the girls competing for the funniest beating story, the craziest crooked cop story, the scariest john story. Just a group of teenage girls entertaining one another, having a riot, shooting the shit about getting beaten, raped, and arrested. Good times.

Within minutes, the CONS side of the paper is a mess of words, mainly ones that describe pain and violence. The mood sobers up a bit as we begin to explore what the exercise means to them.

Isabel's face turns into a frown as she studies the list. "I think there's something really really really wrong with me." She pauses, clearly upset by a disturbing epiphany. "I can look at that list, and see all that bad shit, and it's just mad normal to me. I don't feel shocked or anything. All that stuff, getting raped, pimps, that's . . . you know, the life. That's just what it is. But I don't think it's normal to *think* that. I must be sick or something."

I feel for her. It's scary to realize that your reactions are deadened and even harder to realize that the way you view life might be considered a little odd, or even awful, to others. I use my standard oldie but goodie for these situations. "It's a totally normal reaction to an abnormal situation. You were trained to not feel anything by the people who hurt and exploited you. After lots and lots of pain and bad things happening, it gets to feel really normal."

Isabel objects strenuously. "But I wasn't forced to do anything. I knew what I was getting into. I just thought I was grown. So . . ." Her logic follows. "There must be something wrong with me."

"How old were you when you got in the life?" I ask.

"Eleven." She sees my face and anticipates my reaction. "But I knew exactly what I was doing. No one made me." She's vehement about this.

A few of the other girls agree that they were the same age, one was ten and a half, another twelve. Tonight the *oldest* age of recruitment in this group is thirteen. I decide I'll wait till I get home to be utterly outraged by that.

"Are you the same person as you were when you were eleven? Ten whole years ago?"

"Nah. But that's different . . ." The idea that she "chose" the life is burned into her brain.

I wrap up the group with a bit of a rah-rah speech about how it wasn't ever their fault, that they were children taken advantage of by adults and that they didn't "choose" to be beaten or raped or sold or bought. A few of the girls seem to be letting it sink in just a little, but it's a message they will need to hear over and over and over again. It's a little tough to undo years of damage in an hour and a half, so you have to be grateful for the small steps. We hold hands and close out with a prayer for one another, and I hug all the girls as they gather their belongings.

Isabel waits off to the side. Finally she approaches me. "I still think there's something really wrong with me, though."

"Have you ever heard about child soldiers? In some parts of Africa or the Middle East?"

She nods vigorously. "You know, how they're trained when they're real little, to shoot, kill, stab other people during a war, right?" I say.

"Yup, I saw something about it on TV."

"OK, so if they manage to survive all that stuff, do you think they feel bad about what they've done or seen? Or does it seem normal?"

Isabel is thinking intently. "I don't think they feel bad, probably at first."

"Why, honey?"

"Cos that's what they've been trained to do."

I wait and look at her.

Slowly a small smile begins to spread across her face. "And so were you . . ." I say as she nods in comprehension. She gives me a big hug; it's the most expansive she's ever been with me. "Trained," she says as if sounding the word out for the first time. I nod in agreement. And then she darts out of the door, going home to ponder probably for the first time, how ten years ago her eleven-year-old self was trained to accept the life as normal.

It's confusing in the beginning trying to adjust your view of what's normal to what the rest of the world thinks is normal, particularly when you feel so less than normal yourself. The deep-down beliefs that you've held for so long are hard to let go of. Other people's worldviews seem off, and yours *feels* right, even when you begin to know logically that it's not. It's lonely and frightening in the beginning and you're desperate for someone who "gets" it, who makes you feel a little less crazy.

When I first came to New York, one of the most critical things for me was being around other girls and women who'd experienced the life. It was in a Friday night group at the Little Sister Project with adult women, that I was allegedly facilitating, but in truth I needed as much as everyone else in the room; that became the place where I felt most "normal." We shared a common understanding, remembered similar feelings, and could talk frankly about our experiences without judgment. Those Friday nights with seven or eight women each week made me feel a little less one-of-these-things-is-not-like-the-other. Less of a round peg in a "square" world.

There was often a lot of laughter in the room and to a casual observer, it would have probably appeared that the violence and abuse meant nothing, yet pain and humor aren't antithetical. You had to earn the right to laugh at pain. Jokes about the life are funny only if you've lived it. And in a group of all survivors, everyone had. It was in that room that we could laugh at what we'd once considered normal, laugh at how far we'd come. *Wasn't that shit crazy? Can you believe we're still here?* We'd shake our heads in amazement at some of the bizarre experiences and the ludicrous lies that we'd believed or told to ourselves. It was a relief to make jokes about a john and not have someone judge you, and to laugh about the lengths you'd go to please your pimp without having people look at you like you were crazy. It was in that room that I began to learn and understand the importance of other survivors, how much we needed each other's support.

Over time I learned that there were a lot of people who would judge you, blame you, and try to make you feel lesser, no matter what you did; that a degree, a good suit, and a career wouldn't always insulate you from scorn. But Friday nights in a little walk-up in Spanish Harlem, I learned a little about building some of the insulation myself.

STIGMA

Ah, but let her cover the mark as she will,
the pang of it will be always in her heart.
—*Nathaniel Hawthorne*, The Scarlet Letter

I'm looking rather fly, if I do say so myself. I'm wearing my new Jackie O black suit, with black patent heels and a hot pink patent belt. I'd gotten the suit on sale at Macy's a few months earlier but hadn't had a chance to wear it, as it was a little much for our office in Harlem. It is, however, perfect for this morning's visit to the White House, where a small group of us has been invited to attend a ceremonial signing of the newly reauthorized trafficking legislation.

I spot a friend in the field, Bradley, and we chat excitedly for a few minutes before it's announced that we're being invited into the Oval Office. I walk in and shake President George W. Bush's hand. I find myself feeling a little overcome with emotion, as the weight of where I am and what I'm doing sinks in. We're led in, the president gives a warm and charming welcome, and I find my eyes watering, just a little. I think of President Kennedy and John-John under the desk, FDR, Lincoln, and even Nixon. I think of all the conversations that have been had in this room, the laws signed, the decisions made. I start to well up even more at the thought that in just a few weeks, Barack Obama, the country's first black president, will be sitting in this very office. I surreptitiously touch the side of the desk, just because I can, and fervently pray, *please God-pleaseGodpleaseGodpleaseGod please let me come back here when Obama's in office.*

The president sits down to sign the bill and I find myself directly behind him. I sneak a look at Bradley and he's just as struck by the moment as I am. We make a can-you-fuckin-believe-this face at each other. Clearly neither of us can.

As we prepare for our individual photos with the president, I'm mortified at how incredibly sweaty my palms are and try desperately to wipe them on the side of my skirt. The president does not seem disgusted by my handshake and we take the picture without much incident. It's over in seconds and I walk to the other side of the room where the previously photographed are supposed to stand. Suddenly, Jeffrey Winter, a Republican lobbyist whom I neither particularly know nor particularly like, grabs both my arms in a vise grip. Before I've even had time to register this invasion of personal space, he stage-whispers, "Long way from the street, eh?"

I feel like I've been slapped. Hard. The last thing on my mind today was the streets, the life, or my past—it has been fifteen years. Yet apparently it was the first thing on his. I can feel my cheeks flushing and I'm horrified that he would take this moment, of all moments, to remind me of my past, put me in my "place." How dare he? Unless you'd grown up in the White House, it's a big deal for anyone to be invited to the Oval Office. And yet apparently I'm supposed to be more honored, more grateful, more something because of my shameful beginnings. I'm humiliated and angry. "Take your hands off me right now and please don't say anything else to me."

"What, what? Oh, I can't say that? I didn't mean anything by it. . . ." Jeffrey continues talking, adding insult to injury, and I feel my face getting hotter.

"Don't talk to me. Seriously." I'm aware that my voice isn't quite as low as it probably should be under the circumstances, but I don't care at this point. The moment is ruined for me. We're standing less than ten feet away from the president and I'm guessing that at least a few people in the room, if not the president himself, can hear us. I'm trying to hold in my tears and the only way to do that is to stay angry. Jeffrey, unfortunately, is making it quite easy to do this. "Please don't insult my intelligence," I say under my breath, although at this point we're having a full-blown argument, albeit whispered, in the middle of the Oval Office. I'm thankful that this administration is on its way out, as it's doubtful that I'll get an invite back after this. Fortunately the president is leaving and the event is wrapping up. I just want to get out of there as quickly as possible.

Bradley has caught the tail end of the argument, and knows that something offensive has been said. Once we're outside, away from the White House, I finally start crying. I'm so upset that this will be my memory of this historic White House visit. I vent for a while to Bradley, and then to a few other people on the phone on the train back from D.C. By the time I'm back in New York, I've exhausted most of my anger but I'm still bothered that I'm bothered. I know that most people don't look at me and automatically think of my past, and I know that very few people get an invitation to meet a sitting president, but still, I'm hurt. Despite all my accomplishments, despite the momentous nature of the event, all this person saw was my past. Nothing I did, no one I met, would erase the fact that in his eyes, I was still a former prostitute.

It is rare that I have to feel the sting of that judgment anymore. An ex-boyfriend once threw it in my face during an argument years before; a couple of guys never returned my calls as soon as they found out; there was the occasional insensitive remark at a party where people were unaware of my role; and of course the White House incident. Yet in many ways my openness about my past insulates me. It is in my bio, on the GEMS website, in every Google search of me. I am in a field that values the fact that I am a "survivor"—it gives me, I've been told, a level of credibility that few other people in the field possess. It was frustrating initially and then ultimately unacceptable to be billed as a "former prostitute" at a conference, yet with the girls, my experiences allow me to empathize with them, and to give them hope.

That said, when Governor Eliot Spitzer of New York was busted by a press corps all but visibly salivating over every lascivious detail and fascinated with this entrée into the world of escort agencies and high-priced call girls, the pressure was intense. The sheer volume of cover story headlines featuring the word *hooker*, and the opinions, jokes, and comments that dominated the coverage, the vast majority of which alternately sneered at or lusted after (and sometimes both in the same piece) the young woman who had been bought by then-governor Spitzer, was both shaming and saddening for me and for the girls every morning when we went to buy our bagels and tea.

By the millionth insensitive and rude call that week from the press, I'd had enough. I wanted to lay down the eight-hundred-pound elephant that sat on my neck. The *p* word, the image of a "fallen woman" that inspired scorn and derision, judgment, and often titillation was the last thing I wanted to be identified with. I thought of what a girl in my weekly group had said. "I don't care what you call it, Rachel, sexual exploitation and all that, but to everyone else, we still hos." That week, I felt she was right.

About a week later, another scandal broke that both fascinated and disturbed me. A young memoirist named Margaret B. Jones, who'd claimed a biracial heritage and a hard-knocks childhood in the mean streets of South Central LA, was exposed as a privileged white woman who'd grown up in the rather kind streets of San Fernando Valley. As I watched the story unfold, there was a part of me that felt a little jealous of Ms. "Jones." The luxury of being able to say, "I was just joking; oops, I lied. I was never in the life. In fact I grew up in a great two-parent home, graduated from high school, and went to Oxford, where I decided that to be taken seriously as an advocate for exploited kids, it would be better to create a dramatic backstory." I obsessed over this alternate scenario for several days and imagined conversations with people in the field. How would they respond? Had everything I'd accomplished been judged all along in the context of "She's done so well considering where she came from"?

I toyed with the idea of my imaginary résumé, made jokes about it to a few friends. But beneath the jokes, the yearning to be able to just close the door completely, once and for all, on that chapter of my life was overwhelmingly powerful. If only I could excise the memories, the pain, the having to experience the judgment of other people, the having to "have the conversation" with a boyfriend when you felt the relationship was getting serious, the being a "former" anything. I'd always said that I didn't regret anything and that everything I've been through had made me who I am, but that week I couldn't shake the strong desire to simply make my experiences an imaginary world that I had created inside my head. A chapter that I could unwrite.

The term *prostitute* conjures up so many images, all of them negative. The other words to describe women and girls in the sex industry aren't much better. Growing up, I was enamored of Julia Roberts in *Pretty Woman*, yet I wanted the fairy-tale red dress and diamond necklace part, not the being seen as a hooker, ho, whore, prostitute part. Even when I was working in the club and giving my money to a man, I strenuously objected to the term *prostitute*, so conscious was I of all the baggage and stigma that accompanied it, preferring instead neutral terms like *hostess*, *dancer*, and the German term *anime*. Even as I later came to accept the realities of my involvement in the commercial sex industry, I still couldn't wrap my brain around calling a thirteen-year-old or a fifteen-year-old a prostitute. It denoted a level of choice that just wasn't true. Yet it was the most polite term that I heard girls called when I first came to New York. The word was frequently almost spat out of the speaker's mouth, as if there would be some type of contamination just by saying it.

It was at a youth summit for survivors in Canada in 1998 that I first heard the terminology *commercially sexually exploited child/youth*, a phrase that, while long and challenging initially, spoke most accurately to the experiences and realities of children and youth within the sex industry. It was a phrase that had been adopted by the United Nations and UNICEF and was largely accepted by many practitioners in the international children's rights field. These, however, weren't the people who most sexually exploited children were running into on a daily basis. It was the cops, the social workers, the nurses, the guidance counselors, the family members, the neighbors, the siblings, the judges, the correctional officers who were scornfully calling girls "prostitutes" and treating them accordingly.

One of the statements that we drafted in the Declaration and Agenda for Action at the summit that week was, "We declare that the term *child or youth prostitute* can no longer be used. These children and youth are sexually exploited and any language or reference to them must reflect this belief."

I took this declaration to heart and embraced the terminology for myself and for the girls I worked with. It was clear to me that changing the language would be an integral part of the GEMS mission and philosophy and, over the years, I have argued vehemently for language change, often carefully correcting anyone who misspeaks.

"I'm writing an article on teen prostitutes."

"Oh, you mean commercially sexually exploited youth?"

"No, girls in prostitution."

"Yes, you do mean commercially sexually exploited girls."

"Oh . . . uh, yeah, I guess."

Constantly reframing the issue and changing the language has been imperative in changing public perception and sympathies. It's been a battle particularly with people in the media who feel that using the term *commercially sexually exploited* will confuse their audience. One reporter refused to change his terminology, saying that he felt that the term was "euphemistic." We debated for a while on how *sexually exploited* could possibly be considered euphemistic when it accurately described what actually happened to children and youth, whereas *child prostitute* seemed to denote *who* the child was as opposed to what was being done *to* her. In his article, he went ahead and called them "teen prostitutes" anyway, failing perhaps to understand that it wasn't a question of semantics, that words, names, terminology really do matter.

In my weekly recovery group, inspired, sadly enough, by the pivotal confrontation scene in *Good Will Hunting*, I've decided to discuss the issue of things being "not your fault." We have a lively discussion and I feel like we are making some progress in addressing the issues of blame, and the accompanying shame, that the girls all carry in relation to their past. As usual, I assign homework, trying to get the things we've talked about for an hour and a half to stick even a little. This week's assignment is a writing exercise starting with "They said it was my fault when . . ." I'm hoping that the few girls who actually do the writing will be able to separate the judgment of other people from their own feelings of guilt and unworthiness.

A few days later, Toni comes in subdued, which is uncharacteristic. She works hard to laugh loudly and smile frequently, yet her tears are rarely far from the surface. She carries the shame of her experiences like a heavy weight and gets little support at home. When Toni's mother is drunk she will repeatedly spell out the word *prostitute*, particularly in front of Toni's friends and new boyfriend, who are unaware of her experiences. Toni told her boyfriend that her mother was spelling out *prostate* as she was concerned about a family member having cancer. I'd been impressed with her quick thinking.

Today it's clear that something's wrong. I pat the couch next to me and she plops herself down with a sigh. "What's going on, T?"

"You know that homework you gave us? I wrote mad stuff about everything I went through, like six pages, when I got raped, being in the life, and how people blamed me. I wrote a bunch and it felt good to get it out of my system."

"That's good, hon." I want to be more enthusiastic but something's telling me there's more to come.

"Well, my brother found it."

"Oh." I wince. I know this isn't going to be good.

"He went nuts. Just wilded out on me, cussing me out like crazy and just grabbed me up calling me a dirty ho, a slut, shit like that. The he just started punching me mad times in my face and my head. Look. . . ." She turns her head and lifts up her hair so I can see the lumps left by his rage.

"I'm so sorry, sweetie." I really am.

Toni starts to cry. "I just kept asking him why couldn't he understand what happened, why couldn't he see that it wasn't my fault, but he just kept yelling and hitting me."

She's crushed. Even though she knows that his reaction was wrong, all it's done is reinforce her feelings of guilt and shame. I feel awful. We talk for a long time about her brother's response, her own understanding that she didn't deserve what happened, that she's not to blame. While it calms her down a little, I know that I'm not the one she wants absolution from. She wants to hear it from her mother, her big brother, her friends, her boyfriend, because she's still not convinced that getting raped by an adult when she was fifteen wasn't her fault and that getting recruited by a pimp from a group home at sixteen wasn't her fault. She wants to hear from them that she's not a dirty, disgusting ho, though I'm guessing it will take a long time before that's going to happen. In the meantime, GEMS is her surrogate family, and so we have to keep telling her over and over until slowly it begins to sink in that this was something that happened *to* her. It's not who she is.

In 2000, the Trafficking Victims Protection Act defined sex trafficking as "the recruitment, harboring, transportation, provision, or obtaining of a person for the purpose of a commercial sex act where such an act is induced by force, fraud, or coercion, or in which the person induced to perform such an act has not attained eighteen years of age." Under federal law, there was no need to prove "force, fraud, or coercion" if the victim was under the age of eighteen. There was nothing in the bill that defined these victims as exclusively foreign-born and brought into the United States, so there was some excitement among those of us who were advocates and service providers that domestic girls and women would finally be treated as victims. Yet the implementation and funding of the law left domestic victims out in the cold, and for many years we encountered a frustrating two-tiered system of those who were seen as "real" trafficking victims—internationally trafficked children and women— and those who were seen as "child/teen prostitutes"—girls and young women from the United States. Slowly, the tide has begun to shift and the movement has begun to recognize and, more important, name American girls under the control of a pimp as victims of domestic trafficking.

Identifying any child or youth, girls, boys, or transgendered youth under the age of eighteen in the commercial sex industry as commercially sexually exploited is critical in ensuring that all children and youth who are bought for commercial sex acts are recognized as exploited, even if their experiences don't fall under the definition of trafficking. A sixteen-year-old who trades sex for shelter, or a seventeen-year-old girl who works in a strip club, is commercially sexually exploited; those under the control of a third-party exploiter, i.e., a pimp, are victims of domestic trafficking. Accurately describing the experiences of children and youth in the sex industry is critical to reframing the conversation and shaping public perception and public policy, and most important, goes toward removing the shame and stigma from the victims themselves.

The term "sex work" was created to remove some of the stigma associated with *prostitution* and to perhaps normalize the sex industry and those within it. The term is gaining in popularity and is a favorite of feminists and academics everywhere, yet it's misleading, particularly when erroneously applied to children. It's hard to have much patience with these proponents of the sex industry who, while simultaneously arguing that "sex work" can be empowering, would never dream of having sex for money themselves.

Those advocates for the sex industry who have had firsthand experience frequently fall into two camps. The first argue vehemently that they were not abused, came from middle-class and often privileged backgrounds, had often already attained a degree of educational success, and made an informed decision to do something that is "empowering" and brings them great freedom. This is the Diablo Cody route: A (normally) white, (normally) middle class, (normally) educated young woman chooses to enter the sex industry on a whim just for the experience or to write a book about it. She then leaves, proclaiming how "interesting" the experience was. Of course, these women, and sometimes men, fail to point out that they entered the sex industry with the knowledge that they could, and had the resources to, leave at any time, and therein lies the difference.

The other group is less frustrating than sad. These adults argue that they also made a "choice," but a closer look reveals histories of sexual abuse, running away, poverty, and, frequently, recruitment into the industry at a very young age. One well-known advocate for the sex industry who has frequently glamorized her experiences was actually introduced to the life at the age of fourteen after running away from an abusive home. She was a commercially sexually exploited child "trained," like Isabel, from an early age. Yet because she is not black or Hispanic; because she was not sold on the dark corners of Hunts Point; because she appeared to be on the upper rungs of the "hierarchy" of the sex industry, that much-lauded fantasy world of the escort/call girl, her experience has never been framed as child exploitation or even questioned by the media and general public who continue to enjoy and support the idea that there are some forms of the sex industry that aren't harmful, that women actually like it, that men's "participation" in the industry is inevitable and may actually support the women's career goals. It's ideas like these that rationalize the continued buying and selling of women and girls.

Just like there are some people who are able to use cocaine regularly without jeopardizing their careers, some people who are able to drink and drive without causing an accident, and some people who are able to fight in a war without suffering from PTSD, there are people in the sex industry who may not have suffered any harm. But just because an individual experience has not been difficult, painful, or disempowering doesn't make it true for millions of women and children around the world. The sex industry isn't about choice, it's about lack of choices. It's critical for children and youth, and even for many adult women within the sex industry, that we use language that frames it accurately.

After a week of turning down numerous media requests from reporters salivating at the chance to interview an ex-prostitute at the height of Spitzer-coverage frenzy, I agree reluctantly to go on a *20/20* special with Diane Sawyer. Although I hate to watch myself on television (Why didn't I realize that my eye makeup was too dark? Must they use a graphic of stilettos when introducing me?), I find myself getting caught up in the program itself as they show woman after woman on the streets and in the brothels of Nevada, women whose pain seems to reach through the TV and punch me in the stomach. Here was I, in my carefully applied makeup and "official" black suit, with the title card as I'd carefully instructed to read *Rachel Lloyd, Executive Director, GEMS,* commenting as an "expert" on the perils of life on the streets, in a segment next to "Kayla," who pulls up the back of her shirt to show Diane Sawyer a one-hundred-stitch scar courtesy of a john; Tina, who was once, not long ago, studying music in college, until heroin introduced itself into her life; Brandi, who while a "top earner" at the Bunny Ranch breaks down during an interview; Sarah, who lives in a squat with no running water.

As I watch and listen, with unbidden tears streaming down my face, I know exactly what Tina means when she said she counted in her head through each trick to take her mind off it, what Brandi feels when she hugs the pillow and sobs. Their pain feels so close, so almost yesterday, the memories of counting, of crying, so visceral. I feel the same love for these women that I feel for the girls at GEMS, the same love that comes from a shared experience of a very specific type of hurt and shame that, deep down, will always be a part of me. In my little West Elm–decorated apartment, with my car parked in the garage outside, my two degrees, my ten years of experience in the field, I remember what it really felt like.

As I cried for them, for my younger self, and with gratitude for who I had become, I felt shame welling up. Had I worked so hard to be "more than a survivor" that I'd lost track of what being a survivor really was? Was I so caught up in how far I'd come that I'd forgotten exactly where it was that I'd started? I'd let the media frenzy over "hookers" and "whores" make me want to hide that part of myself, that part I shared not just with these women but with my girls.

I reminded myself how blessed and lucky I was to have people who'd told me that I deserved better, that I didn't have to live in shame all my life. I wondered how I'd been so fortunate, and thought of all the people who had supported me and loved me and helped me heal, and yet my biggest critic, my harshest judge, had always been myself. It was my own voice that for years had shamed me and called me names, and it had been my own internal shame that I'd had to deal with. Over the years I'd learned that somewhere along the line, you had no choice but to accept what had happened; place the blame where it lay, understand the larger social forces, the twists of family and circumstance that had left you vulnerable in the first place. It was ultimately the acceptance, the integration of your experiences into the much larger narrative of your life, that kept you in a place of recovery, that gave Toni's brother and the Jeffreys and the rude reporters of the world less room to hurt you.

I realized that it was owning what I'd been through, not hiding it, that had opened the door to real healing for me. I'd challenged people's expectations of what a sexually exploited high school drop-out could do with her life, and in doing so reminded myself that I was more than anyone else's judgments about me. I prayed that night that Tina, Brandi, and Sarah would have the opportunities to escape, to heal, and to not allow the world around them to tell them that they were tainted, irreparably damaged, that their voices didn't matter, or that no one was listening.

14
HEALING

A father of the fatherless, and a judge of the widows,
is God in his holy habitation.
God setteth the solitary in families:
he bringeth out those which are bound with chains.
—*Psalms 68:5–6*

SUMMER 1997, GERMANY

I wake up ready, but instead of bouncing out of bed, I lie there, savoring my last morning in Germany. This time tomorrow I'll wake up in another country and begin another life. I have no idea what to expect about New York, but I'm excited to start anew somewhere else. Still, my chest hurts at the thought of leaving this place. It was here to this airbase that I came three years ago, barely functional and a broken mess of pain. The airbase has functioned as a cocoon of safety and healing for me, and I'm leaving as an almost unrecognizably different young woman. To me, the military base is beautiful with its rows and rows of neat housing, manicured lawns, dads washing their cars, kids playing out front, and neighborhood barbecues in the summertime. There is no visible poverty, no obvious drug addiction, no homelessness. Everyone is within a certain income level, a specific age bracket, and other than a few bored high school kids who attempt to be daring with their goth or gang member looks, everyone pretty much looks the same, a dubious mix of sporty and JCPenney. Even the apartments all seem to have been furnished by the same decorators, with hideous entertainment units and all the bathrooms decorated with either the Hunter Green or Seashells matching towel sets sold at the PX.

I have, however, grown to recognize that behind the Rockwellian lawns and curtains lies a darker picture of constant infidelity and, often, domestic violence. With the recent advent of the Bosnian crisis, young soldiers and their families who had known only military life in peacetime are now facing separations and fears that the recruiter never informed them about. Yet despite it all, I still love it. The order is comforting, especially in the wake of my turbulent and disordered past. I conform quickly. I decorate my room, choose some of my church wardrobe from the JCPenney catalog, eat Hamburger Helper and processed ham with Wonder bread and mayo, wear socks with my Birkenstocks, and love anything Nike. I am finally just like everyone else. Even though I see beneath some of the facade, most of time I don't want to. I want to stay in this community, where violence is no longer a part of my life. I have a strong attachment to the base, a place that's come to represent and symbolize so much to me, but ultimately it's thinking about the people I'll miss that makes my chest feel like its crushed with grief.

I lie there watching the clock knowing that in a few hours I'll be gone, and tears soak my face. I wish I could say all my good-byes one more time, but I've said them all, other than to the family taking me to the airport.

Cheryl and Samantha, the other nannies with whom I've shared never-ending cups of tea and chatted with about our romantic lives and the gossip on base while "our kids" played together, have both already left for the States. Cheryl left with her boss and was going to continue being a nanny, and Sam was marrying a soldier. Without their adult conversation and support, being a nanny is a little less fun, and I've already begun feeling their absence. One of the challenges of living on a military base is that someone's always leaving.

Finally, I'm the one leaving, having a yard sale with my stuff. I've spent the week making my rounds, taking hundreds of photos, crying and crying and promising to stay in touch forever and ever. Leaving church was perhaps the hardest, despite the fact that my move has been with my pastor's full encouragement and blessing. I don't want to leave the comfort of Victory Christian Fellowship, the place where I've experienced the kind of peace and overwhelming love that I've never felt anywhere else and where I've begun to believe that perhaps God really does love me. It's been through the compassion of many of the people at church that I've seen that love put into action, as I've been given clothing, a job, a place to live, and hours and hours of patient counseling and support. Although I've never fully shared my past, most people know that I've been through some "stuff" and have treated me with great kindness and gentleness. My pastor, and some of the other men in the church, have modeled for me what a "real" man acts like, and I've been shocked and relieved that none of the men, at least the married ones, has ever even come close to stepping across any of my blurry boundaries. In the beginning, I'd even had a crush on my portly, bald pastor, so struck was I by his kindness, intelligence, and obvious devotion to his wife. I'm sure he notices, and the way that he ignores my misguided affection turns into deep respect. He teaches the Bible in a way that I can understand and that doesn't feel misogynistic or disconnected from social justice. I've grown enough at the church that I've moved from hanging out with the little kids in order to hide my severe shyness to becoming the director of the children's ministry, the youngest person ever in the church to be in a leadership role. It feels like the greatest honor of my life and I take it very seriously, probably a little too seriously, if my volunteers were polled. I'm so nervous about being in charge of adults and still so painfully shy that I'm an awkward leader. But I excel at coming up with creative ideas for lesson plans and ways to better the ministry. My role has helped my confidence a little, although I'm still a horrendous public speaker and my good-bye speech consists of four mumbled words and more crying.

It's even harder to say good-bye to Dr. Hall, a guidance counselor at the high school where I've been volunteering for over a year. She has helped me discover my passion for working with teen-agers and allowed me to recognize that I have an instinctual talent for counseling and creative ideas for programs. When I'd originally approached the vice principal with the idea of volunteering, despite the fact that I've never finished high school myself, neither he nor I had a clue what I'd end up doing. I couldn't type, I'd never filed, and I had horrific computer skills. In the face of my earnestness, he reluctantly pawned me off onto Dr. Hall, who within a couple of weeks was giving me *Reviving Ophelia* and a stack of other books about adolescent girls to read. I spent over a year working individu-ally with almost every student in the school on a computer program that helped them identify careers and colleges of interest. For the first few months, I'd pretend to need to go to the bathroom at the beginning of the first day's session and casually ask the students to turn the computer on. Fortunately no one ever figures out that I actually don't know how to turn the computer on myself, and after a few months I pick up some basic computer skills. Learning new skills and finding out that I'm reasonably competent at a lot of dif-ferent things is exciting for me. What started out as something to do for a few hours a week, now that the children I was babysitting were in school, had become almost a full-time job, in addition to the part-time job I held as a cashier at the PX. The principal even offered to create a full-time paid position for me at the school so I could continue this work, a level of validation for my efforts that I don't expect. Throughout the year, it became clear to me that there were students who were chronically absent, and I asked Dr. Hall if I could spend some time focusing on them. In uncovering the reasons behind these students' absenteeism, I'm drawn into more complicated issues: teen parenthood; a girl who's been gang-raped by several soldiers and I'm the first person she's told; a girl whose mother has left and who is now developing into a full-fledged alco-holic under the absent gaze of her father. It's these girls that I con-nect with, rack my brain to think of creative ways to support, and learn some hard lessons with, e.g., never promise that you'll keep a secret without knowing what that secret is first, particularly when it's something like rape that you're required to report to the authorities. Dr. Hall has been my first professional mentor, before I even knew that I needed one, and she has given me so much space to grow that I'm scared of doing this work without our daily check-ins. She tells me she has total faith in me and writes me a beautiful recommendation letter that I read over and over again.

I've been a nanny for the Petersons for the last two and a half years and have loved their three children like my own. Bernadette, a matriarch in every sense of the word, has been like a second mother to me. I've cried and prayed with her many times, learned to cook the best southern food under her tutelage, and tried my best to emulate her as a woman. With her own history of abuse, she's taught me to look in the mirror every day and tell myself that I'm lovable and valuable. She's challenged me to accept love when I didn't even know I was rejecting it. The family has treated me as their own, with Harold even telling people that I'm their oldest daughter, despite the fact that they're black and I'm obviously not. I've learned what it is like to be part of an actual family. We've gone to church together, spent holidays together, gotten on each other's nerves, and ultimately loved each other. When I began dating, they even set a curfew and Harold tried to vet each suitor like a proper father. I bristled against this level of interference, but in some ways I liked the idea of being cared for in that way, even if it was about eight years too late. I'll miss the kids the most and I spend as much time with them as possible before I leave, hugging them tightly, hoping they'll remember me.

The date that Harold doesn't meet is the one I'm most infatuated with. Sam lives in the building behind mine, and is the boy epitome of my feelings about the airbase and its barbecues and lawns. My desire for a normal, suburban family experience translates into the desire for the type of normal teenage relationship that I never had.

We don't have a lot in common and most of the time we talk awkwardly about nothing, but I don't care. Our dating life is relatively chaste and boring, which I love. We watch movies, sometimes at his house till his mother and father come home and make it clear that I need to leave. Sam goes to the prom with another girl that he's seeing and I'm crushed. It's hard for me to accept that I'll never recapture my teenage years, and I don't speak to him for several weeks. I watch him play football from afar and pine away in teenage-girl fashion, writing his name all over my notebook.

Just before I leave, having kissed and made up, Sam and I take a trip to Mainz and walk along the river. It feels fitting to be back in Mainz where so many terrible things happened to me, but this time with my safe and sometimes boring crush. He takes me to McDonald's for my good-bye dinner and the thrill of a "teenage" relationship is beginning to wear off. We pose arms wrapped around each other and ask a passerby to take a picture. I'm disappointed several weeks later when I discover that the picture doesn't come out, but even without the photographic evidence, the image is clear in my mind, me in my pink and white floral dress, him in his ever-present uniform of black T-shirt and jeans, the backdrop of the Rhine at dusk behind us.

I know that I'm about to embark on a whole new chapter and that I won't ever really come home again, not to this time and place. But I'm ready. Bernadette, Harold, Dr. Hall, Sonia, my pastors, the folks at church, Samantha, Cheryl, and even Sam have given me a sense of hope and a sense of self. They've been my family, the community where I've been able to hide and heal, at least enough to keep moving forward. On a small airbase in Germany they've accomplished a miracle. They've loved me back to life.

In psychologist Abraham Maslow's oft-cited Hierarchy of Needs theory, the need for social connection, for community and belonging, are a critical part of any individual's well-being and development. Once the initial needs for shelter, food, resources, and safety have been met, there remains a deep human need for friendship and family, and beyond that, for competence, mastery, and respect for and by others. I hadn't heard of Maslow's theories until I came to New York and studied Pysch 101 in college. Yet I understood that the love and support from the adults around me, the total acceptance and physical affection from my little kids, the ability to try new things and develop skills by volunteering and working, had enabled me to begin my healing process and had left me with a new sense of myself and my abilities.

Most girls, though, aren't fortunate enough to have a sleepy little military base replete with a built-in community to help with the recovery process. They're often still in the same communities, perhaps just a few blocks away from where they were first trafficked, often dealing with many of the same challenges that made them so vulnerable in the first place.

Trafficked girls are also getting many of their needs met in the life, albeit in the most distorted and exploitative fashion. In addition to the basic needs for sustenance and survival, pimps provide a sense of belonging to a family. Being good at making money feels like a level of competence and mastery, and having daily attention from johns can feel like a boost to your self-esteem, even though it's based solely on your ability to provide sex. If you're going to take something away, you have to replace it with something else. Trafficked and sexually exploited girls and young women need a place to hide and heal, but it is not enough to solely provide for their basic needs of food, shelter, and clothing. As I began to create GEMS, I understood that they also need a place where they could feel like they belonged, where they could feel strong and empowered, a place where they could feel loved and valued, even as the struggles remained right outside the door.

Exploited girls need the opportunity to develop new skills, to create a new sense of self. If your entire sense of who you are has been shaped by the sexual abuse and commercial sexual exploitation that you've experienced, it's tough to begin to learn to see yourself in a new way. For girls and young women who've felt "good" only at being in the life, the opportunity to learn new skills and develop hidden talents, whether it's poetry or art or cooking or boxing or finding out that they're a great listener, a good friend, or a supportive peer, can begin to reshape and redefine who they see themselves as.

Yet groups and workshops alone can't support the healing that girls need. People connect to people, not programs. In an effort to develop appropriate boundaries in programs and organizations, we have often shied away from the concept of love as a tool for healing and recovery, yet the human need for appropriate, unconditional love to help in the healing process cannot be ignored. When girls talk about what has made a difference for them, they talk about "that judge who was mad nice," "my counselor who was like my second best friend," or "staff who paid attention to me," not a specific type of clinical therapy or a certain activity that they engaged in at a program. While these services and opportunities are important, they're not what initially gets girls walking through the door and coming back again and again. When their strongest connection to another person, their pimp, is removed, they need to feel connected to someone else. During this scary time, having someone to call at 3 a.m., having friends who have gone through the same thing, and ultimately feeling loved can help to alleviate some of the pain and fear of the recovery process.

Many girls are reluctant initially to come to GEMS when they learn that it's an all-women/girls program. Girls under the control of a pimp have been ruled with a divide-and-conquer model. Everyone competing for the same crumbs of affection and attention is bound to breed intense jealousy and competition, so girls in the life tend to view each other as threats and rivals, which is their pimp's goal anyway. Add to these experiences the already internalized messages of sexism and stereotypes about women and girls—*They're mad grimy/shady, You can't trust females, They'll steal your man*—that many girls grow up believing and it makes it difficult for girls to have genuine and open relationships with other girls. Yet while I've seen my share of fights, clothes stealing, and the occasional boyfriend "stealing" (the girls rarely blame the boys for the cheating), overall I've been moved by the relationships and friendships that have developed at GEMS and overwhelmingly impressed by the way that the girls support and look out for one another.

The *Cheers* theme song, while having the annoying ability to get stuck in your head after just hearing a few bars, actually captures the human need for belonging, community, and understanding in a far more succinct way than any psychologist has ever been able to do:

You wanna go, / Where everybody knows your name, and they're always glad you came. / You wanna be where you can see, our troubles are all the same.

Isn't that pretty much what everyone wants and needs? A place where you feel like you matter, a place where people understand you, a place where you're surrounded by peers?

For sexually exploited girls who often don't have the family structure or support that may be able to provide this sense of community, and for whom this void on some level has been filled by the sense of "belonging" to a pimp, a new type of support system is essential.

There's a host of girls excitedly unwrapping the decorations and beginning to unfold the silver plastic Christmas tree. I'm digging in the decorations box for all our nice decorations, knowing full well that within an hour, every single bauble or piece of tinsel, whether it matches our pink-and-silver color scheme or not, will be crowding the tree. I remind myself not to care that the GEMS tree will look tacky; the point of this exercise is not to indulge my whims but to make sure the girls have a good time. As I'm digging in the jumble of fairy lights and plastic baubles, I see the handmade stars that a staff member who was feeling creative had made several years ago with girls' names and a cutout Polaroid attached to each.

"Ha!" I dangle the stars and the girls pay attention.

"Am I there?"

"Where am I?"

"Ay yo, look at Nadia when she was mad young."

The girls are swapping around the star photos, cracking jokes on each other, trying to remember girls from two and three years ago. The newer girls are trying to get in on the excitement, too. "Who's this one?" "Where's she at now?"

I pull one from the box and my heart stops. It's a picture of Falicia, a GEMS girl who had passed away a few months before from AIDS. Her death at twenty-four had rocked the GEMS community. Her funeral, held by a family who barely knew her, was awful, but we'd held our own memorial service at GEMS that had been funny and beautiful and sad, and ultimately cathartic. Many of the girls had been frightened about their own HIV status, especially those who were already positive. Seeing their peer pass away so young, in 2007, of AIDS, was surreal for them, and there were a lot of difficult conversations with scared teenage girls who were now confronted with the reality of their own mortality. Out of her passing, however, had come a new determination from some of the girls to speak publicly about their status. Just a few weeks earlier the youth outreach team had organized an HIV/AIDS awareness week that had been a huge success, resulting in many more members getting on-site testing. We had honored her memory and her life in every way we knew how to, and I was proud of the girls for the way they'd rallied and worked to find something good come out of the tragedy.

Despite this, seeing her picture on the star throws me. All smiles, she is wearing my wool poncho that had been a bad impulse buy but looked cute on her. All the memories and all the sadness come rushing back. I remind myself that we were her home for a long time, and that she knew that she was loved. I remember how we'd all stood outside after the GEMS memorial, prayed, and together released twenty-four pink (her favorite color) balloons into the air. We'd watched for as long as we could see them, crossing the street to watch them float up, become tiny little dots, and finally disappear into the cloudless August sky. I turn my head away from the girls for a second and wipe my eyes. Jasmine hugs me and I know she misses her friend, too. We finish trimming the tree with Falicia's star perched crookedly on top.

The decorating fever exhausted, the girls settle on the couch. I treasure these moments, the noncrying, noncrisis, chill-out moments when I can simply enjoy them. The conversation soon becomes a GEMS reminiscing session. Talking about the old days is a favorite pastime. "Remember when Rachel walked into the cabinet and fell over and cut her nose wide open and there was mad blood everywhere!"

"Uh, thank you, people. I still have a scar from that!" This does little to quieten the laughter. Now we're on GEMS accidents. In a little while it'll be GEMS fights, and then stories about the GEMS-mobile, my old piece-of-crap car that has a series of stories and jokes all to itself. Just as many of the girls have grown up here, so have I. I was twenty-three years old when I began GEMS and have spent more hours in this office, many of them on this very couch, than I've probably spent anywhere else.

"Rachel, 'member when Sophia sat on a pair of scissors and they went all the way through her thigh and she just pulled them out?"

"How could I ever forget that? I was so freaked-out. I had to drive her to the hospital, singing Jay-Z songs all the way cos that was the only thing that would keep her calm." I pantomime driving and rapping with a bleeding Sophia in the back. The girls are laughing hysterically. They can go on like this for hours. As can I.

My head is full with eleven years' worth of memories involving hundreds and hundreds of girls. It's important to tell these stories so the girls feel like they're a part of history. One of the things I had to learn for myself and have tried to pass on is that you may not be able to choose your family of origin but you can choose your family of creation. We've created our own little family at GEMS with memories and traditions and rituals. For some girls, GEMS may be something that they just need for a season as they create their own families and support systems, a bridge to tide them over when they're in pain and as they slowly emerge as young women. For others, it may remain a constant over the years, a place that always feels like home, no matter how long they've been gone.

One of my favorite things about GEMS at any time of year, but especially at the holidays, is that you never know who's going to walk through the door. Girls who've been gone for years will show up for mac 'n' cheese and the opportunity to relax and catch up with their peers. Girls bring their children, the ever-expanding GEMS extended family of babies, toddlers, and school-age kids, many of whom have literally grown up at GEMS. These kids are now "play cousins" who over the years play together at events and barbecues as their mothers reminisce about the "good old days." At least once a week, there are the screams of "Oh my God," "Look who's here!" and "Ay yo, Rachel—come see who it is!" Girls pretend to look embarrassed by the attention, but they're obviously pleased to be remembered, to be welcomed. We've become the *Cheers* of trafficked girls, the place where everyone's always glad you came.

I'm sitting on the couch, in the middle of an interview with a reporter, when a young woman walks in. She stands by the door, looking at me expectantly. It takes a few seconds to recognize this beautiful young woman as the gangly girl who has been gone for so long. Over the years, I've heard that she's being trafficked to various cities, that she's doing OK, that she's doing badly. I've wondered for a long time when and if she'll ever break free. Looking at her, I can tell that she's back for real, that she's left him and left the life. Tears roll down my cheeks. The prodigal daughter has returned and while we don't throw her a huge feast, we do greet her with a lot of excitement and smother her with hugs. Later I wonder if the reporter thinks we've staged this little reunion. After all, it is quite miraculous for a girl who came to GEMS when she was twelve years old to return at twenty.

Amanda, like many of the girls, wants a complete rehash of what she was like years ago, what I remember about first meeting her. I've got memories of them all, some much clearer than others, but they never get tired of hearing about themselves when they first came to GEMS. "Do me, do me," they'll chorus, as if I'm doing palm readings. I do my best to oblige, struggling sometimes as the sheer number of girls that we see each year increases and my brain feels a little less agile. Amanda, with her outsize personality, I remember very clearly.

"You were always smart, always had a huge personality," I say, laughing. "You were my little entrepreneur. I remember when you wanted to raise money with a lemonade stand. . . . You must've been, what, twelve? Goodness, that makes me feel old." The girls laugh, but it really does.

Jasmine's incredulous. "Really? She had a lemonade stand?"

Amanda's thinking, *I did?*

"Yup, you were so insistent. Wouldn't let me alone until I agreed." As I talk the details come back to me.

"I gave you five dollars and you bought a jug and lemons and sugar and set up that little table we used to have, right in front of the office. You tried to set up on the corner but I told you the beauty salon might not appreciate you sitting outside their door."

"I can't believe you remember that," Amanda says.

"Did she make any money?" Jasmine is fascinated by the whole story, a time before she came.

"Nah, of course not! We spent five bucks and I think she made a profit of about 60 cents. Sitting outside in the hot-ass sun all day, with a little sign you made . . ."

Jasmine and I are laughing hard, picturing Amanda acting like she's in the suburbs sitting on our little block in Harlem trying to sell lemonade amid all the corner-heads, random passersby, and the hustlers doing their best to sell weed.

"I can't believe you remember that," Amanda says again quietly, and I stop laughing long enough to see her crying.

"Oh, sweetie, what's wrong?" Amanda looks at me perplexed. I hadn't meant to make her cry.

"I just can't believe you remember stuff about me when I was growing up." She's sobbing now. I get up and give her a hug and realize the significance that my holding that memory for so many years has for her. For her, it means that she wasn't forgotten, even during all those years when she'd been on the streets disconnected from everyone. It means that she matters. Her healing process is just beginning but at least she feels like she's in a place where she belongs and is loved and is remembered. There's a lot more work to do, but it's a start.

LEADERSHIP

> *But we do know that the women who recover most successfully*
> *are those who discover some meaning in their experience that*
> *transcends the limits of personal tragedy. Most commonly, women*
> *find this meaning by joining with others in social action.*
>
> —*Judith Herman*, Trauma and Recovery

SPRING 1998, CANADA

After having been in New York for only eight months, I find myself representing the United States as a delegate to the first international summit of sexually exploited youth. On the first day of the conference, I'm so nervous that I consider staying in my room for six days and watching cable, but I'm worried that this will get back to my boss, so I decide to tough it out. Since I've never been to a conference before, I have no idea what to expect. It's been organized by Cherry Kingsley, a young survivor of commercial sexual exploitation, who has managed to get support from Senator Landon Pearson, an activist on behalf of children; the United Nations; and various other organizations that I've never heard of but who are apparently important enough to have raised enough resources to support the attendance of sixty young people from all over the Americas who are there to talk about sexual exploitation based on their own experiences.

While I'm slowly overcoming my fear of public speaking, at least in the context of the girls and women I work with at Rikers Island, I'm still painfully shy and have little confidence. At breakfast, I find a girl who looks just as terrified as me. Julia and I latch on to each other and sit together in the main conference room as Cherry takes to the podium to deliver her powerful and inspiring opening remarks. I'm in awe. She's so poised and dynamic. Damn. I want to be her.

Cherry explains that the purpose of the summit is to ensure that survivor voices are no longer silenced, and that our expertise on our own experiences is heard by policy makers and others in power. This seems to me to be a noble goal, although I'm unsure if I have anything of value to add. We participants are asked to choose among several workshops in the visual arts, drama, dance, or something called "the agenda for action group." As all the other groups seem to involve some form of creative expression, which to me translates as pretending to be a tree and making yourself look silly, I choose the last, the most tame and boring-sounding of them all. Julia feels the same way and comes with me.

There are ten of us in the "action" group: three girls from Central America, two guys from Canada, a First Nations girl, Julia, Cherry, and me. Also in our group are important-looking people from the United Nations and from all the other acronym organizations in attendance. There are more of the suits than there are of the youth, and quickly it appears that my wish of remaining silent for the week may come true. The "professionals" seem to be giving lip service to the idea of youth participation and are hogging the microphone, expounding at length on policy and official reports. This doesn't feel relevant to the work I do daily, and certainly has very little to do with my past experiences. All of us survivors are sitting silently when suddenly Cherry, our fearless leader, interrupts one of the speakers. "This isn't what I had in mind, this isn't the point of the conference. You are silencing us again." She's not angry, just firm and unapologetic. The suits stop talking and look chastened. "You get to talk all the time, you're always being heard. This is about survivor voices, not yours. Here . . ." She gets up and begins moving chairs. "You guys can sit in the outer circle and observe; we'll sit in the inner circle and talk." The room is shocked, but

Cherry's instincts are right. Once we survivors are in the smaller circle, the atmosphere changes and slowly we begin to get comfortable. Cherry suggests that we start by simply sharing our experiences. Cherry goes first and her openness and honesty about her struggles break the ice.

And so we tell our stories. One by one, slowly with no interruptions, no sanitized versions, no omissions. We tell how we grew up, how our parents failed us, how we first entered the life, how we felt turning tricks, and how much we hurt on the inside because we couldn't really explain it to anyone. We cry for each person's story, because it's so much like our own and because it's always easier to cry for someone else. My job back in New York is listening to the stories of women in the life but in that role, I'm a listener, always counseling, consoling, being conscious of my reactions, being careful not to make it be about myself. But at the summit I just let all that go and I cry. I don't think I've ever cried this much in a public setting. All around us are the legislators and the policy makers and the United Nations people and yet I don't see them. All I can feel is a circle of nine other people who've been in the life, just like me. I've never felt such acceptance as I do at that moment. Up until that time, I've learned to tell my story in a way that is both funny and compelling and a whole lot of other adjectives that manage to stand in between me and the reality. I've learned to distance myself from the "story" and tell it like it had happened to someone else. But now when it comes to my turn, I just tell it raw and true. Like I'm telling it for the first time, like I'm telling it to myself. It's one of those moments that happens spontaneously, that can't be created and can't be facilitated. It reminds me of a night when I lived in Munich. I happened to be walking past a bar where a few drunken Irishmen were singing "Danny Boy" just as the rain started to fall. Even though they were drunk, their tenor voices were pure and strong. A crowd gathered to listen to the sheer beauty of the music, many of us with faces streaked with tears, even as the rain fell harder and harder. No one could walk away. That same feeling of transcendence is palpable within our little circle. We cry at the sheer sadness of the stories, and yet no one can walk away.

Four hours have gone by as we listened to each other and wept. The other workshops have broken for dinner, and we're still here. And then finally it's over and there's a closeness between us that a hundred "Get to Know You" games couldn't have accomplished. We hug like long-lost siblings reunited, not like the awkward strangers from a few hours earlier. Sharing memories that most people are never privy to, we're a strange clan—male, female, gay, straight, Latin, British/Roma, First Nations, a virtual Benetton ad of kids who all remember what it felt like to be sold for sex. By the end of the week, I've facilitated a couple of the groups, done my first radio and print interviews, stayed up for three nights with Julia and Peter, one of the Canadian boys, drafting and redrafting the Declaration and Agenda for Action that will be the official document to come out of the conference. The first core belief we write down is: *We believe that the voices and experiences of sexually exploited children and youth must be heard and be central to the development and implementation of action. We must be empowered to help ourselves.* Throughout the week, I watch as that belief becomes a reality. On the last night, we present the Agenda for Action at a public forum with about four hundred legislators, policy makers, and nonprofit people. The reaction is amazing, and a few months later, I accompany Cherry as we present the document at the United Nations, where it is ratified by 130 countries. I don't know enough then about the workings of the United Nations to know that it's only symbolic and doesn't really mean anything, so I'm thrilled that words I've written are being taken seriously on an international level.

I discover that week in Canada that I actually do have a lot of opinions on the issue and that people don't think I'm stupid when I open my mouth. Like a novice karaoke singer, now that I've gotten comfortable with the microphone, it's hard to pry it out of my hand. It's an amazing feeling to be an expert on your own life, to have these shameful experiences actually be useful, to feel the shame lifting every time you speak out about what needs to be done to help other victims. My embarrassment at not yet having my GED and my struggles with intense shyness melt away in the presence of other powerful young survivors. I see glimpses of who I might become in Cherry and Julia and Peter, and for the first time I'm comfortable with the reflection.

After my experience in Canada, I knew that I wanted to figure out how to support survivor leadership, both for myself and for the girls I was meeting. I was lucky that when I came into the field in 1997, in addition to Cherry, I had role models like the late Norma Hotaling, who founded Standing Against Global Exploitation (SAGE); and Vednita Carter from Breaking Free. These women and their programs were examples for me of what I could achieve, and of the fact that I didn't have to be limited by my past. I wanted to give the same hope to other girls.

Yet founding an organization at the age of twenty-three, after a year in the United States, was challenging. Founding an organization as a survivor was even tougher. I fought hard to overcome people's perceptions of me, the assumptions they would make, the stereotypes that they would often verbalize. For a while, I took to wearing nonprescription glasses to convey the impression that I was smart and bookish. The glasses didn't help much once people found out about my past. Then the reactions would range from morbid curiosity to unwarranted and inappropriate sympathy to barely disguised contempt.

I realized that one of the most important roles that I could play was to give a face to the issue, to humanize survivors and challenge people's preconceived notions about them. People would tell me "I had no idea," as if I should've come equipped with a warning sign, or at least a scarlet letter. People's perceptions of sexually exploited girls are often based on media depictions of girls in the sex industry, a Lifetime movie version, a *Law & Order* portrayal of a tough girl in stilettos on a street corner, chewing gum and cursing everyone out. The assumption is that these girls must be slow or at least not very intelligent. As I began to speak out at conferences and meetings, countless numbers of people feel the need to tell me how articulate I am. Initially I take it as a compliment, although I soon realize that it's always said with a tone of surprise and a good helping of condescension. One male executive director serving exploited girls compliments me after a meeting for "learning how to dress quite professionally," as if I'd been tempted to turn up in a miniskirt and stilettos. If I'm passionate about an issue, people suggest that my trauma history has made me angry, as opposed to the fact that I might actually be angry because girls are treated outrageously by the justice system. If I'm not angry enough, it's because I'm dissociating. If I don't like someone, especially a man, it's because I have trust issues, not because the person might actually be a total jerk. People ask wildly inappropriate questions during presentations, make crude jokes, and often ask to "see my scars" as if I'm a show-and-tell project.

It's frustrating to continually feel like you're being weighed up against some invisible stereotype, but I work hard to challenge as many of the perceptions as I can. Over the next few years, I overachieve like crazy, graduating summa and then magna cum laude with both a bachelor's and a master's degree, all to prove that I'm more than a story, more than just my past. Often I'm proving it to myself just as much as to others, as it's their low expectations and beliefs about me that I am secretly scared are really true.

Once I start GEMS, I teach the girls to fight, too. They've got to overcome prejudices that are based on race, gender, age, socioeconomic status, and their histories of sexual exploitation. Plus they've got to overcome their own beliefs about themselves, their abilities, their guilt, their shame. Few people they know think that they're capable of being anything, let alone leaders. The girls largely agree. Yet for girls and young women whose voices have been silenced and who have had little to no control over the smallest of decisions, the opportunity to speak out, to create change, and to have leadership roles can be life-altering.

Although I can't take a bunch of girls to Canada and give them the full summit experience, I start a weekly youth leadership group at GEMS to give girls who are interested the tools they need to move into activism. We talk about public speaking, peer counseling, group facilitation, community organizing, and advocacy. We teach them about the global nature of commercial sexual exploitation and trafficking and help them understand the bigger-picture issues: sexism, racism, poverty, the juvenile justice system, the influence of the media. Once they begin to understand that the billion-dollar sex industry that has taken advantage of their vulnerable young lives is supported by racism, sexism, and classism, then they can move from feeling like "bad girls" into an understanding of, and ultimately an acceptance of, what has happened to them. Once their anger is directed outside instead of inside, then it's just a few steps to getting the skills in public speaking, advocacy, peer counseling, and organizing that will help them turn anger into action and, ultimately, self-empowerment.

The idea of asking others to bear witness to trauma is well documented throughout our collective historical tragedies and atrocities. The perpetrators may never be identified, much less brought to justice, and sometimes it's not just individuals but entire systems that have failed the victims. Yet it is well known that sharing the story of what happened in the right and safe context can provide a level of validation, an affirmation that what happened was wrong and that it wasn't the fault of the survivors.

This kind of communal sharing is most productive and healing within the context of a peer support group and with the conviction that good can come from it. Holocaust survivors who testified at tribunals, child soldiers who testified at United Nations meetings, Rwandan genocide survivors who spoke out at local trials, women who have talked to the media after surviving systemic rape in Bosnia all did so with the hope of educating people, sounding the alarm, and ultimately with the vision of bringing justice, if not for themselves, then for others.

We stay at a Holiday Inn opposite the SUNY campus, our hotel of choice as there's a pool and a really good free breakfast. The girls have never been in a sauna before, so there's great excitement. Although there's some fake consternation and a lot of vanity about how they look in their bathing suits, as soon as they hit the pool, they're carefree, playing like little kids. These are the moments I find myself wishing I could freeze-frame, when they get to relax, when the weight of the world seems lifted just for a little while, when they get to be children. These are the moments I wish I could capture for the people whom we're in Albany to educate, for the cops and prosecutors who want to lock these girls up.

After the pool we sit in the sauna, wrapped in our towels. Thanks to Nikki's short towel, I can see the crude, jagged scar that takes up most of her right thigh. A stabbing from a pimp and a lazy stitching have left her with a scar that looks exactly like a child's drawing of one, replete with huge lines crisscrossing the original wound. Sequoia has scars on her face, these neater and better stitched but still apparent on her otherwise smooth skin. I look at Asia, whose upper left arm is tattooed with a huge dollar sign over the words *Daddy's Bitch*.

I think of Letitia, when she graduated from her GED program and she wanted me to tie the balloons around her wrist. As I did, the scores of self-inflicted wounds from several years ago were still clearly visible on her arm and wrist. Or Kendra, whose pimp bought a tattoo machine and proceeded to practice writing his name all over her arms, hands, legs, and chest while his brother and friend held her down. Of Marissa, Tina, Shanae, and so many others with neck tattoos, constantly visible reminders of their abuser's name. Girls with stab wounds, burn marks, permanent markings of the violence. There's a phrase in advocacy efforts against gender-based violence—*making the harm visible*. For commercially sexually exploited children, the harm is written like a road map all over their bodies. "This one, right here, was where he was smacking me with an extension cord and this one, see, is where he burnt me with a curling iron cos I didn't make enough money. This tat is from my first pimp, and this one on my leg is from my second. He wanted his bigger cos he was mad about the first one."

In the sauna, as we sit and relax, or rather overheat, the girls begin to share the stories behind the scars. It's the incongruence that always bothers me the most, the girl who goes from talking about having a crush on Lil Wayne to talking about the adult men who bought her; the teenager who likes making collages with magazines and glitter sharing an account of trauma that most adults couldn't have survived.

It's well known to my close friends, and even to most casual acquaintances, that I'm a certified "Wirehead"—a devotee of the now-ended HBO series. One of its most exquisitely written scenes features the middle school–aged boys who'll capture and then, David Simon–style, systematically stomp on our hearts. The boys sit around an oil drum fire telling ghost stories, like every other pre-adolescent boy has done, yet for these children the stories are based on the multiple murders happening in the neighborhood. They don't flinch when gunshots are heard nearby, yet scramble and run when a bum stumbles out an alley, spooked by their own tales of zombies, as little boys often are. They're world-weary, trauma-tized pseudo-adults who sometimes let their guard slip and allow the twelve- or thirteen-year-old to come out. And the dissonance between their childishness and their forced maturity in the streets breaks my heart. It reminds me of the girls whose stories are not about ghosts and zombies, but about tricks and pimps and rapes and jail.

This dissonance is there at the excited reunions at GEMS, where the girls remember each other from the track, the psych hospital, the detention center, the group home. It's there when nineteen- and twenty-year-olds act like thirteen-year-olds because they never got a chance to. Or when I hear that Monica wanted to go to Build-A-Bear for her eighteenth birthday; see Taisha sucking her thumb at twenty; Joielle playing Dress Up Barbie on the computer; Bianca wanting to go get her pink, fuzzy book bag from a john's house; Evie requesting Hannah Montana school supplies as she attends a trade school at nineteen after eight years in the life; Danielle and her SpongeBob; Sequoia in a pediatric ward with cartoon curtains.

A recent memo in opposition to the bill we're advocating for, the Safe Harbor for Exploited Youth Act, has called the girls "young adults" about twenty times in three pages, despite the fact that the component of the bill that the memo refers to addresses children fifteen years old and under. To hear them defined as young adults is as ludicrous as it is purposefully misleading, but the intent is clear in the other language used: "These are young adults who are very streetwise and who do not obey rules and are not willingly compliant with authority." I look at Asia, Nikki, Sequoia, and Latonia and think how many rules they've had to obey as the property of their pimps. Or, these are "young adults who are on a life path to incarceration anyway," with the not so hidden subtext being that since they'll probably end up in jail later, we might as well just lock them up now. I'm shaking with anger when I read the memo, but I don't tell the girls about it. They're nervous enough without having to be subjected to these offensive and denigrating ideas about who they are and what they deserve.

After the relaxation of the sauna, swimming, and a steak dinner, it's time to work. We sit in my room, piled onto the two beds, notebooks and laptop in hand, brainstorming and preparing for the next day. The girls decide to write their individual speeches, although Latonia, the most experienced speaker of the group and a veteran Albany advocate, only wants to do bullet points. "You never write *your* speeches, Rachel," she points out. I concede the point. I try to encourage them not to read from their speeches, although I know if they have them in hand, the temptation will be too strong. Several of the girls have been through our youth leadership training, so they know the drill and are confident public speakers. They also decide to write a statement together that states their recommendations to make it crystal clear to the legislators what they're asking for and why. As we throw ideas around, I encourage them to think about what makes each of their stories unique and most relevant to the legislation.

Nikki was incarcerated multiple times from the age of thirteen in adult jail and charged as an adult. Sequoia was kept in juvenile detention, as was Asia, who had actually testified against her pimp and yet was still held for two years. Latonia is the only one who wasn't incarcerated, as she was never arrested for prostitution but instead had a PINS case (Person in Need of Supervision) due to her constant running away and was mandated to GEMS. They decide to focus on what works and what doesn't, using the three girls who were incarcerated as an example of how not to treat victims. As they talk, it also emerges that three of the four girls were raped by cops. I tell them not to be scared to tell the legislators. They don't need to be told twice; no one's listened to or believed them about this abuse of power, so the opportunity to tell important people how they were really treated is one they're not going to pass up. They start drafting in their notebooks, Asia quickly filling up page after page with her story.

The following morning, the girls are in and out of my and each other's rooms, borrowing hairbrushes, looking for a belt that'll match. It's a frenzied hour but when it's all done, I'm impressed by the four girls smartly dressed in their professional attire, slacks and button-down shirts. They look like they're off to an internship. We've talked about being able to contradict people's stereotypes of who sexually exploited girls are, and they know that to the Albany crowd, impressions will count.

Unsurprisingly, there are only about ten legislators present when we arrive; a reporter from the Albany *Times Union*; our advocacy partners, Cait and Mishi, from the Juvenile Justice Coalition; and a few other assorted supporters and Albany interns. It's our third year advocating without success for this bill to pass. Still, our hope is that we'll be able to make enough of an impression that these legislators will be able to convince their colleagues to support the bill. I introduce the girls briefly but stay largely quiet; this is about them and their voices, not mine. They've picked the two strongest speakers to go first and last, bookending the two less experienced girls. Their stories, while unique, are frighteningly similar, four girls in succession sharing about the factors that led them in, the pain they experienced during the life, the seduction and then brutality the pimps had used, the anger they felt at the systems that failed them, the way they were treated by the cops, how it felt to be incarcerated when you were the one getting beat up and sold. Even though I know all their stories, have lived through some of these experiences with them, hearing them back-to-back is heart-wrenching.

After Sequoia closes out with a plea to pass the Safe Harbor Act, and the girls take turns reading their statements aloud, the room stays in silence for a minute, punctuated only by the sound of sniffles and noses blowing. I have tears running down my face and am not the only one. There's a sense that something powerful has just happened in this dreary conference room in Albany. Every adult in the room seems to be wondering how on earth we could allow this type of abuse to happen, how these girls, these children could've been failed by so many. It seems inconceivable, ludicrous even, at this moment that these are the girls we choose to punish. Joe Errigo—an assemblyman who looks old enough to be the girls' grandfather—tries to break the silence but his voice falters, and he stops, wiping his eyes. He starts again, his voice thick with emotion. "You are all to be commended." There's a tear rolling down his face now, and he doesn't wipe it away. "I promise you that I will do whatever I have to do to ensure this bill passes."

One of the female legislators gets up. "I want you to know how brave and courageous you all are for giving your testimonies today. You should be incredibly proud of your strength. I also want to tell you that I was a victim of sexual abuse." There's a pause in the room as she says this, and I'm guessing that most of her male colleagues had never heard this information before. I wonder if they'll look at her differently afterward. I wonder if she cares. She seems oblivious to them and is addressing the girls directly. "And I just want you to know, that while it's hard, it's possible to heal and recover and have a good future. Don't let anyone tell you that you can't or that you're not normal." She gestures around at other people in the room. "Just so you know, normal just doesn't exist."

The girls are clearly moved by her honesty and by her revelation. The other legislators commend their courage and promise to fight for the bill, too. We leave elated, and they chatter excitedly in the car most of the way home, until one by one they fall asleep, kids on a long car ride.

A few weeks after our Albany trip, and just three days before the end of the legislative session, I hear news that we may actually pass the bill this year. Then, within a few hours, I get the call that the senate has agreed to pass the bill but with critical changes to the language that make the bill totally ineffective. I'm sobbing on the three-way with Cait and Mishi, crying from frustration, from anger, from disappointment that yet again we've failed to pass the bill and that yet again I have to tell the girls that the folks in power have chosen not to listen to their testimonies of abuse and violence. And so the session ends that week, the bill passes unanimously in the assembly, but nothing passes in the senate. Girls in New York State can still be charged with an act of prostitution even though they're the victims and no amount of compelling stories or empathetic tears have changed that. Six months to wait until the beginning of the next legislative session, six months before we can start fighting all over again.

A year later, one of our Albany contacts, JR, is on the phone debating with me about the need for another youth-led legislative briefing at the capitol.

"It's just not worth it, Rachel. No one's going to come. Besides, at this point, people are either for or against the bill; it's not going to change anything."

"Well, we do it every year and it's important to us and it's important to the girls and I feel pretty strongly that we need to do it, and so do they. They've been bugging me about going to Albany for weeks—it's a huge deal to all of us."

"It's kind of a waste of time, honestly."

"A waste of time? To engage girls in the civic process? Really? To empower them to have a voice? To show them that their voices can make a difference?"

He laughs.

"OK, but don't say I didn't tell you if you only get three people showing up."

"It's fine; we'll do a great job of impressing those three people."

He's almost right, although instead of three it's seven. Not exactly a rousing crowd. There's also no one from the senate, which had been our target audience. Jasmine, Monica, and Kristina do a great job and I give them a good rah-rah speech afterward, but I'm despondent about our chances of getting the bill passed this year. I don't want the girls to know, though, so I try to keep it lighthearted and figure that instead of driving straight back, we'll hang out and get lunch at the capitol and try to make a day of it. After all, the girls had gotten up at 5 a.m. to make it up here in time; the least I can do is feed them.

The weather is beautiful so we grab lunch from one of the many food trucks parked by the Legislative Office Building and sit in the park. Before long I see Shawn, a legislative aide, running across the park, waving a paper in his hand. The girls are excited to see him, mainly because they all have a crush on him. I'm perplexed as to why calm and collected Shawn, whom we've worked with for four years, would be breaking a sweat, running across the park in his suit, looking vaguely manic.

"They've reached an agreement! It's gonna pass!"

I'm floored. He thrusts the paper into my hand. "It happened; they agreed to the language changes." I can't quite believe it.

"We did it? That's cos of us?" Jasmine asks. They're amazed that the wheels of power in Albany move this quickly. We've only just finished our lunch.

I know enough about Albany to know that the briefing just thirty minutes earlier did not cause the legislation to pass that day. There had been a lot of backroom talks and negotiations going on lately, scores of e-mails back and forth arguing over wording and intent. Yet it has been the girls' collective voices and efforts over four-plus years that brought us to this point—all the trekking up to Albany, the testifying at legislative briefings and city council hearings, talking to the press, sharing their most painful experiences.

"Yes, you did it!"

The girls whoop and yell; I'm still half in shock at the timing of it all. After four and a half years of a hard-fought battle, people in power have actually listened to commercially sexually exploited girls and it's happened on the one day that year that the girls are in the state capital. Apparently it was worth going up to Albany after all. I remind myself to call JR and gloat later.

The leadership of survivors in the fight against commercial sexual exploitation and domestic trafficking in the United States is unquestionable. In addition to GEMS, survivor-led programs across the country leading the way in services, advocacy, and training for many years include the pioneering Standing Against Global Exploitation (SAGE) in San Francisco, Breaking Free in Minnesota, Dignity House in Arizona, Veronica's Voice in Kansas, and MISSSEY (Motivating, Inspiring, Supporting, and Serving Sexually Exploited Youth) in Oakland. Clearly, survivors are able to take on leadership roles and excel in them. However, it's also important not to restrict the role of survivors to the "movement" or even to working in the nonprofit world.

Girls need to know that being a survivor doesn't limit them, nor does it ultimately define them. In the beginning, my past is all I really have to go on—I don't have a college degree, experience managing a nonprofit, or any of the other qualifications that most executive directors possess. My ability to connect with the girls is my saving grace, my past the hook that initially drew people in to want to learn more, the thing that makes me "special." Over time I begin to learn how important it is for me to be able to move beyond that role. As I gained real experience, not just "connecting with the girls" but managing budgets, supervising staff, and making the many daily decisions required to run an organization, I learned to see myself as a whole individual, my past just one facet of who I am.

As my understanding of leadership evolves, I try to impart it to the girls. It's the ability to facilitate a presentation or training without even really mentioning your past, and still trust that you're going to do a phenomenal job. It's knowing that you have enough counseling skills to work with a girl in crisis without telling her your own story. It's discovering your skills at other things; writing a proposal, planning an event, overseeing a project—none of which you need to be a survivor to do—that ultimately shows your growth as a leader.

Over the years I learned that youth leadership looks different for different people. Not everyone is a ham like me who enjoys public speaking. Some girls are fantastic writers; some have great programming ideas; for others it may be the opportunity to serve as a "big sister" to other girls in the program. Others may want to make an impact through sharing their creative talents; therefore, there must be multiple avenues and opportunities for girls and young women to share their skills and knowledge and to experience concrete ways of "making a difference."

As a survivor-leader, I hope to see youth survivor-leaders go on to achieve in politics, the arts, science, and business—in any field of endeavor they choose. Learning to advocate in Albany can translate into the confidence to go into the corporate world; counseling peers can spur a career in medicine. Ultimately, as girls begin to find their own voice, power, and strength, they can begin to envision a productive and exciting future. For girls and young women who have experienced such immense trauma and pain, for whom a happy and healthy future seemed an impossibility, the need to be able to envision themselves moving forward, creating a new life, accomplishing and achieving, loving and being loved, being an important part of the world and making an impact on that world, is the true indication of real healing and recovery.

16
BEGINNINGS

In her heart she is a mourner for those who have not survived.
In her soul she is a warrior for those who are now as she was then.
In her life she is both celebrant and proof of women's capacity and
will to survive, to become, to act, to change self and society.
And each year she is stronger and there are more of her.
—Andrea Dworkin, *"A Battered Wife Survives"*

SUMMER 1998, NEW YORK CITY

It's after midnight and yet the air is still hot. It's one of those sweltering New York summer nights that growing up in England has ill-prepared me for. Despite my disdain for the American obsession with Arctic temperatures indoors in the middle of the summer, tonight I am cursing the fact that I can't afford an air conditioner in my apartment. I've decided to sit outside on my stoop and pretend that there's really a breeze. I can't sleep anyway. There's too much on my mind. It's been a year since I came to the States to work with women in the sex industry. My job has just ended, the result of my decision to accept a full scholarship to a private college. I thought my boss would see this as good news, but somehow she wasn't thrilled and gave me an ultimatum, work or school. I'd been under the impression that most people managed to do both simultaneously, but apparently this option is not on the table. It takes me all of about twenty seconds to make my decision. I left school at the age of thirteen and have struggled for years with a sense of inadequacy about my lack of education. I still read voraciously, but I'm aware that there are huge gaps in my learning and that if my life ever depended upon calculating a fraction or a percentage, I'd be in serious trouble. It's not that I think I'm stupid, but I've always wanted a little piece of paper to validate that I'm not. For years I assume that I'd missed my opportunity, until I learn about America's wonderful general equivalency diploma. A few weeks after I arrive in New York, I register for GED prep classes at a local church. My reading and writing skills are fine but math inspires a special kind of terror in me. It takes seven months of twice-weekly math tutoring with the incredibly patient Mr. Robert before I'm ready to conquer the exam. Late one night, just as I'm getting ready for bed, I see an envelope pushed under my door. Inside are the nervously anticipated results, proof that I'm adequate and not stupid. I cry when I read them. Not only have I passed, but I've passed with a really high score. As a missionary making about six thousand dollars a year, I'm permanently broke, but that night I spend my last two dollars to buy a Häagen-Dazs ice-cream bar from the bodega and walk around my neighborhood at midnight, grinning stupidly and having to physically restrain myself from telling every random stranger that it's official. I've graduated from high school at the age of twenty-three.

My scores open the door to an interview with Marymount Manhattan College through their community leadership program, designed for young people who ordinarily wouldn't have opportunities to go to college and who are actively engaged in nonprofit work. It's the perfect fit, and while there are some hurdles about not being eligible for TAP or Pell due to my immigrant status, the director of the program lobbies hard for me and I'm awarded a full four-year scholarship. It would feel like a dream come true, if I had ever dreamed of attending college. After everything I've been through and having been in New York only less than a year, it's hard not to believe that this is a miracle. Now that I've got the acceptance letter in my hand, turning down this opportunity isn't even an option. I'd like to tell my boss to take her ultimatum and shove it, but instead I tell her that I'm going to school and she can make whatever decision she sees fit. She fires me.

So I'm unemployed and broke, and school starts in just a few weeks. I sit on the concrete steps of my building, wondering what on earth I'm going to do. There are people encouraging me to leave New York; there's a job offer in another state from a church that works with homeless people. I try to explain that you don't just trade one set of marginalized people for another. I believe my calling is here in New York, with these girls. People think I'm being foolish. I have no real support, no money, no job, my visa's about to expire, and I have no idea how I'm going to pay the rent on my new apartment. My college degree is still four whole years away.

Yet while my job has ended, my passion for this issue, for the girls, has not; I cannot imagine working with anyone else. I think of Melissa, Jennifer, Aisha, and Katherine, girls I've grown to know and love. Girls I loved from the moment I met them. I think about my girls in Rikers and my girls on the street. I think about Miranda and her comments about my being sent here and I know that she's right. Everything in my life has led me to this point. I think about my journey and what I needed to get out of the life: love, compassion, shelter, clothing, food, kindness, a job. I think about the things that I didn't get but that would've been nice: the ability to be honest about my experiences; an understanding that I was victimized; knowledge about the larger issue of commercial sexual exploitation and how all the things I'd experienced made me vulnerable; and most important, a place where I could talk to other girls and women who'd been through the same things, who would never judge me, who could relate to my experiences. I think about my first year here, and despite the immense challenges and huge learning curve, how empowering it feels to help others, to use my voice and not be silent about my experiences, to sometimes be the expert in the room, to see other young people, like Cherry, Julia, and Peter, as leaders and activists, and how working to create change not just in the lives of individual girls but in the larger system feels amazing. And so I decide to stay and create for other girls the kind of place that I had wanted and needed. It will be like FUBU, for us by us, except instead of sneakers it will be about survivors helping survivors, girls and young women supporting each other, girls being leaders, girls speaking out. I'm not sure how I'll do it but I figure that I'll work that out as I go.

As I walk to the bodega to get an Icee, I think about what I might call my organization. I run into my friend Doug, who is horrified that I'm wandering around so late. I'm babbling on and on and Doug, in his patient-friend role, is listening and offering nods of encouragement.

"What am I going to call it? It has to have a name. Otherwise no one will think it's official." We sit on the stoop sucking on our melting Icees for a few minutes, pondering names. "It has to be like a . . . um, um, what do you call those things that have initials but spell out different words, like ASAP or AWOL? You know?" It's one of the words that I know how to spell thanks to all my reading but am reluctant to say as I don't know how to pronounce it. I simply pretend to have forgotten the word and wait for someone to say it.

"Acronym?"

"Yup, an acronym. All the organizations have those now. It needs to be a good one though, cos I hate those ones that are such a stretch. I want mine to signify something."

We toss names around for a while. "ROSES, Rescuing Others from Sexual Exploitation."

"Nah. I want it to be strong. Not rescuing."

"FLOWERS? Freeing Ladies . . ." Doug offers.

I laugh. "What are you gonna do with that *w*?"

"Ladies Or Women?" We both crack up.

"Seriously, though, I want something that says that girls are valuable. They're important. They're beautiful. I feel like that's the part that no one sees. Everybody looks at them, at *us*, like we're dirty, never gonna be anything. I feel like God sees them, *us*, as beautiful.

All of them." I'm on a roll now. "I've been reading that verse in Isa-iah about laying your foundation with stones, like rubies and stuff. You know the one I mean?" Doug has grown up in the church.

"Yeah, Isaiah fifty something."

"Yep. It talks about being afflicted and tossed with tempest, like violence. But then how God will lay your foundation with col-orful gems. I like that. That's how I think about the girls. It's like their lives have been full of violence but really they're like precious stones."

"How about DIAMONDS or RUBIES or something?"

"GEMS!"

We try out these for a few minutes, making words fit, until I finally decide. "I think it's GEMS, Girls Educational and Mentoring Services.

"Cos if you think about it, to everyone else, they just look like regular old rocks or stones, but to a master jeweler, who can see the beauty and potential in a stone and knows that with some polishing, some care and attention, just like these girls need, that the precious stone, the gem, will come out and be shining."

"That's pretty good." Doug's a fan.

"GEMS, GEMS, GEMS." I try on the name for size. I like it, too.

"The birth of GEMS: on a stoop, eating Icees after midnight, in the Bronx," I declare, gesturing grandly. We both laugh.

It's not until later that night, after Doug has gone home and I've returned upstairs to endure the night in my little oven, that I read the chapter in Isaiah again. The preceding verse, " 'For the moun-tains shall depart, and the hills be removed, but My kindness shall not depart from you, nor shall My covenant of peace be removed,' says the LORD, who has mercy on you," is the verse that a stranger, in a nearby bed, gave to my mother for me in a little hospital in Dorset the night I was born. It's a sign. GEMS it is.

A wise friend of mine, Brad, once tells me in a late-night telephone conversation that it is the job of most founders to learn to embody the mission and philosophy of their own organization. I don't really get what he means and ask him to explain, feeling like I might not want to hear the answer.

"At GEMS, your guiding philosophy is all about seeing girls as beautiful, precious, about empowering them to see that in themselves." I'm starting to see where this is headed and I'm a little uncomfortable.

"Yeah, so . . . ?"

"Well, you really don't see what other people see in you. You're still trying so hard to prove something, to overcome something, still haunted by whatever people have told you in the past, by what people have done, that you can't accept how beautiful and special you are. It doesn't matter what you accomplish, it's never enough. You see and believe it for all the girls. You just don't believe, not really, not deep down, about yourself." He's hit a nerve. I'm not sure what to say but his words stick with me for a long time and I do my best to work on this new idea—valuing myself like I value the girls, accepting myself like I accept them, not blaming myself, integrating my experiences, being happy with who I've become. It's a process, a long one that I'll mess up at multiple opportunities, until slowly I begin to find a little balance, a little peace of my own.

In my thirties, I reach a stage where I decide that given my family history, I don't want to drink anymore, not even a little bit. Not even if I think I can "handle it." I ask a friend who's sober if he misses drinking and he tells me, "Yeah, sometimes. But I feel closer to being whole." I write his words on a Post-it note and work to embrace this notion of wholeness, taking sobriety seriously and working on some of the things I've worked so hard to hide over the years. I'm watching *Celebrity Rehab with Dr. Drew* one night, one of my few reality TV guilty pleasures, when they show a group of children who've been affected by their alcoholic and substance-abusing parents. The children speak frankly and painfully about their longings for a real family, their confusion at coming second to a drink or a high, and their fervent wish for things to be OK with Mommy. *They're just babies,* I think, as tears stream down my face. *They shouldn't have to go through this much pain at that age.* And that's when I realize their ages, twelve, thirteen, fourteen years old, and I see myself. For the first time, I have real compassion for myself, for the childhood that I didn't get to have. It's the same compassion that I've been able to give the girls for years, always seeing them as children and young people who deserved so much better. I cry a lot that night for the ten-year-old, the twelve-year-old, the fourteen-year-old Rachel, and for the years that got lost, and yet after the tears, I can feel it. I'm a little closer to being whole.

Over time, I realize that beginning with meeting the girls at Rikers, to understanding trauma, to addressing the control of pimps and the harm done by johns, to dealing with the stigma of being a "survivor," to changing public perception, to creating a new type of leadership, it has been about my own journey and my own healing as much as it's been about the girls, the issue, the movement. I wonder if this makes me a selfish person, and then realize that this kind of thinking is probably a little counterproductive to the whole idea of loving myself. Yet while GEMS may have originally been my way to work through my own pain, over the years it has become its own entity. It's not just about me anymore; it's become a community of girls and women, of supporters and allies, an organization that has affected systems and changed lives.

SUMMER 2008, NEW YORK CITY

There's great consternation conveyed through text messages from my staff. THE T-SHIRTS HAVE NOT ARRIVED!!!! We'd designed hot pink (GEMS colors) fitted tees with a huge Girls Are Not for Sale sign on the back. As I drive down the West Side Highway, working myself into a lather about the unreliability of T-shirt vendors and feeling like the day is doomed, I have to take a deep breath and remind myself that today we are celebrating the passage of the Safe Harbor Act. After over four years of an emotional roller coaster of advocacy, we have actually won. We're making history, changing state law; girls will be protected, not punished. I decide that in the grand scheme of things, T-shirts may not be the most critical thing. Yet as I round the corner to City Hall Park, all I can see is a sea of hot pink. The T-shirts evidently have arrived. I take it as a sign that all will be well with the day.

The weather is beautiful, and the girls are having a blast. It seems everyone's brought a camera, and they are taking countless pictures, posing, directing each other like Jay Manuel on *America's Next Top Model*. "No, move closer. Do one with your hands on your hips."

"Tiff, you turn around so I can see the writing on the back. No, the *other* way. The back." Dramatic sigh. "Jen, you face the front. Now stand next to each other."

Seeing them excited reminds me what we're doing here. I breathe deeply again and decide to relax and enjoy the day.

The program starts. It's our third annual New York State End Commercial Sexual Exploitation of Children Day. This year, the mood is giddy. Some of the girls kick off the event by taking the mic and talking about how proud they are that the bill has passed. Then Assemblyman William Scarborough, our original champion in the assembly, talks about his commitment to the issue, and how after years of driving by girls on Jamaica Avenue and Queens Boulevard and turning his head, he began to understand that they were children and they were victims. There's a short round of speeches, lots of applause, and I find myself in tears.

Normally I'd stay and eat lunch with the girls but I have to get to Brooklyn within the hour. With a couple of other staff members, I drive over to the Brooklyn Museum, where the event is to take place. We take our seats in the audience and wait anxiously through a series of interminably long speeches and a painful rendition of Mariah Carey's "Hero" delivered off-key. Mercifully, the song finally finishes, and I know it's the part that we've been waiting for. There's Sequoia in a white cap and gown, looking totally radiant and stunningly beautiful. My heart swells. She walks up to the stage and I see her being hugged by a teacher; she's clearly nervous. I send her mental blessings and try to impart confidence from my seat thirty feet away. The principal is talking about the school spirit. "And now," she says, "someone who exemplifies that spirit, graduating senior and class valedictorian . . . Sequoia Thomas." We're on our feet, screaming, going nuts. Her cheering section is composed of GEMS staff; Cait and Alex, her Legal Aid lawyers; her mother, her sister, her therapist. People who've shared the journey with her. Sequoia sees us and seems unsure if she should be happy or mortified that we're so vocal. To save her from further embarrassment, we sit down, although I'd rather listen to her whole speech on my feet, yelling *woo-hoo* at the top of my lungs. I listen to her describe herself as a lotus that has grown in mud and has evolved into something beautiful. I think about her in a hospital bed and about all the struggles she's been through. Seeing her now on the stage in her cap and gown, I am overcome with pride and admiration for her courage and determination.

We race back to Manhattan for the last leg of the day, getting stuck in Friday rush-hour traffic on the FDR. Running late, I jump out of the car and throw my flats on so I can run the three blocks from the parking garage to the Fordham University campus where we're having a public presentation of our newly written white paper on survivor leadership, fittingly titled *From Victim to Survivor, From Survivor to Leader*. It is a youth-led research project on youth empowerment and leadership wherein the girls had been trained by a grad student to interview each other on their experiences. I'd had the task of weaving all their comments and themes together, and I'd stayed up for three nights in a row, drinking endless cups of tea and a bunch of Red Bulls, in order to get it finished. Reading what the girls thought about GEMS, about the ways we tried to support them, about the skills that they'd learned, the confidence and self-esteem that they'd gained, was revelatory. I knew that we'd helped girls over the years because I got to see the progress and growth in individual girls' lives firsthand, but reading quotes like *Some people know what proper love and care is, and I know because of GEMS and I get that every single time I come here*, and *I used to have no self-esteem at all. Like I want to look for a job but if the restaurant looked fancy I wouldn't walk in there. GEMS gave me a lot of self-confidence. It also gave me the position to be a leader and I can help other girls feel the way I do now* made it real in a whole other way. Although the girls had been given pseudonyms, it wasn't hard for me to tell just who was who. Their personalities, their strengths, their interests came shining through, and I sat crying as I read page after page. It wasn't just that they were glad they'd come to GEMS or that we'd been helpful to them in various ways, it was the fact that the very things I'd envisioned and worked to create—a community that was safe and nonjudgmental, a space where survivors could gain strength from each other, programming that felt empowering, that taught them that their voices were important, that they didn't have to be ashamed—was all here, in line after line of the girls' own comments.

Tonight, five of the girls are presenting the paper to a roomful of over two hundred people. I know that the deputy commissioner of probation, the assistant commissioner of child welfare, and people from the mayor's office are all here, a miracle in itself. We're all nervous but we huddle for a minute, pumping each other up, saying a heartfelt prayer, gripping hands tightly.

The panel begins and the girls each take a theme to present on, reading from the white paper, then using their own experiences to illuminate each section. I'm bursting with pride, watching them

handle the questions from the audience with poise and thoughtful responses. When one seems stuck, the others jump in to help.
I watch them whisper to each other, pass the mic back and forth.
"You should take this one, Jasmine." "Why don't you share about
going to Albany, Kristina?"

As I watch these smart, self-assured, confident, strong young
women, I think of the day I met each one of them; the experiences
that we've been through; the tears, the frustrations, the leavings
and the coming-backs; the practicing for the GEDs; the sharing in
group; the late-night car rides home that turned into hours-long
counseling sessions; the trips to the emergency room, court, the
precinct; the celebrations over birthdays, graduations, and just the
small daily achievements of hanging in there in the face of so much.
The girls receive a thunderous and long standing ovation. They're
beaming. I'm still trying hard not to cry, proving Monica's recent
assertion that I'm the most "crying-est staff." Her statement was
pretty funny to me, given all the times I want to cry and don't and
the tears the girls have never seen, but I agree with her, I do have a
tendency to choke up at the happy stuff, the proud stuff, the warm
and fuzzy stuff. Today has been the most incredible conflation of all
of that, so I feel like I deserve a break for crying today.

Once the public portion of the evening is over, the tears so close
to the surface really begin to flow. Julie sees me close to falling apart
and grabs me by my elbow. I'm too overwhelmed to explain what
I'm feeling. Outside the fresh air does little to stop my tears. It's
everything all rolled up into one. It's the culmination of ten years
of struggles, the fulfillment of the vision I had long ago on the steps
of my building in the Bronx. It's seeing these amazing girls develop
into strong young women, and having other people see and validate
what I'd always believed about them. It's passing the first Safe Harbor law in the nation that will change things for victims in this state
and eventually across the country. When the girls come out of the

auditorium after being mobbed by the supportive and now enamored audience, they immediately come over. We're standing in a small huddle and I'm struck by how right this feels, how much I love every knuckleheaded last one of them. "I gotta tell y'all—I wouldn't change a single thing, not a moment, wouldn't take away one bit of my life, of being in the life, cos I wouldn't have ended up here with y'all." I'm trying to hold back the tears, yet they're rolling. "And you, all of you, make every single thing worth it. It was all worth it, to know you and to be lucky enough to be part of your lives."

"You mean that?" asks Monica, crying too.

"Yes, more than anything. I love you all so much—this is where I was always meant to be."

There's so much strength here in this circle of hugs and tears. Tomorrow there'll be another crisis. Someone will come in late and have to be written up, new girls with new pain will show up, some still attached to their trafficker, others struggling with the early stages of leaving, girls who'll go missing in the coming weeks, girls who'll be arrested and treated badly. There are millions of perceptions to change and more hurdles to jump in the courts. But I figure for one night, I'll just relax and stop fighting. We did good. After years of one step forward, ten steps back, today has felt like a hundred steps forward. Today's been all about survivor voices, survivor achievements, survivor leadership, a stunning affirmation that offers a rebuttal to all the people who didn't believe in us, in me, in any girl who has been sexually exploited. It's one of the best nights of my life. I'm frequently proud of these phenomenal girls and young women. Tonight, I decide to actually be proud of myself.

One evening, I'm sitting at the office chatting with a couple of my older girls, both of whom have been around for years. For some odd reason we're talking about tanning beds and I admit that yes, I've been on them a few times.

"I don't believe it. Not you," Ashley exclaims.

"*Really?*" Jasmine cannot believe her ears.

The girls both look at me as if I've just admitted to suffocating kittens. I know the health issues are bad, but still, they're horrified.

"Goodness! Why are ya'll making such a big deal out of this?"

They're still in shock apparently as it takes a few minutes for either of them to get beyond, "Because" or "You know."

Finally Ashley is able to articulate their keen sense of horror.

"You're too empowered to tan," she says. Jasmine nods in agreement. Both of them deadly serious.

"I'm what?" I can barely talk, I'm laughing so hard. Eventually I catch my breath. "That's the funniest thing I've heard all year. Have y'all ever met me?"

I think about my insecurities, my challenges over the years to accept myself, my well-known vanity and obsession with shoes. I start laughing again, but they look a little miffed that I'm not taking their point seriously.

"You're so, you know, confident and together, and you know, all that stuff. . . ."

And finally I get it. To them, I'm the grown-up, poised and in control. Although I barely ever feel like a grown-up, especially as I forget to pay a parking ticket or spend four hours trying to locate a shoe in the mess that doubles as my bedroom, I realize that finally I'm "that chick," that woman that I wanted to grow up to be. Dr. Hall mentoring in the guidance counselor's office. Bernadette being a strong and confident working mother. Cherry Kingsley presenting in Canada. I'm not the girl who came to New York too shy to speak in meetings, thinking everyone on the street could look at me and just tell. I'm not the girl who thought getting hit was normal, or who believed that I had to settle for mediocre in my personal relationships. I'm not waking up in the middle of the night screaming, or crying with shame every time someone says something hurtful.

I've still got a lot of growing to do, but it's nice being seen at least as someone who's over some of the early hurdles and has emerged confident and secure.

"Thank you," I tell the girls, and they seem pleased that I'm getting what they mean. "I do think it would make a great T-shirt, though, *Too empowered to tan.*" Just the thought of it makes me laugh all over again.

That night, I think about the mistakes I've made, the hard lessons I've had to learn both personally and professionally, the times when I was counseling girls and heard myself give advice that I desperately needed to hear for myself. I think about some of the girls who are now twenty-three and realize in hindsight how young and totally unprepared I was to start a nonprofit at that age. I had so much growing up to do, growing up that happened right alongside the girls. I think of how broken and damaged I was, even when I thought I wasn't, and all the healing that happened in fits and spurts, painfully and awkwardly. I think of how much my confidence, my sense of self, my capacity to love and trust has grown. I think of everything that I've learned from the girls and how blessed I am to have founded GEMS and to have had GEMS find me. People would often ask, "Did you ever imagine that it would be like this, a decade later, when you started it?" And the truth was, I did. I knew that we were going to change things. I knew that young women had the power, and that survivors could be leaders and that we would create a safe space and a home for girls, and we would create programs and counseling and health care, and all the things we've been able to do over the years. But I didn't know how much I would get out of it, and I didn't know how much of a family the girls and women at GEMS would become. I had no idea just how much I'd enjoy walking through the doors every day to learn from and grow with some of the smartest, funniest, strongest, most resilient girls I could ever hope to meet.

ACKNOWLEDGMENTS

This is definitely the hardest part of the book to write. In thinking about all the people who have not only supported me in the last two years of writing but also all the people who have supported me and believed in me over the years, which allowed me to even get to this point in my life, I'm overwhelmed with the enormity of love and kindness I've been shown. If I were to acknowledge all of the individuals who have touched my life in one way or another, knowingly or not, it would fill the pages of a whole nother book. So . . . if you have ever been kind to me, said an encouraging word to me, helped me in some way, taught me something or prayed for me . . . I'm sincerely grateful. Thank you.

A special thanks, too, to anyone who has supported GEMS over the years, especially those who've donated money and resources and ensured that we could continue to build a place of safety and support for our girls and young women. Thank you.

While I'm well aware that this is not an award show, I really do want to thank God for blessing me and for His amazing grace that saved a wretch like me. I'm so grateful to be found.

Thanks to my mother for supporting me in telling my story. I love you much and always, and I'm so glad we have the beautiful relationship that we have now. I'm proud of you and thankful that you're my mom. Truly.

To my grandma, the late and great Jean Lloyd, who always believed in me and who gave me my stubbornness, my sense of humor, and my ability to cook a mean roast dinner. I miss you always.

To my wonderful and wise editor at HarperCollins, Gail Winston, for all of your support and faith and, of course, patience. Thank you so, so much for believing in me. And to Jason Sack, assistant editor and phone buddy—thank you for answering all the millions of questions I had and for keeping me on track.

To my agent, Elizabeth Sheinkman, at Curtis Brown. Thank you for your support and encouragement.

A thank-you to everyone who's ever told me, "You should really write a book," but especially to David Henry Sterry, who told me lots and lots of times and inspired me to actually do it. Thank you to Janice Erlbaum for giving me real-life author advice. And thank you to all the amazing writers I've read over the years who taught me so much and inspired me with the power of their words.

A huge and heartfelt thank-you goes out to my friends and surrogate family, who not only deal with me on a regular basis and still love me but who put up with my grouchiness after spending numerous sleepless weekends in a hotel room in Jersey, writing and drinking way too much Red Bull, and who dealt with my general and frequent whining about writing a book—thank you! Your support and encouragement helped me keep going.

A special thanks to Senior Clinical Director Julie Laurence and Fiscal/Admin Director Yvette Velez, who've not only been holding it down at GEMS for years but who have held me down and always had my back. From fiscal meetings in my car to driving down to D.C. in the middle of the night, never-ending streams of crisis calls, all-nighters in the office, Popeyes, Starbucks, Jamal's, FDR park BBQs, Christmases and Thanksgivings, watching the girls grow up, laughing, crying, smoking too many cigarettes . . . and that's just the stuff that's printable. We've made it through so much, and GEMS, and I, could never have made it without you. I love and appreciate you both more than you know . . . fam!

Thank you to my assistant, Elizabeth Gaines, for being an amazing assistant and friend. I couldn't have gotten through the last three years without you. In fact, I'd still be driving around somewhere, lost in Jersey. I wish you so much happiness in your new life.

Bridgit Antoinette Evans, so happy to have you in my life as a sister and friend and to be on such a wonderful journey with you. Aries all the way!

My big sister Lisa Goldblatt Grace, director of the wonderful My Life, My Choice program in Boston (and erstwhile author). Thank you for so much, for . . . everything. Don't know what I'd do without you.

Ruben Austria, executive director of Community Connections for Youth, thank you for over a decade of friendship, *Miss Saigon* sing-a-thons, and your prayers and support. You've held me down, son!

Bradley Myles, executive director of Polaris Project in D.C. and all-round supersmart guy. Thank you so much for your friendship and support and all our late night chats. I'm really grateful for you.

Cait Mullen, the architect of the nation's Safe Harbor law—I miss our trips to Albany. You're an incredible advocate, great lawyer, and a wonderful friend. Thank you for being in my life.

Priya Swaminathan and David Schisgall, thank you for making our documentary *Very Young Girls* and for knowing that we could truly begin to shift perceptions about our girls. Thank you for your continued friendship, love, and support. You are two of my favorite people.

Thank you to my readers, Julie, Brad, Lisa, Bridgit, Ruben, Priya, Pamela Shifman, and Teresa Tomassoni. Thank you for being so excited and for so much encouragement.

To my "grandbaby" Juston. I love you more than you could ever know and am so happy to be in your life.

To H. Thank you for being my sober role model and inspiring me. For real, for real.

To Scott and Gail. Thank you for being there for me and for all your support. It has changed my life.

A huge thank-you to all of the GEMS staff who do phenomenal work every single day. I'm so grateful to work with such an amazing group of talented, smart, funny, dedicated women. You have all made my dream a reality.

And finally, a very special thank-you to the girls and young women who trusted me to tell their stories and have shared their lives with me. I'm scared to name any of y'all cos there's no way to name everyone, and God forbid I leave someone out! Y'all know there would be some drama over that. So . . . please know how much I truly love you and how special you all are to me in your own unique way. I hope you can see through these pages how much you've all taught me and inspired me. This is for you.

To learn more and to support GEMS' work with girls,
please visit our website at:
www.gems-girls.org

If you suspect that someone you know is a victim of
human trafficking, call the National Human Trafficking
Resource Center hotline at 1-888-3737-888.

NOTES

PROLOGUE

10 *1.2 million children and youth*: UNICEF. Child protection from violence, exploitation and abuse. http://www.unicef.org/protection/index _exploitation.html.

11 *200,000 to 300,000 adolescents are at risk*: Estes, R. and N. Weiner. 2001. The commercial sexual exploitation of children in the U.S., Canada and Mexico. Philadelphia: Center for the Study of Youth Policy, School of Social Work, University of Pennsylvania.

1 : LEARNING

15 *"Child sexual exploitation is the most hidden form"*: Ibid.

2 : RISK

33 *the number of children and youth at high risk for recruitment*: Estes and Weiner. Commercial sexual exploitation.

39 *"Between 1984 and 1994, the homicide rate for black males"*: Levitt, S., K. Murphy, et al. 2006. How bad was crack cocaine? The economics of an illicit drug market. Washington, D.C.: National Bureau of Economic Research.

39 *In 1984, there were 16,230 children*: Reinharz, P. 2000. No, the neighborhoods haven't healed themselves. *City Journal.* Winter.

40 *The murder rate in 2007*: "New York Law Enforcement Agency Uniform Crime Reports 1980 to 2005." http://www.nyc.gov/html/nypd/ downloads/pdf/crime_statistics/cscity.pdf on the Web page http://

www.nyc.gov/html/nypd/html/crime_prevention/crime_statistics
.shtml, which shows the 17-year change from week-to-date 2010.

40 *Nationally, over thirteen million children*: Douglas-Hall, A., M. Chau, et al. 2006. *Basic facts about low-income children: Birth to age 18.* New York: National Center for Children in Poverty, Mailman School of Public Health, Columbia University.

40 *Over half a million children*: Chau, M., A. D. Kinsey, et al. 2006. On the edge in the Empire State: New York's low-income children. New York: National Center for Children in Poverty, Mailman School of Public Health, Columbia University.

41 *There are currently over 15,000 children*: New York City Administration of Children's Services. Statistics and Links. http://www.nyc.gov/html/acs/html/statistics/statistics_links.shtml (accessed August 10, 2010).

41 *75 percent of sexually exploited and trafficked children*: Gragg, F., I. Petta, et al. 2007. New York prevalence study of commercially sexually exploited children. Rensselaer, N.Y.: New York State Office of Children and Family Services.

44 *For a time, one of the most*: Smalley, S. 2003. This could be your kid. *Newsweek.* August 18.

3: FAMILY

64 *Like all forms of child abuse*: Centers for Disease Control and Prevention. 2005. Adverse childhood experiences study: Data and statistics. Atlanta, Ga.

65 *"Incest is boot camp for prostitution"*: Dworkin, A. 1997. Prostitution and male supremacy. In *Life and Death.* New York: Free Press.

65 *sexually abused prior to their recruitment*: Widom, C. S. 1995. Victims of childhood sexual abuse—Later criminal consequences. Washington, D.C.: National Institute of Justice, Office of Justice Programs, U.S. Department of Justice. Finkelhor, D. and A. Browne. 1985. The traumatic impact of child sexual abuse: A conceptualization. *American Journal of Orthopsychiatry* 55(4). Silbert, M. 1984. Treatment of prostitute victims of sexual assault. In *Victims of Sexual Aggression.* New York:Van Nostrand Reinhold.

4: RECRUITMENT

72 *"I ain't gotta give 'em much"*: Jackson, C. ("50 Cent"). 2003. "P.I.M.P." In *Get Rich or Die Tryin'.*

79   *For victims of sex trafficking*: S. 3061: William Wilberforce Trafficking Victims Protection Reauthorization Act of 2008. Retrieved August 10, 2010, from http://www.govtrack.us/congress/bill.xpd?bill=s110-3061.

82   *"allowed herself to be entrapped"*: Gorham, D. 1978. "The maiden tribute of modern Babylon" reexamined : Child prostitution and the idea of childhood in late-Victorian England. *Victorian Studies* 21:3.

5: PIMPS

88   *Snoop brags about his pimping*: Toure. 2006 America's most lovable pimp. *Rolling Stone* 14. December.

89   "Wait I got a snow bunny": Three 6 Mafia. 2005. "It's Hard out Here for a Pimp." In *Hustle and Flow*.

6: JOHNS

108   *A University of Pennsylvania study*: Estes and Weiner. Commercial sexual exploitation.

108   *113 men who purchased sex*: Durchslag, R. and S. Goswami. 2008. Deconstructing the demand for prostitution: Preliminary insights from interviews with Chicago men who purchase sex. Chicago Alliance Against Sexual Exploitation.

109   *"My . . . hasn't she grown!"*: FHM. 1999. Britney Spears cover issue. July.

109   *hundreds of thousands of websites*: Ropelato, J. Internet pornography statistics. Retrieved August 10, 2010 from http://internet-filter-review .toptenreviews.com/internet-pornography-statistics-pg11.html.

109   *In the CAASE research*: Durchslag and Goswami. Deconstructing the demand.

111   *A Canadian commission found*: Special Committee on Prostitution and Pornography. 1985. Pornography and prostitution in Canada. Ottawa: Canadian Government Publishing Center.

112   *Another study put the estimate*: Lowman, J. and P. Dillon. 1998. Life on the streets is dangerous. *Surrey Leader.* May 17.

112   *"I picked prostitutes as my victims"*: Gary Ridgway (the "Green River Killer") in a statement to the court in which he pled guilty to murdering forty-eight women and girls, 2003. http://www.cnn.com/2003/LAW/11/05/ridgway.statement/.

7: VICTIMS

115 *"The majority of rapes"*: Rennison, C. M. 2002. Rape and sexual assault: Reporting to police and medical attention, 1992–2000. Washington, D.C.: Bureau of Justice Statistics, Office of Justice Programs, U.S. Department of Justice. August. NCJ 194530.

131 *"In New York City, good victims"*: Vachss, A. 1993. Sex crimes: Ten years on the front lines prosecuting rapists and confronting their collaborators. New York: Random House.

8: COPS

133 *"Larger social forces have"*: Bortner, M. A. and L. Williams. 1997. Youth in prison: We the people of Unit Four. New York: Routledge.

140 *"As long as black women"*: Cobb, W. J. 2004. Nelly, Portrayals of Women of Color, and Bone Marrow. http://jelanicobb.com/content/view/20/30.

140 *"There are certain rules"*: Bright, M. 2002. The vanishing. *Guardian*. December 15.

141 *"A Nexis search of major newspapers"*: Johnson, M. and A. Johnson. 2002. Alexis gets little notice; Utah girl widely covered. *Milwaukee Journal Sentinel*. June 15.

141 *"It would have been difficult"*: Fountain, J. W. 2002. Hope lingers in Milwaukee for youngster's return. *New York Times*. June 27.

142 *"her precociousness may have"*: Fenner, A. 2004. Sad farewell to Tyisha, *New York Daily News*. July 14.

142 *"fun-loving," "sweet," and "caring"*: Hutchinson, B. 2004. Sad songs for slain teen. *New York Daily News*. August 3.

143 *"The lanky and sour Nicolette"*: Kaufman, L. 2004. Determining the future of a girl with a past. *New York Times*. September 15.

144 *she's headed to Rikers*: New York is one of three states that sends sixteen-year-old children to an adult correctional facility.

9: STAYING

152 *"One of the first books"*: Herman, J. 1992. Trauma and recovery. New York: Basic Books.

155 *"Psychologist Dee Graham identified"*: Graham, D.L.R. 1994. Loving to survive: Sexual terror, men's violence, and women's lives. New York University Press.

157 *"all unequal power relationships"*: Clark, L.M.G. and D. Lewis. 1977. Rape: The price of coercive sexuality. Toronto: The Women's Press.

163 *his concentration camp experiences*: Bettelheim, B. 1943. Individual and mass behavior in extreme situations. *Journal of Abnormal and Social Psychology* 38.

163 *the former slave clearly*: Equiano, O. 1789. The interesting narrative of the life of Olaudah Equiano, or Gustavus Vassa, the African. Vol. 1. London.

10: LEAVING

180 *A study done by Dr. Melissa Farley*: Farley, M., I. Baral, et al. 1989. Prostitution in five countries: Violence and post-traumatic stress disorder. *Feminism & Psychology* 8(4).

11: RELAPSE

192 *After years of watching girls*: Prochaska, J. O. and C. C. DiClemente. 1983. Stages and processes of self-change in smoking: Toward an integrative model of change. *Journal of Consulting and Clinical Psychology* 51.

12: UNLEARNING

198 *one in four women*: National Institute of Justice and Centers for Disease Control and Prevention. 2000. Extent, nature, and consequences of intimate partner violence. Washington, D.C.: National Institute of Justice, Office of Justice Programs, U.S. Department of Justice.

198 *half of the two hundred teenagers*: Boston Public Health Commission. 2009. Public Health Commission surveys youths on dating violence. March 12. Retrieved August 10, 2010 from http://www.bphc.org/Newsroom/Pages/TopStoriesView.aspx?ID=60.

13: STIGMA

217 *"The recruitment, harboring, transportation"*: S. 3061: William Wilberforce Trafficking Victims Protection Reauthorization Act.